VANCOUVER

SECRETS OF THE CITY

VANCOUVER

SECRETS OF THE CITY

Shawn Blore

ARSENAL PULP PRESS

VANCOUVER

ARSENAL PULP PRESS
103-1014 Homer Street
Vancouver, B.C.
Canada V6B 2W9
www.arsenalpulp.com

The publisher gratefully acknowledges the support of the Government of
Canada through the Book Publishing Industry Development Program for its
publishing activities.

Book design by Lisa Eng-Lodge
Production Assistant Judy Yeung
Editorial Assistant Laura Lemay
Cover photo Trudy Woodcock's Image Network
Printed and bound in Canada

Efforts have been made to locate copyright holders of source material
wherever possible. The publisher welcomes hearing from any copyright
holders of material used in this book who have not been contacted.

CANADIAN CATALOGUING IN PUBLICATION DATA:
Blore, Shawn, 1966-
  Vancouver: secrets of the city

  Includes index.
  ISBN 1-55152-091-5

1. Vancouver (B.C.)—Guidebooks. I. Title.
FC3847.18.B56 2000   917.11'33'044   C00-910920-X
F1089.5.V22B564 2000

c o n t e n t s

acknowledgments

It's a characteristic of secrets that the best ones are never written down, but passed on by word of mouth from person to person. Thanks, then, to all those who opened up their personal hoards of secret knowledge and chipped in with whispered contributions, small and large. Some are worthy of special mention, including Jim Sutherland who, when he was with *Vancouver Magazine*, first brought Vancouver secrets to the light of day those many years ago, as well as Sarah Reeder and Nick Rockel and Jamie Maw and everyone else who spent time in the *VanMag* tribe, and who helped keep up the flow of secrets. At Arsenal Pulp Press thanks goes to Robert Ballantyne for his help on the first edition, Laura Lemay for her huge contribution to this second version of the *Secrets* opus, and Brian and Blaine (you know who you are) for their help at all times. Graphics guru Lisa Eng-Lodge made both *Secrets* editions things of beauty to behold. Finally, thanks to the numerous librarians and helpful bureaucrats at various levels of government whose names, alas, will have to remain a secret.

One name does need to be known, that of my wife Alexandra de Vries, whose support – sorely tested now and again with demands, at 6 am, for yet another proofread – has been unwavering.

introduction

Vancouver is one of those cities that doesn't know what it wants to be when it grows up. What would be typical urban haste in other places is, in Vancouver, tempered by the encroachment of the natural environment. We want to be an urban centre, but Mother Nature just won't let us.

In pure economic terms, while Vancouver was once dedicated to natural resources, it now tries to charm dollars from film production and new media enterprises. In fact, we've noticed that cameras and computers are taking over. Certainly this is true of the new Yaletown highrises, the converted Gastown lofts, and certain downtown spaces in between.

Unlike older cities in the east that are burdened by history, Vancouver is not tied to any particular past, and continues to change and shift. At times the changes seem to be a result of whimsy, as if the city was changing for no other reason than it can. But don't be wary of such changes, because keeping track of Vancouver's growing pains is what *Vancouver: Secrets of the City* is all about.

It's a nerve-wracking thing to publish a book. We did our best with the first edition of *Vancouver: Secrets of the City* in 1998, certainly, packing it full of some of Vancouver's best secrets – underground tunnels, secret passageways, hidden beaches, and covert rifle training grounds – and more useful ones – hidden hikes, secret spas, little-known patios, unknown restaurants, and the dates and times of late-night gatherings of lingerie-clad hedonists. But when we finally sent the book out – alone – to fend for itself in the great wide world, we had no idea what to expect.

Gratifying then, that *Secrets I* zipped through three printings. What was intriguing was the range of uses to which the book was put. We expected most buyers to be locals, curious about the seemier side of their own city. And while many purchasers were local, a surprising number were from out of town. One woman e-mailed with her story: she special-ordered the book from a bookseller in San Francisco, and upon arrival in Vancouver used it as her sole travel guide. She spent a happy weekend, book in hand, poking about for secret tunnels and hidden landmarks, eating in obscure restaurants and sleeping in an out-of-the-way spot somewhere on the East Side. Best trip she'd had in years, she said.

So for *Secrets II* we've offered more. Of everything. More history, more scandal, more tunnels (!), hidden landmarks and unknown shortcuts, as well as lots more stuff to seek out and explore on your own. Happy hunting.

Secret tunnels, hidden rooms, unmarked graveyards, lost plans, buildings with a past: they're all right under your nose. Vancouver is rich in secret sites, if you know where to look.

Photo: Blaine Kyllo

Secret Source of Tourist Fraud

The Gastown Steam Clock is one of the least secret things in the city. It sits wheezing on Water Street, surrounded most days by a claque of camera-toting tourists madly clicking away at what the plaque declares to be the "World's First Steam Powered Clock." What a crock. The clock, in fact, is driven by electricity, and has been for most of its existence. True, when first built by Vancouverite Ray Saunders, the timepiece did indeed derive its motive power from steam. But the system was tricky, requiring constant fidgety adjustments. After five years of near-constant tweaking, Saunders gave up and threw the switch on the auxiliary electric motor. From then till now and for the foreseeable future, the whistling bits of steam have been just for show. But don't tell the tourists. They'd just go home upset.

Photo: Blaine Kyllo

Trying to get a drink anywhere in Yaletown – without the bother of ordering the requisite token chicken wing or nacho plate – one could be forgiven for wishing Vancouver would finally grow up and join the 21st century. Better yet, that it could go back to the 19th. When Yaletown got its start in the 1880s, there was not a single law concerning the sale or consumption of liquor. In fact, there were no laws at all. The settlement sprang to life when the railway workers – who'd been living up the line in the Fraser Canyon town of Yale – loaded their houses, kitchen sinks and all, onto the CPR flat cars and headed west for the newly established port of Vancouver. Arriving more or less where the Roundhouse now is (across from the ultra-yuppie Urban Fare where even a glass of white wine can't be served unless accompanied by a full meal and three affidavits of sound character) the workers lifted their homes down, plunked them on the surrounding hillside, and thus was Yaletown born.

It was a wild and woolly place – outside the limits of Vancouver proper, and thus ungoverned by the city's laws, unpatrolled by its constabulary – and full to bursting with booze and whores and establishments where one could enjoy either or both. Alas, the uptight forces of law and order expanded their lines of control and absorbed old Yaletown. The houses were all knocked down to make way for warehouses around 1910. The only structure remaining from the original Yaletown is the Yale Hotel, which was shifted up the hill from to a new location at the foot of Granville. And though the location has changed, on your average Saturday night the clientele looks much the same.

MASONIC TEMPLE

Though innocent looking on the outside, the small brick building at 301 West Cordova Street has a closeted and cabalistic past. When it was constructed back in 1888, the ground floor was ordinary commercial space, but the upstairs was the ultra-private territory of Vancouver's first Masonic lodge. The Masons were a shadowy, secret society of well-placed men who at one point were thought to control the entire city. (Their fortunes much reduced, they now occupy a concrete bunker of a building on West 7th.) The venture into real estate marked a bit of a change for the temple's builder, Capt. James van Bramer, who up to that point had been a nautical man. Van Bramer, in fact, had been captain of the *Sea Foam*, the first steam ferry to regularly make the trip back and forth across Burrard Inlet. He was also the first captain to watch his ferry sink, when the *Sea Foam* exploded and burned to the waterline five years later.

It's a Bust

The Georgia Medical-Dental Building was once one of the city's favourites. Designed by the same McCarter and Nairne team that also produced the Marine Building, the 15-storey Art Deco tower was bedecked with intricate panels and bits of medically-themed statuary. When plans surfaced in the late 1980s to redevelop the site, there was a massive hue and cry, but before the preservationists could say "frieze," the old edifice was gone completely. Or almost completely. In designing a replacement, architect Paul Merrick paid tribute to the past by putting the four famous nurses that once crowned the Medical-Dental part-way up at the corners of his own Cathedral Place. These, however, are merely replicas, recast from the original moulds. Out back of Cathedral Place, the Medical-Dental's original terra cotta panels have been preserved in the lobby of the Canadian Craft Museum. And for true verisimilitude, peer inside Cathedral Place's ultra-Gothic lobby where the head of one of the original statue nurses sits encased in splendid isolation, a constant obstacle for the Garden Deli's noon-day rush of diners.

Gastown Gallery

Photo: Mandelbrot

When the Magasin building at 332 Water Street was renovated, several Gastown notables opted to have themselves immortalized as plaster gargoyles. From left to right as you face the building are: Dr. Lee Poulus, one-time owner of the Old Spaghetti Factory; John Levin, one-time owner of Brother's Restaurant; painter Jean-Paul Chason; developer Howard Meekin; Ray Saunders, builder of the Steam Clock; and model Blanche Macdonald.

Tower of Power

When the late afternoon sun strikes the building at 999 W. Hastings Street, it glows as if it were made of gold. Which it is. Yup, there's aurum in that aura. Within each glass panel lies a molecule-thin film of the finest gold powder. How much is it worth? "Not enough to make it worth melting down the broken glass," says the architect, Frank Musson.

Lost Airport

Photo: City of Vancouver Archives

Blame it on the booze. An airport, being a rather largish sort of thing, is usually fairly difficult to lose track of. Yet though there was once an entire airbase down near Jericho Beach, thanks to alcohol consumption (or lack thereof) the entire establishment has now vanished without a trace. The Jericho Beach Air Station, as the base was called, was established largely at the behest of Her Majesty's Customs, who wanted to stem the rampant smuggling of Canadian hooch south to the thirsty U.S. Flying boats – many of them hand-me-downs from the U.S. Navy – were rolled down concrete ramps on a daily basis to English Bay where they flew off into the wild blue yonder. By the late '40s, with both war and prohibition a thing of the past, there was little reason left to keep the airbase going; the only remnant today is the large, flat concrete pier on Jericho Beach, a relic of the concrete aprons where flying boats once rolled on and off. And also the yacht club next door, upstairs at which is a rather good greasy spoon – licensed, of course, so it's always possible to get a drink.

More Than Just Tires

Though it's now the land of yupps and gupps and other young health club types, the area around Burrard and York Street in eastern Kitsilano was once of a very different character. Early on, this was the Vancouver Sikh ghetto, complete with a full Sikh temple located around the corners of Burrard and York. 'Twas here in September of 1915, in the aftermath of the *Komagata Maru* affair, that angry Sikhs seeking vengeance tried to shoot down alleged government informant Bela Singh. In retaliation, Singh drew his own gun and shot two of his assailants dead. That aside, the neighbourhood thrived from the turn of the century until the early 1950s, when civic officials re-zoned the land as industrial. The temple came down, replaced eventually by a famous Canadian autoparts supplier.

Secret Names

Jericho Beach

The name Jericho has nothing to do with the dusty West Bank town with the faulty masonry. It's actually short for Jerry's Cove, the name given to the area by early settler Jeremiah Rogers. Rogers himself is immortalized by a pub on Fourth Avenue.

Minoru Park

In a fit of unholy Colonial ass-kissing, city fathers in 1909 named Richmond's central greenspace after one of King Edward's favourite horses, Minoru.

Lulu Island

Dance hall sensation Lulu Sweet stopped in at New Westminster to entertain the troops back in the 1860s. The site of this sophisticated showgirl drove chief land commissioner Colonel R.C. Moody to such a peak of gallantry that he grandly offered to name a flat bit of river delta after the sweet young miss. Lulu's reaction went unrecorded.

Main Street

Main Street

The only tri-lingual street in town, Main is English at both ends, and Punjabi and Chinese at different parts in-between. Interestingly, the Chinese characters on the street signs translate as "Street of Tung People." In Chinese terms, the Tung dynasty was the last truly civilized era, setting a standard to which all latter-day urbanites have aspired.

Dollarton

Why Dollarton? In the heady days of World War I the Dollar Mill opened near the waterfront to serve a booming war economy. The town that grew up around it became known as Dollar Town, or just Dollarton. If you search in the grass at the far end of Cates Park Road, you'll find a curious circular structure, the last remaining sign of the mill.

Old Shoreline

There's no surer bet than waterfront real estate. Unless, of course, you bought on Vancouver's Grove Crescent — a delightful little crescent at the base of a wooded hill overlooking False Creek — in 1910, and some other large and powerful entity — say, a railway — came along 10 years later, filled in the creek and covered it with tracks and sidings, leaving you with a bit of land on a street — now called Atlantic (just off Malkin), fronting on a railyard.

lost plans

Since the very first settler arrived, there have been those – inspired by the natural beauty of the surroundings – who have come up with grand plans and dumb schemes for improving the city of Vancouver.

And I See a Host of SUVs and 4x4s....

Vancouver has never wanted for industrious movers and shakers looking for ways to improve upon nature's handiwork. One of the most eloquent – and least successful – was 1930s mayor Gerry McGeer, who outlined his plan for a massive parkway scheme with biblical flourish in his inaugural address in 1935:

"I see the city of my boyhood dreams surrounded by one of the world's most marvellous driveways; one commencing at Chilliwack and coming down the south shore of the historic Fraser.... I see great boulevards flanking Marine Drive around the University Section, past the bathing beaches, adding beauty, use and purpose.... I see the driveway swinging through Stanley Park and across the Lions Gate, and following Howe Sound to a great national park built around the attractions of Mount Garibaldi. I can see that driveway extending as time goes on over Hollyburn Ridge and along the North Arm of Burrard Inlet ... back to Chilliwack via Harrison Hot Springs.... It would be a driveway some 250 miles in length that would change a wilderness of water and mountain grandeur into one of the most inviting and picturesque parks men have yet been privileged to enjoy."

Spanish Banks Airport

At a lecture given in downtown Vancouver in the early 1960s, the then-mayor of Los Angeles remarked – with that endearingly naïve boosterism with which Americans seem genetically programmed – that if Vancouver worked hard and played its cards right, it too might someday become another L.A. The audience burst out laughing.

It must have puzzled the poor mayor. L.A. as a city was about movement, about getting out and going places. Its iconic structure – next to the freeway grid – is the control tower at LAX, the city's aerospace on-ramp.

Vancouver was about the exact opposite, about staying and being. All Vancouverites really want to do is plunk themselves down and enjoy the view. Besides, in a city in a valley surrounded by mountains, with nothing over the ridgeline but 3,000 miles of snow, just where is there to go exactly? As for space-age bits of civic infrastructure dedicated to movement, there were none.

Not for a lack of trying, of course. In 1958, the Vancouver Airpark Committee put forward a multi-million-dollar proposal to dredge and pave Spanish Banks for a close-in city airport. That plan never achieved lift-off, but in 1962 the concept was back, this time with the full backing of the *Vancouver Sun*. "Revival of the Spanish Banks airport plan," said the paper of record, "is proof that good ideas don't die." The generations of beach volleyball players who have frolicked there since should be glad that every now and again, the *Sun* had been known to get things wrong.

L i v e r p o o l ,   B . C .

For the city's first settlers, all that nature surrounding the city was a sure sign of backwardness. Vancouver, they thought, should be a city of dark satanic mills, like the BC Sugar warehouse on the waterfront – six storeys of prison-cell windows and grimy red brick. To the city's early elite, this kind of belching redbrick factory was the ultimate icon of progress

The very first drawing of such a mill appeared at the bottom of an 1870s subdivision plan for the West End, on which the same early booster inked in a name expressing all his hopes for the metropolis-to-be: City of Liverpool.

The CPR insisted on "Vancouver" instead, but that didn't kill the dream. By 1912, with the Panama Canal bringing the markets of Europe and the U.S. within economical reach, Vancouver's industrial takeoff seemed

A Clerical Error

Ever notice how the streets named after trees seem to progress in alphabetical order as you go from west to east (i.e. Arbutus, Cypress in the west, Fir and Hemlock in the middle, Spruce and Willow to the east)? Only a few interlopers like Larch in the far west and Ash to the east seem to mess up the pattern. In 1885, when Canadian Pacific Railway surveyor Laughlan Alexander Hamilton laid out the street grid on the portion of the city owned by the railroad, his original intention was to have all the names progress in alphabetical order. Unfortunately, when he passed his list of names on to an underling, the papers got shuffled about, messing up the arrangement. By the time the mistake had been discovered, it was too late.

A reflecting pool and fountain make Cathedral Place on Dunsmuir Street one of the city's most relaxing public spaces, at least to judge by the number of indigent men who gather to pass the day and night in extended bouts of relaxation. What they may not know, however, is that they're slumbering over thousands of kilowatts of hydro power. The park sits atop BC Hydro's main downtown substation. The columns in the plaza double as exhaust vents, and the pool water is part of the substation cooling system.

imminent. Thus it was that the plan for a new Kitsilano Point Terminal popped up, featuring eight massive new piers and over 20 factories marching across what is now the Planetarium's lawn. Even more ambitious was the 1912 Vancouver Harbour and Dock Extension Company plan for Richmond, which turned the entire coast of Lulu Island into a breakwater, pier, and factory complex worthy of Hamburg.

Only one of these schemes ever went through: the 1913 deal allowing the Canadian Northern Railway to fill in the whole east end of False Creek, from the Main Street bridge to Clark drive. Even here the promised hotels, factories, and deep sea shipping facilities never materialized.

Still, dreams die hard. Later, would-be Liverpudlians proposed putting a Ford assembly plant on Kits Point. And in 1928, the Vancouver Terminals Company produced a revised and expanded scheme for Spanish Banks, featuring an aerodrome, 1,000-foot breakwater, 1,500 acres of industrial fill, 20 new deepwater piers, and dozens of smoking, red-brick factories. The then-separate city of Point Grey voted to approve the plan, but when Vancouver and Point Grey amalgamated in 1929, the new Vancouver council ixnayed the scheme.

The promoter was livid. "It is a malodorous mistake on the part of pretty town planners that for all time the entire waterfront must be gummed up and reserved for hot dog and fried onion joints, and allocated as a pleasaunce of yellow sands for tourists and ladies in scant attire and the like. WE WANT BUSINESS."

Brave New World Indeed

In his 1931 novel *Brave New World*, Aldous Huxley described a world in which alpha-class professionals occupied the prime real estate, while labourers, tradesmen, and others gamma-class specimens kept to suitable enclaves elsewhere. It turns out, however, that Vancouver Town Planning Commissioner Arthur G. Smith had beaten him to the punch.

"The wise foresight which Point Grey has used in planning at an early stage in its growth," wrote Smith in 1928, "should provide Vancouver with one of the most desirable residential districts ... on the continent, while those who have to gain their livelihood by manual labour should find in Hastings Townsite, and in a replanned East Vancouver, a place where they can build up modest homes which differ only in size from that of their more opulent employers."

If there's a note of triumph in Smith's words, it's because Vancouver's better classes had dreamt of such an arrangement since the city's founding, but until the advent of that new-fangled tool – zoning – in the 1920s, they had always lacked the legal tools to enforce it on the ground.

By the early '50s, unfortunately, it'd become clear that some of the gamma-workers just weren't conforming to the vision. In Strathcona – which the alphas had decided should become industrial land – the unwanted Chinese and poor white residents were stubbornly refusing to vanish.

In the booming 1950s, the city had plans for a downtown of gleaming towers and swooping freeways. The urban blight down in gamma-land Strathcona was a serious threat to the vision. "Blight is contagious," said a 1956 City of Vancouver study. "When it is found only in a few isolated structures, it can be cured quickly and easily; when it infects a whole district, it begins to threaten the economic base of the entire city, and only the most drastic and expensive remedies will suffice."

The cure – by noted urban expert Leonard Marsh – called for the entire neighbourhood to be razed, then replaced with block after block of Moscow-issue apartment towers (diagram below). True, a poll of residents revealed that over 90 percent of residents said they would never live in such a building. That, Marsh noted, was likely because they lacked the education to appreciate the opportunity they were being offered. Certainly his plan had made provisions for children –

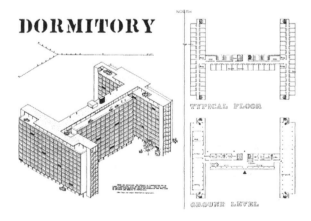

DORMITORY

Lost Subdivisions

Where is there a more likely place to gather than your own neighbourhood? And what could be more secretive than an entire community or three that, for one reason or another, do not appear on any Vancouver map?

Poor Old Cora Brown

Urban planners hate suburbs. Sprawling, car-dependent, land-hungry blight in their view. Given a Shakespearean bent, most planners would wish that these too, too solid things would melt into air. But only once has it ever happened. Located near current-day McDonald Park on Sea Island, Cora Brown was once a thriving little suburb, until the feds decided they needed a third runway at Vancouver International. Houses were expropriated – compensation being inversely proportional to the owner's access to a lawsuit-threatening lawyer – then bulldozed and left alone for 20 years until, in the early 1990s, the Airport finally got around to creating that third runway. The only remaining sign of Cora Brown's forever-lost picket fences are the different-coloured patches of grass, and the occasional exotic tree.

Finn Slough

Not only does this community not appear on any map, but it vanishes with every tide. Richmond's last true houseboat village floats on a tidal inlet south of Steveston Highway in one of the remaining agricultural bits of Richmond. To take a gander, take No. 4 Road to Finn Road, park, and look around. (Residents are generally quite tolerant of camera-toting tourists, but show restraint.) Finn Slough is extremely picturesque — not to mention picture friendly.

Cypress Estates

A rough-and-tumble kind of place, but not without its charms. For his 1970 shot-in-Vancouver film *McCabe and Mrs. Miller*, director Robert Altman built an entire frontier town in the Capilano Canyon. The film was remarkable for a number of reasons. It marked the return after several decades of big-time stars (Warren Beatty, Julie Christie) and a serious director to Vancouver. The infrastructure built to service Altman's film formed the kernel that grew into the city's now-burgeoning industry. Finally, and not least significantly, *McCabe and Mrs. Miller* marked the world film debut of ex-cop and local semi-celeb Terry David Mulligan. After filming wrapped, the western town was transformed through the magic of two-by-four studs and stucco into the modern-day subdivision of Cypress Estates.

they could play in the covered dirt area beneath the buildings, which Marsh had thoughtfully raised on pilings. He had also made provisions for the many single men in the area, designing a single massive tower to house them all.

For once the lack of federal interest in Vancouver proved a blessing. The only part of the scheme that ever received funding was the McLean Park housing project. The massive single men's dorm came to life only in the work of Vancouver artist Stan Douglas. For his 1998 video installation *Win, Place or Show*, Douglas recreated one of the dreamy modern interiors envisioned by Marsh, and filled it with two of the trapped and angry men who would have wound up living there had this ghetto in the sky ever come to be in the real world.

Ceremonial Georgia Street

In 1912, Vancouver's City Beautiful Association brought famed English landscape architect Thomas Mawson to town and asked him to do something with Georgia Street and Stanley Park. The resulting plan was a bizarre and magnificent cross between Versailles and Trafalgar Square. Coal Harbour was filled and covered with carefully cropped playing fields. Lost Lagoon was tidied up into a perfect circular lake, with a museum on one side, ceremonial gardens and stadium on the other, and in the middle a fountain with a 100-foot-high column topped by "some local historical character such as Vancouver or Cook." Georgia Street Mawson transformed into a kind of Champs Elysée leading from Lost Lagoon to a great city square in the heart of downtown.

Much as it stirred Vancouverites' hearts, Mawson's plan was nipped quickly in the bud by an unlikely coalition of tax-shy businessmen, leaders of the district labour council — who strongly suspected that once the park and playing fields had been sufficiently improved, certain classes of people would no longer be welcome — and the turn of the century equivalent of the Friends of Stanley Park defenders — who feared Mawson's call for a "judicious thinning" of the "abnormally luxuriant" trees.

Secret Steps

In 1969, untold millions tuned in to watch as astronaut Neil Armstrong first spoke these immortal words: "This is one small step for a man. One giant leap for mankind," then leapt backwards to the surface of the moon. Armstrong became a hero of the age. A mere eight years later, however, only a handful turned up to watch as Armstrong made another small step, this time into a square of wet cement to mark the opening of Vancouver's Harbour Centre observation platform.

Fortunately a visual record of the occasion still exists. A photograph hung by the bar in the observation deck shows Armstrong, flanked by a pair of Herb Tarlick characters, pulling his booted foot from a square of wet cement and giving it into the eager hands of an Asian shoeshine boy.

The cement impression has also been preserved. It sits alone, unmarked and unloved, in the stairwell by the emergency exits. No one can quite figure out exactly what to do with it, according to a Harbour Centre spokesperson. They had to move it to the stairwell because the tourists kept tripping over it.

Stonehenge II?

When future archaeologists dig through the rubble of this once-proud city, they will undoubtedly conclude that the fountain in Leg-in-Boot Square was one of our holiest shrines. Consider this: in the courtyard below the fountain, symbolic marking lines have been set into the cobblestone using red brick. Twelve of these lines radiate out from a single source like a compass rose. The cardinal directions of the compass exactly match the orientation of the city's street grid. What's more, a larger 13th line, which slashes across the other twelve at an oblique angle, joins up with the fountain's central wellspring to form an arrow which points directly towards the twin peaks of the Lions on the North Shore. Every last building of the new Concord development has been carefully designed to preserve this sightline from the fountain to the mountain. Finally, this same line, when extended through downtown, passes straight through the heart of the Vancouver Stock Exchange.

A MITE OVERCOOKED

One of the artifacts housed in Vancouver's Maritime Museum is a hearty sea biscuit, baked when Victoria was still queen and as fresh today as when it was first issued to a hungry mariner 132 years ago in 1864. The date is known with such exactitude because the sailor who got the hockey puck-like biscuit marked the date on it in India ink, and later passed the hard tack on to his descendants as an heirloom.

Indeed, mariners would do almost anything except eat these little bricks of alleged bread. Recently, the Maritime Museum discovered another hardtack biscuit, this one dating back to 1823. It had washed up on an Arctic beach after a shipwreck, then been recovered again when sailors from another wrecked vessel washed up on the same beach nearly a decade later. Even then, hungry, weary and thousands of miles from home, the shipwrecked crew preferred to leave the little biscuit uneaten.

Wishing to discover the source of these biscuits' incredible longevity, the Maritime Museum had them analyzed under a scanning electron microscope. The secret ingredient turned out to be thousands upon thousands of small insects — flour mites — ground up and baked right into the fine fresh dough. Them's good eatin'!

LOST CEMETERY

Beneath the road that encircles Stanley Park lie the graves of some of Vancouver's earliest settlers. Pioneer Cemetery, as the graveyard was called, covered virtually all of the land between the Nine O'Clock Gun and the Brockton Point Light. The remains of sailors, settlers, and Natives were brought to the cemetery by boat and buried beneath flimsy split cedar crosses. The last corpse was buried in May of 1888, the same year the road went in.

Photo: Dominic Schaefer

Far, far below the roses and rhododendrons of the VanDusen Botanical Gardens lies the vast and echoing chamber of an abandoned water reservoir, constructed in the heady boom years before World War I. The subterranean concrete vault once stored three million gallons of city drinking water, but it was drained and – supposedly – sealed in the early 1970s. That might explain the stubby beer bottle – possibly a '70s relic – but not the recently chewed-up glove.

The Air Up There

In Vancouver, even the air can be sold at a profit. In return for the rights to the airspace over top of Christ Church Cathedral at Georgia and Burrard, the developer of the neighbouring Park Place complex agreed to pay the church $300,000 a year for the next century. Beats swampland in Florida.

secret tunnels

Photo: LaBounty & Jahl

Post Office Tunnel

The main post office has its own secret escape route, a 2,400-foot concrete passageway that runs from Georgia Street all the way down to the former train station on Cordova. Equipped with an extra-long conveyor belt, the tunnel was designed for the high-speed transfer of special delivery train-mail. When it was opened in 1959 it was possible to move a mail-bag from the train station to the post office in under nine minutes. But within a few short years, airplanes had shunted trains aside, so the tunnel was mothballed. Lately, though, the multi-million-dollar boondoggle has found a new function as an eerie location for film crews in need of a secret command post, Nazi bunker, or alien hideout. Just below the escape hatch at the Cordova end of the tunnel, there's a small graffito commemorating the shoot by the TV series *Highlander*: "Duncan McLeod was here."

Quirky Museums

Everyone knows the Art Gallery and Science World. Serious museum nuts know about Hastings Mill Store on Point Grey Road. But how many know about these little gems?

Photo: Mandelbrot

The Vancouver Police Centennial Museum

A macabre little musée featuring murder weapons, scenes of the crime, and the occasional mock-corpse.
240 E. Cordova St., 665-3346

The *HMCS Discovery* Museum

To a civilian, Deadman's Island looks like a tidewater mudflat with a posh bar and clubhouse. To the navy, it's a ship, the *HMCS Discovery*. If you can sneak onboard (the *Discovery* is off-limits to all but naval types), there is a small museum, just off the drill deck, that contains pictures of naval life since 1890, artifacts, equipment, and crests.
Stanley Park

B.C. Golf Museum

Located in the little Tudor shack (a former clubhouse, actually) by the bus loop near the gates to UBC, the Golf Museum has a library and research archives, as well as exhibits showing the technological development of the sport and profiles of greats from B.C.
2545 Blanca St., 222-4653

UBC Zoological Museum

Birds, bugs, fish, plants, and slime: whatever you're into, chances are the Zoological Museum has a sample. The Ichthyology Collection, for example, has over 800,000 fishy specimens, not to mention a database searchable by name, taxa, morphological features or habitat. Each of the various collections is housed in a different room, each with a different curator. Viewing is by appointment. *Biological Sciences Bldg., 6270 University Blvd.*

Vertebrate Collection:
15,200 birds, 1,400 reptiles, 17,000 mammals. *822-4665*

Entomological Collection:
600,000 specimens of *coleoptera* (beetles), *diptera* (flies), and *hymenoptera* (bees and wasps). *822-3379; www.insecta.com*

Ichthyology Collection:
Fish and more fish. 800,000 specimens. *822-4803*

Chinatown Tunnels

Rumours of Chinatown gambling dens with underground escape routes and secret tunnels linking Gastown brothels have circulated in the city for years, popping up now and again in novels and memoirs of life in Chinatown. Engineers with the City of Vancouver pooh-poohed these tales, until in 1996 a BC Gas crew working on Alexander Street cut through the pavement and discovered air where there should have been roadbed. A startled construction worker reportedly jumped down through the gash in the asphalt into a passageway six feet in diameter, stretching at least 30 feet in either direction. One city engineer speculated that the tunnel may have been used for smuggling contraband from the docks, which once lay on one side of Alexander street, out through the basement of the Europe Hotel, which still sits on the other. Alas, the tunnel's discovery was also its undoing. City work crews returned that September and resurfaced the whole block, filling in whatever passage had remained.

The only Chinatown tunnel still in existence – at least so far as is currently known – extends underneath Carrall Street from the Sam Kee building on Pender. Access to the tunnel is via a tiny winding stairway. Though once home to baths, toilets, and barber chairs, the little passageway is now, alas, deserted.

Downtown Tunnels

"Deep underground tunnels – the kind you read of in mystery and detective novels – now link the Hotel Vancouver with the Medical-Dental Building and the Hotel Devonshire." So said the *Province* on October 22, 1942. Taking their cue from the "advanced technology of Soviet Russia," the managers of the three buildings teamed up to heat their buildings with common steam heating systems. The boilers were located in the basement of the Hotel Vancouver. The tunnels – 36 feet below the surface of the city's busiest street – housed the pipes carrying the pressurized steam. Two of the three buildings have since been demolished, but what about the tunnels? According to city engineers, there are all kinds of things lurking in the city's depths that they know nothing about whatsoever.

UBC Tunnel

Five feet wide and 200 vertical feet straight into the ground – these are the dimensions of a tunnel dug on the campus of the University of British Columbia way back in 1936 by the Vancouver and Districts Joint Sewerage and Drainage Board. Its purpose was to divert water away from the fragile cliffsides, thus preventing a repeat of the spectacular landslide that created Second Ravine. To ensure the water didn't build up too much speed, the sides of the tunnel are lined with a six-inch spiral flange, which also provides a convenient handhold for would-be climbers. The only trick? You have to find the tunnel first.

Capilano Water Tunnel

On the northern side of Stanley Park, at the junction of Stanley Park Drive and Pipeline Road, there is a pavilion, unmarked except for the letters GVRD. Within its walls, a tunnel drops nearly 130 metres straight down into the soil and rock, passing below First Narrows and coming up on the far shore near the Capilano River. At seven feet in diameter, the passageway is plenty big enough to walk through, were it not for the millions of litres of water coursing its way through from the Capilano Watershed to thirsty consumers in Vancouver.

Gastown Tunnel

Beneath the oft-trod streets of Gastown there lies a lonely tunnel. The multi-level passageway runs underneath Cordova from the parking garage of the former Woodward's department store into the Woodward's building itself. The upper level is for humans, the lower level houses the now-defunct conveyor belt system used to bring meat and other supplies in and out of Woodward's. This little tunnel hasn't seen much use since the store closed, but it is much loved by location scouts. Duncan McLeod, on yet another *Highlander* shoot, dropped by once and decided the underground passage would be a delightful place to chop off someone's head.

UBC M.Y. Williams Geological Museum

The highlight of this museum is the reconstructed skeleton of a lambeosaurus, a hooded dinosaur from the upper Cretaceous found in Alberta in 1913. In addition, there are another 39,999 items, many of them minerals of scientific interest and aesthetic appeal. *Geological Sciences Bldg., 6339 Stores Rd., 822-2449*

Chinese Cultural Centre Museum and Archives

Photo: Robert Ballantyne

The first Chinese-Canadian museum anywhere, featuring an art gallery on the main floor, a museum on the second, and an archive for those wishing to dig up the secrets of the past. *555 Columbia St., 687-0282*

The Trev Deeley Motorcycle Museum

Located in the Trev Deeley warehouse (near Ikea) in Richmond, this highly specialized museum is a Harley lover's dream, with everything from a 1913 proto-Harley to the latest in Harley hogs. Also on display are Nortons, Kawasakis, Hondas, bikes from BSA, and a number of 1940s Indian motorbikes. Rarest of specimens is perhaps the 1926 Excelsior Super X, from Chicago bike maker Schwinn. Best of all, admission to the museum is free. *1-13500 Verdun Pl., Richmond, 273-5421*

Canadian Craft Museum

Hidden away behind the '80s gothic of Cathedral Place is small gem known as the Canadian Craft Museum. Duck inside the museum lobby and there are relics from Cathedral Place's past at the Georgia Medical-Dental Building, including a number of terra cotta panels. Display-wise, the museum is dedicated to exhibiting and preserving fine craft and demonstrating its social relevance, be it in glass, wood, metal, fibre, paper or mixed media. Not what one would have thought a hard-sell in a knick-knack-happy town like Vancouver, but on most days the Craft Museum is surprisingly crowd-free, perhaps due the sheer trickiness of finding the place. During business hours, you can sneak in through Cathedral Place, while after hours you can hop up the eight or ten steps from Hornby Street. The best and most secret way, however, is to head round to Burrard Street, clamber up the small waterfall opposite the SkyTrain station, sneak through the grove of Ponderosa pines, and boom – you're out in the middle of a formal baroque square, smack in front of the Craft Museum. *639 Horby St., 687-8266*

Cleveland Dam Tunnel

Running 200 metres along the west side of the Capilano Canyon, this concrete passageway contains a pipeline that takes excess water from one side of the Cleveland dam and funnels back into the Capilano River on the other. The tunnel is just large enough to slouch through, and is lit with electric lights for the convenience of GVRD staff who make regular inspections. For the rest of the tunnel-curious public, the biggest barrier to gaining access is not the fences, locked doors, or remoteness of the site, but the total inflexibility of the Workers' Compensation Board.

Central Park Tunnel

Say you had a pipeline with lots of water, and a water reservoir with comparatively little, and the only thing preventing you from bringing the two together was the city's favourite park. Now, you could damn the torpedoes and run the pipeline right through the park, ripping up the earth and cutting down hundreds of trees in the process, but this being Burnaby – and Central Park – some tree-mad Burnabyite would likely track you down and beat you to death with a club of mountain hemlock or western red cedar. Alternatively, you could run the pipeline along the streets around the park, but the ensuing traffic disruption would be enormous and, this being the Lower Mainland, some irate Honda driver would likely track you down and beat you to death with a KLUB®.

So you do as GVRD engineer Tim Jervis did, and dig a tunnel, 825 metres long, 1.2 metres in diameter, eight metres below the ground, from the tennis courts on Patterson Avenue, beneath the horseshoe pitch and public pool, and over to the far edge of the park on Boundary. You give the pipeline project a nifty name like the Westerly Transfer, get some positive press in the local papers, and let the politicians worry about the $5.2 million bill.

VGH Tunnel

Looking for a quick way to get from 12th Avenue and Laurel up to 28th? Well, you could take the surface route, and hope that with all the traffic nowadays the 16-block trip doesn't take a lifetime. Or you could swim. Hidden beneath Laurel Street is a new but never used underground pipeline running 2.2 kilometres underground from Vancouver General Hospital south to the BC Women's Hospital on 28th. Constructed in 1995 at a cost of $4.5 million, the 45-centimetre diameter passageway was meant to, well, what is was meant to do depends on who you talk to. The construction company says it was built so the heating plants at the two hospitals could be joined up and consolidated. The hospital plant manager says it was built only as an emergency back up system for the Laurel Pavilion. The hospital planning manager says the tunnel was intended to provide steam heat to the as-yet-unbuilt VGH tower. Whatever its purpose, for the moment the sizable underground passageway sits unused and unloved, filled with a solution of water and anti-corrosion chemicals. So if you find yourself getting chased by bad guys in the basement of the VGH, you could always grab an oxygen tank, a face mask, and some medical tubing, slap it together *MacGyver*-like, and dive in.

Highbury Interceptor

Ah, the fortunate West Side. Blessed with parks and ocean and homes that are still among the priciest in the country, the West Side is also home to one of Vancouver's longest and deepest underground passageways, the Highbury Interceptor. Running from Highbury and 4th Avenue in Kitsilano all the way downhill to the Fraser River, the Highbury Interceptor is more than four kilometres long and in places nearly a kilometre below the earth's surface. Sewage and rainwater from Boundary Road and points westward run first to the Interceptor, and then out to the sewage plant on Iona Island. At regular intervals, GVRD sewer inspectors get to hop in the boat moored at the Kitsilano end and drift gently down through the darkened caverns to the Fraser River.

Secret HQs

With most commercial real estate in Vancouver, chances are there's a sign out front to let the casual passer-by know what's going on inside. Not these three:

CSIS

4720 Kingsway, Burnaby
Most secret of all, perhaps, is this nondescript building in the Metrotown mall, the Pacific outpost of the Canadian Security Intelligence Service, Canada's answer to the CIA. What does CSIS do exactly? The CSIS spokeswoman wouldn't say. However, should you ever want to snitch on some of your more dubious friends and acquaintances, she did point out the local CSIS contact number: 528-7400.

Fall from Greatness

Photo: Mandelbrot

MasterCard Processing Centre

1745 West 8th Ave.

This unsigned and unlisted brick-red building has the architectural feel of a prison, with narrow recessed windows of one-way glass, and a sweeping surveillance camera on the roof. Inside, vast amounts of cash are tracked and transferred.

B.C. Centre for Disease Control

655 West 12th Ave.

Well, there's a sign outside B.C.'s own hot zone, but that's because you don't want to know what's going on inside. This is the spot where all the various bacilli, viruses, and other virulent and debilitating buggies are caught, isolated, and kept so they can be studied to find out what makes them tick.

The Dominion Building, at 207 West Hastings Street, across from Victory Square, contains its own sad and tragic secret. For a time at the turn of the century, the terra cotta-clad structure with the three-storey mansard roof was the highest in the empire and the pride of its architect, J.S. Hellyer. Within a year, however, the Sun Building across the street took away that title. Worse, Hellyer tripped on the treads of his prized trapezoidal staircase, and fell to his death.

A Monumental Room

Vancouver's Terry Fox monument has few admirers. It stands lonely and forlorn at the foot of Robson, looking like a top-heavy Chinese pagoda. Its top half is so big and blocky, you'd swear there was a room inside. Which there is. To get in you have to open a trap door in the roof of the parking garage one floor down, then climb up through one

Photo: Mandelbrot

of the monument's two supporting pillars. What's inside? Computers, theatre lights, control switches, and film projectors, all unused. The original concept, according to architect Franklin Allen, was to project images from the Marathon of Hope onto the back-projection screens that form the room's walls. BC Place built and equipped the monument's projection chamber, and then changed their minds. They didn't like the idea after all.

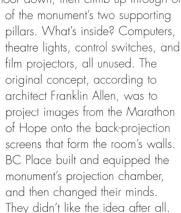

big ticket houses

So what's Greater Vancouver's ritziest enclave? Near the beginning it was certainly Shaughnessy, though Point Grey and SW Marine had their supporters, and then West Van seemed to be taking over, and now it seems to be Shaughnessy again. As the eldest of the group, Shaughnessy certainly has the best selection of dirty secrets, but here's a selection from all four:

4769 West Second
Recent Assessment (2000): $5,736,000

West Point Grey appears to be the favoured haunt of VSE promoters seeking social validation. Whether that's because of the views, the proximity to water, or the relative ease of dumping a WPG mansion when bankruptcy or a trading ban looms is difficult to say. What is certain is that the late Murray Pezim bought this house, which features two swimming pools, two steam rooms, a tennis court, a ballet exercise room, an elevator, wine cellar, five bedrooms, and a gourmet kitchen with walk-in cooler — just down from the *Gone with the Wind*-style mansion (Recent Assessment: $5,040,000) at 4707 Belmont that once belonged to Nelson Skalbania.

Nelson relinquished Tara to wife Audrey as part of their divorce settlement, just before the rest of his empire did an Atlanta and burned to the ground. The Pez sold his place for a miserable $5.5 million in 1991, just after selling the B.C. Lions and just before getting hit with a one-year trading ban from the VSE.

1402 McRae Avenue
Recent Assessment (2000): $4,207,000

This Tudor-revival mansion was built in 1912 for Walter Cameron Nichol, founder and publisher of the *Province* newspaper and B.C. lieutenant-governor for much of the 1920s. It is currently owned by Toni Bentley, widow of Canadian Forest Products founder Leopold, and mother of Canfor's current president Peter. Featuring dark, broad eaves and half-timbered walls surrounding an exquisitely manicured English garden, the house seems to bespeak its original owner's need for social acceptance, and his desire to keep his secrets to

Big Ticket Condos

Ever wonder how much a luxury hi-rise condo in Vancouver would set you back? Here are some of Vancouver's ritziest rises:

Kingswood
As its name suggests, the exuberant Kingswood at 1596 West 14th Avenue aims to be a castle-in-the-sky. Each suite features over-the-top features like hand-set marble flooring, 24-karat gold-plated bathroom fixtures, hand-painted domed ceilings, or — Idaho being taken — your own private elevator. Up at the very top, the two-storey penthouse unit is listed for $6,250,000. The suite offers a stunning view of the city and while the hoi polloi in other spots might well be enjoying the same view, it's a safe bet they can't do it from within the realm of a jetted pool in the private roof-top cabana, while one's minions, lackeys, and assorted hangers-on can frolic among themselves in the rather less secluded hot tub.

CONDO CLEARCUT

Nearly everyone knows the Eugenia building, if not by name then by the sight of the lone oak tree that sprouts from the penthouse of the Beach Avenue tower. Architect Richard Henriquez's design harkens back to the days when Vancouver was little more than a clearing in a clearcut. The stone wall surrounding the tower reproduces the foundations of the four pioneer houses that once occupied the site. The pin oak on the penthouse patio reaches the same heights as the soaring firs that stood on the shores of English Bay before the axe-men came. A few tree stumps even lay scattered around the foot of the tower. Unlike the originals, these stumps are concrete.

himself. A phenomenally successful businessman, Nichol, like many self-made men, had much less success relating to his children.

Son Jack, in particular, seemed far more interested in spending the family wealth than in learning how it was made. In 1924, the jazz-age playboy wandered down to a party at the 3851 Osler Street home of Freddie Baker. The next morning, Baker's Chinese houseboy found the body of twenty-two-year-old nanny Janet Smith lying dead in the basement. Jack Nichol's name was brought up frequently among the list of likely culprits. Thanks to the efforts of his father, however, young Jack was never charged or even seriously investigated. Some years later, whether from guilt or simply from the stress of spending the family fortune on a life of dissolute hedonism, Jack was committed to psychiatric care. From his private room he was said to call out from time to time, "I know who the murderer was!" No one listened, and the case was never solved.

4857 Belmont Drive
Recent Assessment (2000): $5,951,000

Henry Kaiser was a giant of his age. Born a shopkeeper's son in Iowa, he pulled himself up by his bootstraps to become an industrial titan, the head of Kaiser Steel, Roosevelt's right-hand man in the industrial effort of World War II and, as the creator of the Liberty ship, the only grandfather-of-a-future-Vancouverite (how's that for obscure) ever to be immortalized in a Bugs Bunny cartoon. Alas, what is found in the father is oft lost in later generations.

Henry's grandson, Edgar Kaiser Jr., was more interested in French fries than steel. In 1987, the Spud Stop king built a 21,000-square-foot mansion on this three-acre property and filled it with rare and expensive paintings and *objets d'art*. A little over a year later, on Christmas Day 1988, a fire that started on the Christmas tree burned the house to the ground. It turns out that although there was an indoor pool, there was no sprinkler system.

Kaiser's wife Judith Dee left him while the ashes were still smoldering, receiving $15,300 a month in maintenance payments. The ruin of a house Kaiser sold off for a dollar. It was later rebuilt by one Mohammed Mohseni. In 1998, Kaiser applied to have his ex-wife's maintenance payments reduced, claiming that his net worth had fallen from $32 million in 1988 to a mere $4 million.

1920 SW Marine Drive
Recent Assessment (2000): $5,000,000

Like many a well-respected family, the Reifels made their money in the liquor business, distilling then distributing the demon rum to the demon Yanks south of the border. The elder Reifel – Harry – made a name for himself at a customs inquiry when he complained that he'd paid over $100,000 to the Liberal Party in order to change its mind on prohibition, and hadn't received his money's worth.

Photo: Heather Dean

In 1931, son George built Casa Mia on 20 acres of land, just down from his little brother Harry's place (Rio Vista, 2170 SW Marine Dr., $3,637,000). Persistent rumour suggests that tunnels connect the two estates, both to each other and to the flatlands on the Fraser where the family used to launch their rum-running expeditions.

130 South Oxley
Recent Assessment (2000): $6,972,000

Is it a bird, is it a plane, is it an *X-Files* location? It's only the UFO-like home of Flora Bosa and her husband Nat, the developer of Citygate and other Vancouver properties. Those expecting an alien-breeding facility beneath the round green roof and ring of porthole windows that top this odd-looking structure are in for a disappointment. There's nothing more exotic than a swimming pool, in a room with huge glass walls and a sweeping view of English Bay, where Bosa no doubt entertains his developer buddies – who all carry electronic organizers and cellphones, who converse in incomprehensible codes like FSR, DCLs, Dus, and "negative absorption," and who always seem to have with them at least one exceptionally attractive earthling of the blonde female variety. Okay, so maybe it is an alien-breeding facility. The rest of the ultra-modern, open-plan home – including a five-car garage and chimneys cast in the same curving lines as the outside fence – serves only as the abode of the man frequently called "the smartest man in real estate."

Quebec Place

England, in the darkest days of World War II, took down all of its street and road signs in order to confuse the expected Nazi invaders. The USSR during the Cold War did much the same; entire cities of vital strategic interest were disappeared from the map. That being the case, the question becomes just what is there on Quebec Place that's so all-fire important? Not Quebec Street – that well-marked north-south thoroughfare that runs through the heart of the city – but Quebec Place, a small, secluded, unmarked street, hidden a block or so west of the barrage of antique shops and ethnic restaurants on yuppifying south Main. Never heard of it? Not surprising, considering it doesn't appear on a single city map. Indeed, so cleverly hidden is this little enclave that unless you're personally escorted on site, there's little or no chance of actually finding it. What's there to justify such seclusion? City officials aren't saying, possibly because, of the two houses that make their home on Quebec Place, at least one is owned by a ranking member of the City Hall nomenclatura.

Rose Street

The East Side's Shangri-La. Nearly impossible to find, and so charming it's difficult to leave once you're there. This one-block street lies between Napier and William Streets, two blocks east of Victoria Drive. It harbours a tribe of people with a taste for renovated older houses done up in brilliant colours, with riotous flower gardens front and back. Tell a relative before you set out, just in case you don't return.

Stephens Street

This short stretch between West 4th Avenue and Broadway harbours the city's finest remaining collection of Craftsman-style houses. Houses on opposite sides of the street at 2220 and 2221 were made famous as the lair and target of Richard Dreyfuss's and Emilio Estevez's spying in the movie *Stakeout*.

Hawks Avenue

Strathcona's an interesting kind of place. Younger neighbourhoods like Shaughnessy or Killarney were built exclusively for one class or another. In Strathcona, however, no one yet knew in which direction the city would develop, so tenements and quite substantial homes came to exist side by side. The result is a street like Hawks Avenue, where the 500-block has working man's hovels, restored and painted brilliant colours, just down from the string of Edwardian middle-manager's houses in the 700-block.

1690 Mathews Avenue
Recent Assessment (2000): $2,454,000

Controversy is nothing new to Glen Brae, one of the most spectacular houses in Shaughnessy and the current home of the Canuck Place hospice for children. There was a time in the 1920s when the mansion was the most notorious spot in all of B.C.

It had all begun so well. When the mansion was built for lumber baron William Tait in 1910, the local press gushed over its expensive and unique appointments – the dance floor sprung with seaweed; the fence of thistle-shaped wrought-iron, imported from Scotland. But Tait was to enjoy his house for less than 10 years. After he died, his widow found the mansion too expensive to maintain, and in 1920 she moved out, leaving the estate completely empty.

Photo: City of Vancouver Archives

Enter the Ku Klux Klan. The Klan began making inroads in Canada in the early 1920s so when Klan organizer Major Luther Powell arrived in Vancouver in October of 1925, he didn't lack for attention. 500 people showed up for the Klan's first Vancouver meeting on October 12, 1925 at the North Vancouver Agricultural hall.

Attendance had swelled to 2,000 by the second meeting on November 13 in the ballroom of the Hotel Vancouver. Some were merely spectators, but a sizable number paid the $10 fee and joined up as Knights of the Klan.

Powell went looking for a local headquarters. Glen Brae was still empty, and the widow Tait was more than happy to have a tenant. So it was that in the late fall of 1925, the grandest mansion in the richest neighbourhood in the entire province became the site of the Imperial Palace of the Kouncil of the Kanadian Knights of the Ku Klux Klan. Twice a month, men dressed in sinister-looking white hoods would assemble in Glen Brae.

That is, until late 1926, when the King Kleagle himself, Major Powell, went south to Louisiana with a goodly portion of the BC Klan's treasury. Lacking money to pay the rent, the Klansmen were evicted. And although they tried to carry on, moving to a new office at 304 Georgia St., they lost momentum and, by 1930, the BC Klan was dead. In the meantime, however, Glen Brae had been occupied by an equally childish and potentially destructive group of people: it had been rented out as a kindergarten.

hotel histories

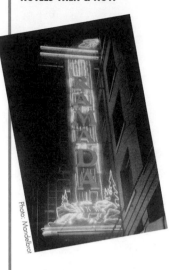

Photo: Mandelbrot

There are, in the whole length and breadth of the civilized world, about 100 hotels that rate five-diamond status from the American Automobile Association. Vancouver has three of them, more than any other city in the world, New York included. And not only is the service exceptional at these and other Vancouver hotels, so too are the secrets:

How Bubba Takes Up Space

Photo: courtesy Waterfront Centre Hotel

Talk about an entourage. Accommodating U.S. President Bill Clinton and all his various aides, advisors, flunkies, and functionaries for the four-day APEC conference in November 1997 required fully 431 of the Waterfront Centre Hotel's 489 guest rooms. Of those, 431 were occupied by the President and friends: 54 were earmarked for the Secret Service; 55 were set aside for White House communications; 13 were needed by the State Department; 42 were taken up by the Secretary of State; 17 were used by the U.S. trade delegation; 58 were required for White House staff; and 192 were for members of the press and the APEC coordinating office.

We're lucky he didn't take more. According to a source, while the President waited for the hotel elevator after returning from a golf game with Jean Chretien, he was heard to make the following remark to one of his secret service agents, "We had to call the game. The Prime Minister lost Saskatchewan and Manitoba to me on the first two holes. He didn't want to throw away any more of the country."

Famous Faces on Georgia

The Crowne Plaza Hotel Georgia has to its credit a notable string of firsts. It was the first and only Vancouver hotel to play host to two future English kings (Edward,

For years the SRO (single room occupancy) hotel was a Vancouver tradition. In exchange for a bed, a sink, and a toilet down the hall, residents handed over a steady $325 a month. The tavern selling cut-rate draught on the ground floor vacuumed up any money left over. Owners got sort of rich, poor folks got sort of housed, and the approximately 12,000 SRO rooms gave the city's downtown eastside its slightly seedy aura of decay. Everyone was sort of happy. But with the recent gentrification of Granville Street and the downtown eastside, owners have been tossing out the poor folks, slapping on some paint, replacing the bar with a coffee shop or nightclub, and reincarnating their once-proud fleabags as mid-priced hotels. The following is a guide to some of the more recent transformations:

Prince of Wales, and his younger brother George, on August 18, 1927); the first to break the colour bar back in the 1950s by allowing in Louis Armstrong; the first place ever to give Jimmy Pattison a job (as busboy); and the first hotel ever to have a murder attempt broadcast live from the hotel coffee shop. That last event occurred on September 23, 1968, when an argument broke out between VSE stock promoter Jimmy Hill and another man named Danny Cackle. Cackle left in a huff, returned with a .38 and pumped five bullets into Hill. Radio host Jack Webster, who was broadcasting from an upstairs studio, rushed down with a portable unit and began describing the scene: "My God! It's Jimmy Hill. He's dead. No, he's alive, I see him moving!"

Other notable Hotel Georgia guests have included John Barrymore (1935), The Beatles (1964; actually, the Fab Four only used the room as a decoy so they could flee fan-free to Seattle), Maria Callas (who insisted on a piano in her suite), Princess Elizabeth and Prince Philip (1951), and Katharine Hepburn (who wanted fish every night at midnight).

Hotel Noir

When there are nefarious transactions or shady dealings to be done, the Vancouver hotel of choice seems to be the Westin Bayshore. Why this should be so is not exactly clear. The hotel itself is really quite nice, and its setting – on the shore, by the park – is closer to the Riviera than to Raymond Chandler's L.A. Perhaps the pattern was set just a few months after the Bayshore opened, when a guest gunned down a city policeman and the hotel's assistant manager.

There are other examples. In 1971, notorious American recluse Howard Hughes holed up in a suite in the Bayshore for four months, until some less-than-subtle questions from Revenue Canada convinced him to move on. In 1990, then-B.C. premier Bill Vander Zalm chose the Bayshore's hotel bar as the place to pick up $20,000 in cold hard cash from Taiwanese real estate developer Tan Yu. What the money was for, the Zalmster wouldn't say.

Not even time or distance seems to weaken the pattern. In 1998, when noted aging libertine Hugh Hefner decided to send out his latex-covered Playboy Bus on a continent wide quest for a new photographable playmate, what site did he choose, of all the places on earth, from which to begin the search? The parking lot of the Westin Bayshore.

The Dome of Doom

The Dome of Doom on top of the five-diamond Pan Pacific Hotel exerts a powerful influence on the city of Vancouver. Coming into the city along the Stanley Park causeway, it's the first thing that appears: 12 metres high, 19 metres around, a great green hemisphere riding high above the sails. When the recent Coal Harbour development was designed, entire skyscrapers were moved about just to preserve this corridor unobstructed. So what's inside the dome to make it worth such a fuss? Dust, elevator equipment, and a fully functional but now incomprehensible computer that used to run the light show that used to blaze out from the dome across the city. Oh, and some pigeons.

The Pan Pacific gets its fair share of the beautiful people. Robin Williams stayed there during the shooting of *Jumanji* (he apparently had everyone hoarse with laughter). So did Luciano Pavarotti (ditto, but drop the laughter). For its greatest examples of customer service, the hotel even prepares little anecdotes for internal circulation. The following are actual examples, given in the hotel's own words:

Groupie Care: A woman friend of a professional athlete who'd been staying at the hotel thought her room had been taken care of by her friend for another night. It had not. When she realized she was alone in the city with nowhere to go she had a meltdown in the lobby. Unfortunately, the Pan Pacific was fully occupied, as it often is. So the hotel booked her into another hotel … and paid for it.

Grumpy Care: One night a VIP decided his pillow was not fluffy enough and became quite agitated. Unfortunately the in-house seamstress had gone home. So a young woman employee took apart a pillow, stuffed extra feathers in – despite her allergy to feathers – and got the VIP his fluffier pillow. She ended up puffy-eyed with allergies. The VIP never knew what it had taken to make him happy.

A Sting for Four Seasons

Discretion is the watchword at the Four Seasons, another five-diamond hotel. Reports about guests and visitors are almost impossible to obtain, unless of course they happen to be entered in evidence in B.C. Supreme Court. Such is the case with Glen Sebastian Burns.

A 19-year-old from North Vancouver, Burns was the target of an undercover RCMP investigation into the brutal murder of his friend Atif Rafay's parents and sister. Police were working on inveigling him into a life of crime, in the hopes that he would soon feel safe enough to confess any past crimes to his new criminal buddies. On the night of May 6, 1995, the two undercover cops had a bit of theatre planned for Burns. They brought him to a suite in a luxury hotel room. Minutes later another cop dropped off a duffel bag full of cash. They all sat down to count it.

It took awhile, as there was $250,000 in all. That done, they shared some beers, relaxed, and like old friends, started to shoot the breeze a bit. Burns began to tell them of his plans for a film, a semi-autobiographical account of criminals who get away with their crimes. The room was wired, so the police got all of it on tape. And though he didn't confess that night, it took only a few more meetings before he did. The scene of that first bit of police theatre: Room 2510 of Vancouver's Four Seasons Hotel.

A Grand Problem

Photo: Blaine Kyllo

Showbiz can be such a headache. The luxurious Westin Grand Hotel opened in April 1999, right next to Vancouver's new Broadway-style music hall, the Ford Centre for the Performing Arts. The location was considered a key selling feature — not only were rooms and lounges were given musical names, but the building itself was shaped in the form of a very large grand piano. Unfortunately, shortly after the Grand opened, the Ford Theatre closed, a victim of impresario Garth Drabinsky's crash-and-burn-and-only-escape-jail-by-the-skin-of-your-teeth school of business management. Fortunately for the folks at Westin, the fundamentals were still good. The Grand is also within easy walking distance of GM Place, Yaletown, and the Robson Street shopping area. When the time comes for remodelling, the Westin could even take inspiration from the across-the-street Public Library, and reshape itself in the form of a great big book.

A Tall Order

Photo: Blaine Kyllo

What's black and white and seen all over? The new Wall Centre Tower, which at 48 storeys pokes its slender see-through head well above every other high-rise in the city. And why, you may ask, is the glass clear for only the top 24 floors, while below that it's black as pitch? The usual reasons: ego, pride, politics, and bad note taking.

As originally designed by architect Peter Busby, the tall, narrow tower was crystal clear from top to bottom. That was the plan, model included, that convinced Vancouver City Council to relax its normal 30-storey height limit and instead allow the Wall Tower to soar up 400 feet.

City Hall thought the clear glass was an integral part of the design. Developer Peter Wall had even given city bureaucrats a little sample piece of clear glass to scratch and sniff and peer through, as if to assure themselves that Wall had nothing up his sleeve. But as it turned out, Wall himself much preferred black glass – the kind found on limos, aviator shades, and the two high-rise towers he'd already built on the same site. So when it came time to build, he gave instructions to plate it black.

The building was a third done before anyone at the city noticed, at which point city planners had a small but serious conniption. But as it tuned out, the happy planner in charge of dotting i's and crossing t's had clearly forgotten to specify the exact glass colour. As for the sample, it had vanished. Legally, the city had no recourse; while planners and politicians hopped madly up and down, Wall kept the black glass going up.

Why did he stop? When asked, the city and Wall mouth platitudes about win-win situations and the spirit of good-natured compromise. Of course, though it lacked any legal recourse, the city might well have made Wall aware of its other forms of influence, such as the ability to deny him building permits for so much as a lemonade stand for the rest of his natural life. At which point the intrinsic beauty of clear glass no doubt became much easier to see.

HISTORY REPEATS ITSELF

See Borneo natives. Experience the sunrise atop Manchu Picchu. Touch rainforest blowguns, and quiver at the sight of shrunken heads. For years, all this and more awaited at the Museum of the Exotic World. Located in the front two rooms of Harold and Barbara Morgan's lime green house on Main Street, the museum featured hundreds of photos and curios from Harold and Barbara's three-plus decades of world travel. Harold was both curator and tour guide. When grounded by a bum heart some years ago, Harold collected up his photos and keepsakes, put them inside gold gilt frames, and hung them up over every square inch of available space. As you stepped into the main gallery Harold would flick off the TV and regale you with tales of distant lands, with the highlight of any visit coming with the story of Harold's visit to the Centaur people, a little known tribe from the southern reaches of the African continent. If you stayed more than ten minutes Harold – whose memory was not what it once was – would tell the story of the Centaur people twice.

Harold, alas, recently set out on the greatest journey of all. His prized collection of oddities is taking a much shorter trip. Wife Barbara recently put the entire collection up for auction. The winning bidder was the Museum of Anthropology, which planned to photo-document the exhibit and then store it away in crates someplace in the dark end of a warehouse. When it came time to hand over the $3,000 winning bid, however, it was discovered the chief anthropologist had gone walkabout. So the auctioneer contacted the first runner up, Alexander Lamb (of antique fame), who was delighted to add the Exotic World collection to his existing Wunderkammer store *(3271 Main Street)*. The vanished anthropologists – now returned – plan to catalogue and document the collection in its old and new settings. New to the exhibit, and much anticipated by Exotic World aficionados, are Harold's entire collection of 8 mm films and audio cassettes. Visit and see Harold looping endlessly.

Vancouver – Paris. Paris – Vancouver. Thousands of similarities immediately jump to mind. Well, okay. One does anyway. Stand at the base of the Arc de Triomphe and look out in any direction and you'll see kilometre after kilometre of open boulevard cutting arrow straight through the heart of Paris. The boulevards are the work of Baron Haussman, a 19th-century aristocrat who chopped up much of medieval Paris in order, he said, to make the city both more beautiful and more functional. Critics, including Emile Zola, noted he was also knocking down an awful lot of poor folks' homes, while simultaneously clearing out a nice broad path for squads of cavalry and truncheon-swinging soldiers. That rioting mobs of working class folks from these same tenements periodically threw barricades across the narrow streets and took control of the central city was said to be entirely coincidental.

To see Vancouver's version of the Champs Elysée, stand on the south side of the Harbour Centre observation deck and look south. Seen from above, Richards Street appears as block after city block of parking lots. In the 1920s and '30s, Richards used to boast big Edwardian homes, the abode of the working-class folks who staffed the port and nearby railyards, sent their kids to the Central School, and played lacrosse on the public park that is now the parking lot opposite the Beatty Street Armoury. In the early '50s, a powerful city bureaucrat decided that downtown was not the place for people. The working class homes were rezoned and then razed to the ground, transformed by legislative fiat into parking space. The people themselves moved elsewhere. That these were the same folks who in 1938 had had come out *en masse* to watch and partake in the Vancouver's great Post Office Riot was said to be entirely coincidental.

Photo: Ian Lindsay/Vancouver Sun

Arthur Erickson, Vancouver's most famous architect, is a mass of contradictions. The one-time prophet of a massive East Side freeway (don't think of it as a road, he told doubters, think of it as a large building that just happens to have a road on top) doesn't even drive himself. The life-long prophet of cities that were *Larger! Taller! Denser!* (10 million people is just the beginning, he once said of Vancouver), Erickson has lived most of his life in a secluded little cottage in the far off reaches of Point Grey. Most confounding of all, the man who was commissioned in the early 1970s to give Vancouver a new civic square – a place where the great masses could meet and gather – doesn't much like the masses. "I wonder what it is about the middle class I hate so much?" he wondered aloud to his one and only biographer.

The resulting civic space – Robson Square – shows all these contradictions. A green and elegant refuge in the heart of the city, Erickson's garden and square are defended from the prying eyes of the bourgeoisie by a deep ditch and a high concrete wall. Access to the gardens and the adjacent sunken square is limited by a series of convoluted, confusing, forbidding and sometimes downright dangerous stairways, doors and walkways. Few among the common folk ever make it in. Indeed, Vancouver's civic gathering place has been notably described as a spot where on a sunny day in the middle of the lunch-hour you could dance a jig naked while setting off rescue flares and smoking the world's largest joint without anyone ever noticing.

Perhaps the first and only time Robson Square saw crowds was on opening day in October of 1978, when the elite of civic and provincial politics gathered to declare the $160 million, publicly funded project open. The only one missing was Arthur. He'd gotten a lift to the ceremony – Erickson riding shotgun and providing the directions. They made it down into the underground parking garage, but the multitude of levels and elevators and exits and stairways defeated even the designer himself. On his way to the grand opening of his great civic square, Arthur Erickson got lost.

Secret Vistas

In a city with as many dedicated view junkies as Vancouver, finding a spot to contemplate the mountains and sea in something approaching splendid isolation can be quite a challenge. The observation platform at the Harbour Centre offers a great 360° perspective, but you have to fend off the persistently perky tourist guides. The parking lot at 10th and Sasamat offers a great view of Simon Fraser and, on a clear day, Mount Baker, but only if you can filter out the sounds of necking teenagers. All is not completely lost, however. What follows is a shortlist of semi-private public places to contemplate the vistas:

Vancouver Public Library

When architect Moshe Safdie unveiled his Colosseum-like design for the new central library, it included a luxurious roof garden where, at least in his artist's renditions, members of the public could wander amidst the trees and luxurious shrubs like so many latter-day Christians. The building is now a reality, and the garden is there, but the public, alas, has been fenced out. That's not to say the downtown library doesn't offer some splendid views, you just have to know where to look. On the Georgia Street side of the building is a set of double-glass doors embossed with the provincial seal. Go through them and take the elevator up to the 8th-floor offices of the Labour Relations Board. Step out and through the single glass door on your right, and you're on a large and nearly private downtown balcony, just one floor below the off-limits rooftop garden. On the north side, a curved colonnade frames views of the downtown core. Wander over to the south side and there are even more impressiveviews, both of Queen Elizabeth Park and the city's west side. Look down through the glass ceiling of the library atrium and you might even see your friends hanging out in the building's main concourse, a full seven stories below. Stick out your tongue, just for fun.

tips for bookworms

There are lots of secrets to be uncovered at the Vancouver Public Library at Georgia and Homer. Here are a couple of them:

Web Feats

One set of letters (www.vpl.vancouver.bc.ca) combined with two sets of numbers (library I.D. number and your phone number) provides the key to a vast array of information: 17 different databases and directories, including the CBCA (Canadian Business & Current Affairs) and Canadian NewsDisc, both of which will give you access to full text online articles from newspapers and magazines from across North America; the full text of the *New York Times* for the most recent 90 days; Quick Facts, a database with instant answers to pressing questions; and the Community Organization Directory – your link to Vancouver associations of mushroom sniffers, Esperanto speakers, Nude Creative Anachronists, and other kinkier groups.

Roping Them In

A little known treasure hidden away downstairs in the children's section the main library is the Harvey Southam Children's Program Room. The large circular chamber is hung with original artwork of prominent B.C. children's book illustrators including Ann Blades, Celia King, and Ron Lightburn. Topping off the space is a skylight that gives a spectacular view of the library. When not roped off, the room is most often used as a storytelling spot for groups of children. Still untold is the full tale of how namesake Harvey met his end, but then neither is that exactly a tale for children. Call for reservations as events fill up fast (331-4045).

art for the people

Modest Differences

Danish visitors to the Stanley Park seawall might be forgiven for thinking Copenhagen's *Little Mermaid* has a twin in the form of the Elek Imredy statue *Girl in a Wetsuit*. On closer inspection, however, it becomes evident that the two bear no relation to each other whatsoever. Being native to the sea, the mermaid wears no mask. Being Danish, she also wears no clothes. The demure Canadian wetsuit girl has both. That's not to say the *Girl in a Wetsuit* isn't interested in reproduction. Hidden away in the bowels of the Maritime Museum's storage room on Kits Point is an exact fibreglass mold that would allow her to clone herself, completely asexually.

Artistry is Fleeting

Down on Wreck Beach – just to the right of the semi-permanent concession stands – is a rock with a few small smidgens of some off-colour substance. Is it the work of a passing seagull, or the remains of some illicit Wreck Beach ritual best left unmentioned? No, it's art.

In 1969, American artist Robert Smithson, now considered the founding figure of "Earth Art," visited Vancouver for an exhibition at the Vancouver Art Gallery. While he was here he executed an outdoor work called *Glue Pour*, consisting of a large bucket of bright orange glue, which he dumped over a slight incline at Wreck Beach and allowed to solidify after 10 or so feet of flow. Most of the work was washed away after several seasons of Vancouver's heavy rain, but touches here and there remain. Smithson also proposed a much larger work called *Glass Covered Island*, which would have dumped tons of broken waste glass on a small island in the Strait of Georgia. A public uproar ensued, and the project was cancelled. Most of the arguments focused on potential harm to seabirds. Smithson, who was killed in a plane crash in 1973, remains a canonical figure in contemporary art.

Marine Building

On the ground floor of the Marine Building is a two-storey arched window done up in stained-glass looking out over the harbour. It's nice, if a trifle gaudy. Eighteen and a half floors up there's something better. When the Marine Building was built in the late 1920s, it was architecturally acceptable to leave the stairs half outside. On each landing, an open stone archway looks out over harbour. The only thing between you and a fabulous view of the North Shore are a few irregularly spaced wrought iron bars, now the better part of 100 years old.

Photo: Blaine Kyllo

Photo: Blaine Kyllo

St. Paul's Hospital

For this substantial downtown refuge, enter through the Burrard Street entrance (directly opposite the Burrard Motor Inn), turn left past the CNIB Tuck Shop, and pop into the elevator just before the information booth. Go up to the 4th floor, then follow the little cup-and-saucer signs that supposedly mean cafeteria, but really lead to a vast rooftop garden, complete with a fountain, rock garden, little benches for contemplating life, and thick laurel hedges where — at the right time in the evening — hundreds of little songbirds come back to nest and sing.

YWCA Downtown

This is likely the least visited rooftop garden in the city, thanks to a complicated internal structure of elevators and stairwells that make it impossible to reach if you're actually using the Y's facilities. For random passers-by, however, it's dead easy. Walk into the Hornby Street facility, take the elevator to the 5th floor, and walk out into the sunshine. If you couldn't afford a room at the Y itself, you could probably camp out here for several weeks before anybody noticed.

On the curbside on Homer Street between Drake and Pacific, six metal receptacles sit atop cracked concrete pedestals (above). They were created by artist Marc Lewis, and placed on the street as part of the city's public art program. Three of the receptacles are time capsules; they contain relics of western civilization, like the works of Karl Marx, old socks, and copies of the *Vancouver Sun*. The other three receptacles hold trash. The trick lies in discerning which is which. Meanwhile, around the corner on Pacific Boulevard, artist Alan Storey has installed a dynamic piece of art that, on first glance, looks suspiciously like a set of air vents (below). And so it is. But behind the metal slats, cylindrical fan blades inscribed with letters of the alphabet spin round, flashing out messages letter by letter. It's been said that when one peers down at the spinning metal wheels, the Oracle at Concord seems to flash out the following bit of wisdom: C-O-N-D-O -S . . . L-E-A-K. If true, it's hardly a secret.

Photo: Blaine Kyllo

The Lost Explorer

Poor Christopher Columbus. He could find his way from the Azores to the Caribbean and back, but he couldn't navigate the tricky shoals of political correctness in modern-day Vancouver. A few years ago, the city of Genoa, Italy offered to build a Columbus monument in Vancouver to commemorate the 500th anniversary of the explorer's voyage of discovery to the new world. The city hemmed and hawed. "Commemorate"? "Discovery"?

After much delay, the city settled on what it thought was an appropriate location – an isolated spot by the Skytrain tracks in an unfashionable section of Clark Drive, overlooking the industrial lands by Great Northern Way. In 1996, 504 years after Columbus sailed the ocean blue, a monument was erected, a statue of the admiral himself looking out towards the sea, surrounded by a little semi-circular colonnade. Within months, all reference to Columbus had been obliterated. A new spray-painted legend read: "500 Years of Genocide."

The statue has since been removed from the Clark Drive location, and is to be reinstalled elsewhere. Exactly where is the secret.

Love's Labour Lost

Sculptor Beatrice Lennie was blessed with an ability to please all comers. Some of her best work was done on commission for the oligarchs at Shaughnessy Private Hospital, but when asked to carve a panel commemorating the wartime cooperation of the U.S. and Canadian labour movements, Lennie knew how to produce. The finished product is a fabulous example from the now-lost school of socialist realism. It shows square-jawed workers holding the tools that made the weapons that made the world safe for democracy. Actually, it shows quite a lot of the weapons too: great fleets of bombers flying off to beat the hell out of the fascist oppressors of the working man. Alas, in this cold and cynical age, no one seems to want the sculpture anymore. It hangs above the entranceway of what used to be the Labour Temple at 307 W. Broadway, but is now the home of cut-rate fleece and Gore-tex merchant Nadex Sports.

Totem Pole Sightings

The grove of totem poles at Stanley Park is on every tourist's hit list, and most are also aware of the excellent collection of poles out back of the Museum of Anthropology on the UBC

Photo: courtesy UBC Museum of Anthropolgy

campus. Serious pole afficionados with hefty wallets and a yen for a pole of their own can visit Douglas Reynolds Gallery (2335 Granville Street) or Eagle Spirit Gallery (1814 Maritime Mews); prices start at $1,500 a foot. For those who just like to look, here are some other sites, many of them listed in the book Looking at Totem Poles by Hilary Stewart:

Writing on the Wall

Photo: Blaine Kyllo

Museum of Anthropology

6393 NW Marine Dr.

In 1962, a Bill Reid totem pole was raised at the entrance to the Museum of Anthropology. Nearly 40 years later, it had become too fragile to stay outdoors, and was replaced by "Respect to Bill Reid Pole," designed and carved by Haida artist Jim Hart. The wolf image, at the base of the new pole, represents Reid and his clan. After a bit of restorative work, the Reid pole is to be raised in the Museum's Great Hall.

VanDusen Gardens

West 37th Ave. & Oak St.

Two poles stand at the entrance to the gardens, one carved by Art Sterrit, the other by Earl and Brian Muldoe. Both are in the Gitskan style. The most intriguing of the pair tells the story of a woman's battle with Baboudina, Chief of the Mosquitoes, and his deadly crystal proboscis.

Plaza of Nations

750 Pacific Blvd.

Three poles — two by Earl Muldoe, one by Walter Harris — all in the Gitskan style. Points for spotting the kidnapped maiden at the top of one of the poles.

Following the excellent advice of Edgar Allan Poe, the Vancouver Art Gallery decided to hide this piece of public art in the plainest possible view. In this case, that meant putting the piece — an inscription by New York artist Lawrence Weiner, which reads "placed upon the horizon (casting shadows)" — on the entablature of the gallery's Georgia Street façade. Meaning is always a tricky question with non-representative artwork. Pontificating on the significance of Weiner's work, Chicago art critic Benjamen Buchloh commented thusly: "The particular function of his work was the restoration of the real conditions of discourse which underlay the accumulation of mythical object on display inside the museum. Its placement in an urban architectural setting insured a public mode of address, and its particular material pointed to the extension of the conditions of imperialism from economic to aesthetic matters." Just what does that mean? It's a secret.

Hidden Meanings

Time was, an ambitious young man heading for the B.C. coast was told to pick himself up a grammar book of Chinook. They weren't hard to find. In the 1800s, four separate London publishers offered concise books of Chinook grammar, along with Chinook dictionaries and teach-yourself-Chinook phrasebooks. What had begun as the language of a small tribe at the mouth of the Columbia River had grown into the lingua franca of the coast. In fact, in the early decades of the 20th century, Chinook looked set to make the transition from mere trading pidgin to the native tongue of a large number of coastal Natives, but then, well ... missionary schools ... loss of culture – you know the rest. Down in Drake Street

43

plaza, an art installation by Henry Tsang, entitled *Welcome to the Land of Light*, recalls a bit of those old days. The piece consists of two identical messages posted one atop the other on the plaza guardrails. The top message is in Chinook, the bottom one in English. Those with talent for languages can puzzle out some of the words. Our favourite: "Hee hee," meaning laugh.

Empty Throne

Photo: Blaine Kyllo

In a tiny green space near the foot of Hornby Street, sandwiched between the Burrard and Granville Street Bridges, there sits a great stone table – over 10 meters long and so high that a person standing can just peer over the edge and see onto the surface. This emperor's banquet table is flanked on either end by two enormous concrete chairs, like the thrones of absent giants. What's the secret message behind this bit of sculpture? Possibly, nothing – just another obscure piece of Vancouver public art occupying park space. But it's also possible that this installation has something to do with the presence next door – at 888 Beach – of the city's most powerful bureaucrat, the man who more than any other responsible for the forest of highrises now lining False Creek. Possibly, the sculpture is his subtle message to those who have questioned just who is in charge of the city of Vancouver: in answer to the question "Who Rules Here?", the sculpture makes succinct reply. "I do."

Langara College

100 West 49th Ave.

Carved by student Don Yeomans in the Haida style, this pole eschews the traditional myth motif and goes instead for a theme made timeless through generations of student café conversation: existential angst of the should-I-follow-my-head-or-my-heart variety.

Maritime Museum

1905 Ogden Ave.

Completed in the province's centennial year – 1958 – this 100-foot-high pole is an exact replica of one shipped to the UK and presented to Queen Elizabeth. Both poles were carved by Mungo Martin in the Kwakiutl style. Man at the top is a chief standing on a beaver.

Douglas Border Crossing

Mungo Martin pole done in Haida Style is a replica of a pole from the Skedans village in Haida Gwaii (the Queen Charlotte Islands).

Heritage Park – Musqueum Native Reserve

Stan Greene pole done in the much more representative style of the Coast Salish people. Somewhere on the same sight are the reburied remains of villagers found during archaeological excavations on the Musqueum site.

Psychology Building, UBC

2136 West Mall

Art Thompson pole depicts the whaling tradition of the Nuu-chah-nulth people. The guy on top holds a dorsal fin in either outstretched hand, symbolizing — like the hash marks on a fighter plane's nose — two successful kills.

Native Education Centre

285 East 5th Ave.

Pole carved in the Nisga'a style by Norman Tait, with the assistance of his brother, son, nephew, and cousin. Surrounding the portal on the bottom of the pole are four faces, each carved by one of the assistants. Master carver Tait chose to represent himself with the wolf cub being held in the paws of Black Bear.

CBC Building Plaza

700 Hamilton St.

Chief carver Richard Hunt expressed his feelings for Jane Wilson of the CBC's PR department by representing her on the Kwaguitl-style pole as a Dzunukwa, the all-black Wild Woman of the Woods. Perhaps as a concession to her modesty, however, Hunt dressed the normally naked Wild Woman in a skirt and allowed Bear to discreetly cover her chest with his paws.

Photo: Blaine Kyllo

Rooms Without a View

Photo: City of Vancouver Archives

Among the city's strangest and most deeply secret places are the twin cable rooms beneath the south approach to the Lions Gate Bridge. In these bombproof underground bunkers (shown here under construction), the two 61-strand cables that hold up the bridge unwind in gigantic canary-yellow spirals attached to the bedrock. The Department of Highways has keys to the rooms, but shy away from publicity because of the terrorist potential.

Defence Secrets

Twice this century, the powers-that-be have been sufficiently panicked to erect gun emplacements to guard the port of Vancouver. In 1914, one set of guns — a pair of four-inch naval cannons — was considered sufficient, mounted on the Stanley Park cliffs above Siwash Rock. At the outbreak of World War II, authorities went whole-hog, installing no less than three batteries: one on Point Grey, one on Brockton Point in Stanley Park, and one on Point Atkinson in Lighthouse Park. No shots were ever fired in anger, unless you count the time in 1943 that the overeager gun crew lobbed a pair of shells at an unidentified fish boat. The Point Grey emplacement is still there, built into the foundations of UBC's Museum of Anthropology.

Transportation

Photo: Blaine Kyllo

Secret shortcuts. Hidden train rides. Unknown tunnels. Vancouver is a city at the end of things – the Terminal City – the place with connections to everyone and everywhere, via modes of transport both physical and ethereal, public and obscure, legal and less so. In Terminal Town as elsewhere, the fastest route from A to B hangs on knowing who to ask, and where to look.

A Sweeping View

Hidden away at the bottom of Yale Street, in an obscure corner of the city's unfashionable east side, is absolutely the best place to stand and watch the rail yards, the cruise ships, the freighters, and the whole vast sweep of the city's working port – and almost no one knows about it. For although the viewpoint masquerades as a pedestrian walkover – from Commissioner Street up and over the railway tracks to Wall Street – it does not appear on any map. To find it, drive along Wall past a series of small parks until you find the one named Meditation Park, at the bottom of Nanaimo Street. Get out of the car and stroll confidently down the slope to the northeast corner of the park – carrying on even though it looks like an unfenced drop-off – until you see a set of slightly rickety steps, partially hidden by a thick bramble of blackberries. Wander down the steps and out across the old-style railway trestle, complete with creosote-soaked beams and structural railing made of wrought-iron. Look out and enjoy the view. Look down at the trains sitting side-by-side on the four parallel railway tracks. Pretend you're Steve McQueen and drop down onto a boxcar. Mind the pigeons.

Free Ride

Photo: Blaine Kyllo

Vancouver's first ever motorized ambulance – purchased in 1909 – was the pride of the city, and a joy to the volunteers who had begged and cajoled for the money to buy it. According to a contemporary witness, on its first trial run, "It ran over a man and killed him, in front of old Fader's grocery store at Pender and Granville, where the Bank of Montreal is now." The unfortunate bystander – an American tourist – got the dubious honour of becoming the ambulance's first passenger, winning a one-way trip to the city morgue.

Misses Not So Near

Strange, but there's an art to crashing a car. Especially if you're doing it on camera for the benefit of a hotshot Hollywood director. Even trickier, as ICBC can attest, is the art of not quite crashing your car. Especially when the near collision is with a plane.

Cut to Abbotsford Airport, where *The X-Files* second unit is filming a segment that calls for Mulder and Scully to speed down an airport runway, narrowly avoiding a collision with a low-flying Cessna. The director – tortured genious that he is – wants shots from inside the car as the plane buzzes over, missing them by a few scant feet. The pilot – an experienced water bomber jockey – says "can

do." But on the night of the shoot, on the very first take, a gust of wind causes the plane's landing gear to slam into the top of the car, crushing the roof and bursting out the windows. Fortunately for Anderson and Duchovny, the shots from inside the car were captured using remote-controlled cameras.

A Royal Ride

Vern Bethel's 1939 McLaughlin Buick is one of a kind. Literally. It was hand made by General Motors' Canadian (McLaughlin) division for the Duke of Kent's wartime tour of Canada. After the war, the three-ton beauty served in other capacities – even briefly as a taxicab in Victoria – until Bethel picked it up in 1972, and brought it back to his shop on First Avenue near Cambie.

He's fixed it up since then, so much so that when the Queen and Prince Philip were looking for a ride during the opening of the Commonwealth Games in Victoria in 1994. In fact, given that Charles and Diana also used the car for the opening of Expo, Bethel's McLaughlin has now safely transported three generations of British Royals. And what's the performance like on a 1939 McLaughlin? Not as speedy as a good black Mercedes, but then it handles better through the tunnels.

10 LIKELIEST PLACES TO CRASH YOUR CAR

Looking to put a ding in Dad's car? Here are the places to go (or, better, avoid): the 10 top accident locations, as supplied by the Vancouver Police Traffic Services Department:

1. Stanley Park Causeway
2. 49th Ave. and Knight St.
3. Burrard and Georgia Sts.
4. 33rd Ave. and Knight St.
5. Cambie St. and SW Marine Dr.
6. 100 E. Hastings St.
7. Broadway and Clark Dr.
8. 49th Ave. and Oak St.
9. Burrard St. and Pacific Blvd.
10. Broadway and Rupert St.

OUR LADY OF THE TRAFFIC JAM

Commuters are not often given to acts of piety. Indeed, to judge by word and deed and gesture, the average driver is more likely wishing or being wished a one-way trip to Hades. But perhaps such comments aren't to be taken *ex-cathedra*. Inside the cathedral commuters are blessed, at least to judge by the stained glass at Christ Church Cathedral on Burrard. Look up at the panel at the far northwesterly corner (the one closest to the First Narrows) and you can see an image of St. Nicholas standing guard over the Lions Gate Bridge. The Lord, it seems, will have no truck with sinners; likewise are the queue jumpers damned (and them that travel slowly in the fast lane, though the sign sayeth slower traffic keep right).

CAR AND READER

Say you've picked up an original 1974 two-stroke Trabant station wagon and you need a copy of the original East German service manuals in order to fix the tranny. Odds are, you need your head examined. But if the doctors declare you fit, then you may – just may – find your what looking for at Wilkinson's Automobilia *(2531 Ontario St., 873-6242)*, an amazing emporium of all things auto-related. Run by brothers Bill and Ted, Wilkinson's stocks books, magazines, videos, new, used and out-of-print service manuals, as well as a sizable selection of models, Matchboxes, and Hot Wheels.

Fast Ferries Fiasco

Photo: Ric Ernst/The Province

What's the secret to not selling a $200 million set of brand new aluminium fast ferries? Well, you could do like the folks who ran the Pacificat program, and design boats too delicate to withstand the sort of seas regularly experienced in your target markets. You could further sales-proof your ferries by adding in a two-level, roll-on roll-off design customized to BC Ferries' loading ramps, and useless to everyone else in the world. You could ignore the voices – internal and external – that point out not only these faults but also the fact that the underpowered engines will cost way too much to operate, and are liable to rattle themselves and the ferries to bits if run at anywhere near the promised top speed. But the true test of a sales-proof ferry program is the willingness on a moment's notice – say for instance, when the foreign heads of state were visiting Vancouver for the 1997 APEC conference – to force the shipyard to weld the various available ferry bits together (Plans? Who needs plans?) in order to create some recognizable semblance of a ferry that can then be shown to the visiting hotshots. The parts will then have to be pulled apart again, engendering endless mechanical problems, doubling construction costs, and generally guaranteeing a product so expensive and problem-prone that no one but your own provincial government will ever be able or willing to buy it. That's the secret of a successful ferry fiasco.

Strange the way parks and politics come together, at least in the case of the Stanley Park causeway. In the 1920s, when the Guinness family – of beer and British Properties fame – first proposed putting up a bridge and running a road through the park, official Vancouver's reaction was outraged horror. Still, the brewery folks persevered, lubricating local political circles until in the midst of the 1930s Depression, a fishy little deal was finagled whereby Vancouver would get a miserly little patch of westside green called Tatlow Park, and the folks at Guinness would get to multiply their West Van property holdings many-fold by putting up Lions Gate Bridge and then ripping a great gaping tear through the centre of Stanley Park.

Ah but that was then, you say. Fast forward 60 years, however, and see how little has changed. In the summer of 1999, while the province was planning to widen the bridge, Parks Board chair Alan Featherstonaugh, in a rare and suicidal act of courage, stood up and said that under no circumstances would he allow the province to chop down some 200 trees in order to widen the Stanley Park causeway. His fellow Parks Board commissioners – all members of the same Non-Partisan Association – backed him up. So did the NPA councillors who controlled city council. Come the election that November, they all said they were against any widening of the causeway.

This was strange, considering the NPA is otherwise very cosy with the kinds of folks – property developers, for example – who stood to benefit from increased road capacity to the North Shore. Even stranger, no-widening champion Featherstonaugh wasn't on the ballot. Seems the NPA had felt it best if he took a break from politics. After the election – which the NPA won – Parks Board commissioners and city councillors suddenly had a change of heart. A much wider causeway, they thought, would be a good idea after all. Of course, this thought occurred to them all only well after the election.

Travel Back in Time

Vancouver is a major transportation centre, so it's not that surprising there are a number of homages to transportation, past and present, some of which are pretty unusual:

S.S. Samson V Maritime Museum

The vintage sternwheeler on display here was retired from service as a snag puller in 1980. On board you can find illustrations about the old sternwheeling days on Fraser River.
Westminster Quay Public Market, New Westminster, 522-6890

Britannia Heritage Shipyard

For old-boat aficianados: a working shipyard specializing in wooden boats.
5180 Westwater, Richmond, 718-1200

Canadian Museum of Flight

Bombers, biplanes, jets, and a gift shop, all hidden away in Hangar #3 at the Langley Airport. *5333-216th St., Langley, 532-0035*

Vanterm Public Viewing Area

Ever wondered what goes on inside the Port of Vancouver? So do the Mounties, but they at least can ask the Hell's Angels. For the official story, however, visit Vanterm's public viewing area, which boasts a bird's-eye view of a working container terminal, along with a full-sized container in cutaway and an audio tour.
Vancouver Port Corporation, 666-3226

3 Secret Masters

Vancouver's restive populace is ruled not by law, or fate, or justice, but by the will of three Secret Masters. Ensconced in his cubicle at the north end of Lions Gate, the Bridge Master peers down through hidden video cameras upon the hapless commuters on the Stanley Park causeway and North Shore. He is the arbiter of the merciful centre lane, which he dispenses to those with whom he is pleased, and takes back from those with whom he is wrath.

Nought enters or leaves Vancouver's port without permission from the Harbour Master, whose lofty office occupies the 23rd floor of the less-than-remarkable Granville Square complex at the foot of Granville Street.

Most secret of the three is the Traffic Master. Squirreled away in a locked room on the second floor of city hall, the computerized Traffic Supervisory Control System governs each of the city's 600-plus traffic signals. The all-powerful operator decides which lucky commuters get to return home, and which are red-lighted into traffic-jam purgatory.

Sneaky Driving Secret

Down Burrard St. along the waterfront

Say you're downtown cruising past Planet Hollywood when a call comes in on the cell phone. It's the crazed maniac who kidnapped your pet rabbit and he wants you at the corner of Hastings and Main in three minutes or the bunny gets it. Then the traffic report comes on over the radio: major blockages all through downtown. What to do? Blast down to the foot of Burrard Street, turn left by the Marine Building, swoop down the ramp past the float planes, and you're onto Coal Harbour Road, a little used stretch of blacktop running along the waterfront. Scream underneath the Waterfront Hotel and along side the railway track to the overpass at Portside Park, then up and over the tracks, past the No. 5 Orange, and you're there in time to blow away the bunny killer and make the world safe for democracy.

Sneakier Driving Secret

Underneath the CPR Station on the waterfront

Say you're in Gastown, and you want to deke into downtown around the blocked-up tour bus traffic. Nothing simpler. Just past Maple Tree Square, turn right on Carrall Street, then left again into the alley. Bomb along up the alleyway (keeping a careful eye for the occasional IV user), and then – here's the fun part – underneath the tower at 100 Granville, through the Pacific Press parking lot, and up and out the parking garage ramp beneath the Gateway to Gastown sign. You're now on Cordova Street, heading east.

Sneakiest Driving Secret

Howe Street Underpass

Say you're stuck in a slow-moving jam on Howe Street. If you're near the Pacific Centre, there's hope. Pop down the parking garage ramp at Dunsmuir (below), then plow on past the signs saying turn left. You're into the Howe Street Underpass, a single-lane car tunnel that extends a full kilometre underneath Howe, all the way to Nelson Street.

Photo: Blaine Kyllo

Watch for the speed hump – whump! – wave to the prisoners being dumped off at the law courts loading dock – Hi, guys! – then accelerate up the cement ramp and – boom – you're back on Howe, four blocks further along, and on the other side of the street.

51

MORE
secret tunnels

Horseshoe Bay Tunnel

First you see it, then you don't. Driving west on the Upper Levels Highway, the West Vancouver section of the BC Rail line bobs and weaves tantalizingly in and out of view. Then in Upper Caulfeild, it disappears completely. It's not magic. The line has just ducked in to the Horseshoe Bay tunnel, a 1,500-metre opening blasted from the solid granite between Upper Caulfeild and Horseshoe Bay. BC Rail engineers went to the trouble of building the tunnel because it replaced four switchbacks, three kilometres of track, and one great big timber trestle that had already been built over Nelson Creek.

Lonsdale Tunnel

As you step out of the SeaBus, on North Vancouver's Lonsdale Quay, you tread atop a tunnel. Built in 1928, this 492-metre concrete box-tube runs below West Esplanade Avenue, from St. Andrews Avenue to Chesterfield, connecting up the CNR track with that of BC Rail. Access is difficult, dangerous, and probably illegal, but those who make it in are rewarded with a view of a long dark hollow concrete tube, dappled here and there with spray-painted messages, and filled with the cardboard encampments of one or two intrepid members of the permanently un-housed.

PACIFIC STARLIGHT DINNER TRAIN

Will that be Art Deco, or Dome Car? Departing North Vancouver every night at 6:15 p.m., the Pacific Starlight Dinner Train offers an elegant escape to an earlier age, with three-course meals and choice of rolling stock. Return trips to Porteau Cove start at $83.95. Taxes, tips, and dome cars cost extra. Twice a month in the spring and summer, the train offers a murder-mystery ride, offering a better-than-even chance of getting killed.
BC Rail Station, 1311 West 1st St., North Vancouver, 1-800-363-3373 or 984-5500 (in the lower mainland)

The Secret Source of It All

In France, all distances to and from Paris are taken from the foot of the Cathédrale Notre-Dame on the Ile de la Cité, the heart of the ancient realm. In the holy Mormon capital of Salt Lake City, street addresses indicate a building's distance from the altar of the mighty Tabernacle. And then there's Vancouver. Here, the city's magic centrepiece is Gassy Jack Deighton's Globe Saloon, erected on what is now Maple Tree Square in 1867. Deighton's drinking hole defines the city's unit block. From the 1885 survey onward, all streets to the left of the saloon were designated East, and those on the right side, West. As he must have dreamed all along, the loudmouth saloon keeper is now and forever more directly in the centre of it all.

Thornton Tunnel

The history of B.C. politics is written on the ground, and sometimes underneath it. The recalcitrant voters of West Vancouver never once put a Socred in office during the long reign of his wackiness, Premier W.A.C. Bennett. Their reward was the PGE railway – now known as BC Rail – that runs across their rolling lawns on the tony West Van shoreline. The good burghers of Burnaby – loyal Socreds through four elections – got a tunnel. Built in 1969, the Thornton Tunnel runs for 3.2 kilometres beneath the streets of North Burnaby, connecting the Second Narrows railway bridge to the Burlington Northern line on the far side of the Lougheed Highway. At its deepest, the tunnel is a full 45 metres below the surface. An unmarked sign of gratitude.

Skytrain Tunnel

Photo: Blaine Kyllo

Back in 1985, when the folks from BC Transit needed a way to get their nifty new Skytrain tracks through downtown to the waterfront, they cheated a little and cut a deal to use the CPR's pre-existing Dunsmuir Tunnel. That's hardly a secret – thousands of happy suburbanites ride those rails daily. What is a secret is that BC Transit didn't use the whole tunnel. A substantial disused section (now the property of Concord Pacific) extends beneath downtown. Musty and forgotten, it's employed for storage, occasional film shoots, and not much else. In fact, a Concord Pacific spokesperson says they'd rather people didn't even know the tunnel exists. Sorry: the big double doors that mark its eastern terminal are clearly visible in the side of the cliff below Beatty Street, near GM Place.

Burrard Bridge Castles

Photo: Blaine Kyllo

How many times have you rolled across the Burrard Street Bridge, looked up at the mock castle structure over the span's centre, and wondered what's behind the stained glass windows? Actually, not much – a room with bridge maintenance bric-a-brac, mostly. Until not so long ago, however, part of the space housed the equipment for an elevator that was to take passengers down to what is now the seawall on the north side. The rails for the intended lift are still inside Pier 4. For reasons unknown, the elevator was never built. Stairs inside the piers at the south end of the bridge were finished, but then bricked off after several incidents of late-night crime. Graffiti artists who penetrate bridge defences will find circa 1930 railings and stair treads made from brass.

10 Busiest Bus Routes

Photo: Blaine Kyllo

Taking the bus is usually convenient and always environmentally responsible, which is difficult to remember when you're stuck in a sweaty, crowded one. Here are the routes to beware:

Route #	Route Name	Weekday Boardings
9	Boundary/Alma/UBC	45,400
8	Fraser/Granville	31,800
20	Victoria/Downtown	27,000
22	Knight/MacDonald	24,200
3	Main/Downtown	23,600
99	Lougheed Mall/UBC (B-Line)	23,200
10	Hastings/UBC	23,000
41	Joyce Stn/Crown/UBC	21,600
15	Cambie/Downtown	14,100
16	29th Avenue Stn/Arbutus	14,100

GROUSE MOUNTAIN HIGHWAY

So you want your sweetie to catch the sunset from the top of Grouse Mountain, but the $36 Skyride fare (for two, return) seems a bit steep, and you're reasonably sure that the Grind in high heels is a poor prelude to romance. So drive. Just because it's a mountain peak doesn't mean you can't get there by auto. Take the hidden service road, accessed from the top of the Mountain Highway in Upper Lynn Creek. The grade isn't steep enough to really require a four-wheeler, and what few potholes there are offer no real obstruction. The barrier at the beginning is a bit of a snag, of course, as is the likely fine for unauthorized entry when you reach the top.

Zooming east along the Georgia Viaduct is the best place to contemplate perhaps the most intriguing of the city's might-have-beens. Leaving downtown, looking down from the elevated causeway at the slowly regenerating urban wasteland, it feels like you're driving on an American superhighway. Which you are.

When it was built in 1970, the Georgia Viaduct was meant to serve as the lynchpin of a series of no less than five major urban freeways: one heading east along either Adanac or the Grandview Highway (they weren't quite sure), two running parallel south along Main and Quebec Streets, one snaking in along new waterfront landfill to around Howe Street (at which point it would head north over a new artificial island in the harbour and over a third crossing to the North Shore), and one following along the south side of False Creek to Burrard Street, and then south through Kitsilano and Kerrisdale to Richmond. Chinatown, where the freeways came together, was set to be demolished and replaced by the mother of all clover leafs.

Back to the present: you come off the viaduct and slow to an impatient 60 kph on Prior Street, and suddenly you're back in Vancouver. What happened? When word of the freeway plan hit the streets, the streets — particularly in Chinatown — erupted in protest. Arthur Erickson was all in favour, saying Vancouverites shouldn't think of the freeways as freeways, but rather as buildings with roads on their roofs. Everyone else was opposed, including a young activist by the name of Mike Harcourt, the Man Who Would Be Mayor.

Such was the public outcry that the freeway plan was stopped. Three decades later almost everyone is grateful, except the original designers — but then they made the mistake of not keeping their plan a secret.

RIGHT OF WAY IN PIGEON PARK

Stand in Pigeon Park at the corner of Hastings and Carrall Streets and — if the drug merchants will give you half a moment's peace — look first towards the northeast, and then turn around and look towards the southwest. Note how the building corners for blocks in either direction seem sliced off, almost as if an implacable force had come with a great cleaving knife and shorn a path through the heart of the city's old downtown. In a sense, that's what happened, for the strange oblique slash marks the right of way of Canadian Pacific's now abandoned rail line. (In the Vancouver of days gone by, the CPR was the next best thing to an implacable force.) The trains are gone, but the city is preserving the right of way as a possible future Greenway.

secret right turn shortcuts

These driving tips for getting there faster are brought to you courtesy of the cab drivers of Vancouver:

Eastbound on Prior

Say Adanac is clogged, and you're using it to get to Clark anyway. Leave Adanac on Malkin, bomb along past Strathcona Park – being careful to wave to the community gardeners or any street pros working the boys from the warehouses – jog north on Raymur to William, then north on Vernon past the Yellow Cab guys, up the hill by the railway tracks and voilà, you're on Clark, four lights on and light-years ahead of the game.

Southbound on Granville at 71st

Heading south on Granville en route to Richmond? That nasty no-left-turn sign at 71st making you miserable? Don't despair, just do as the taxis do. Turn left into the Shell gas station at the corner of Granville and 71st and then out of the parking lot again onto 71st towards the Oak Street Bridge and the endless delights of Richmond.

A SHORELINE DRIVE

Want to go for a drive by the seashore? Try West 2nd Avenue, just south of Granville Island. From the Granville Bridge to Main Street (where it becomes Great Northern Way) and then up to Clark Drive, this road parallels the Burlington Northern Railway tracks, which run along the original False Creek shoreline. As you zoom up towards Clark Drive, you traverse the mouth of an old watercourse which used to run all the way up to Trout Lake. Its name is commemorated by the park on your left: China Creek.

Northbound on Main at Terminal

The light at Main and Terminal is atrocious, the kind of thing you want to bypass entirely. If you're heading east, you can. Just leave Main at Industrial, go north on Western past Southern and Central, east on Northern, north on Station, and you're onto Terminal, having boxed the compass – bypassing a light known to take seven minutes at its worst – and avoided an encounter with a mob of squeegee kids.

QUICK EXIT

Ask Mayor Philip Owen. The biggest perk to being Vancouver's mayor is not the free cell phone, nor the travel junkets to Surrey and Richmond, nor even the big comfy mayor's chair. The biggest thrill is getting to use the executive elevator. The unmarked lift runs from the sixth floor – preserve of senior city mandarins – down to the sub-basement parking, with a stop, of course, right by the mayor's third floor office. According to city hall insiders, the secret elevator's most important function is as an escape route, allowing the mayor and mandarins to duck the angry crowds that sometimes descend looking for blood.

Northbound on Clark at First

There are other gas stations in town through which one can cut, either to bypass a light or deke past the guy in front of you, but they all have attendants with the unfortunate habit of complaining about such things. But the Commercial Gas Bunk station at Clark and First is self-serve. So serve yourself.

Photo: Blaine Kyllo

secret ways to leave downtown by land, sea, and air

Okay. So you've just been torn from a restless sleep by a tremendous thunderclap only to find a dead man slumped on a chaise lounge on your hotel room balcony. You didn't kill him, but the police'll never believe it, because you've only just narrowly escaped being hanged in your native North Carolina for a similar suspicious death, this one involving your husband. You've got to get out of town. Farfetched? This was exactly the premise of Raymond Chandler's 1948 set-in-Vancouver screenplay, *Playback*. Chandler's heroine had to stay and face the music, because the authorities sealed off the regular road and rail links, and she didn't know about these somewhat less traditional methods for exiting the city.

Sea

Photo: Mandelbrot

Freighter

How do those sailors on those huge freighters moored in the harbour make it ashore? Generally, they abandon the ship in a little orange lifeboat and motor over to the public wharf at Granville Island. That's not to say you couldn't hitch a ride back, except, of course, that stowaways are generally tossed overboard once found.

Water Taxi

The Burrard Water Taxi *(east of Canada Place, 293-1160)* serves Vancouver and Indian Arm 24 hours a day, seven days a week; can pick up and drop off to any marine location. $99 an hour. Corpses extra.

Speedboat

In the Granville Island Harbour right next to Bridges Restaurant, Granville Island Boat Rentals *(682-6287)* is

Unusual Ferry Trips

Photo: Mandelbrot

The fleet of the BC Ferry Corporation is an icon of B.C. tourism, and an idyllic means of getting to Victoria, Nanaimo, and the Gulf Islands. But there are other ferry routes to try out, too:

Paddle Wheeler River Adventures
Westminster Quay Public Market, New Westminster, 525-4465
The only working paddlewheeler on the Fraser, the *MV Native* makes the run from New West up to historic Fort Langley. Enjoy food and live music along the way, then take the ferry back again, or bring along your bike and cycle back.

Coast Salish Boat Tours
Toivo Hutikka, Scowlitz Band Office, 826-5813
Pioneered by UBC's Dr. Michael Blake, this tour sets off from Fraser Valley

near Kilby. Sto:lo (Coast Salish) guide Toivo Hutikka will take you to Native pit houses and middens that are more than 2,500 years old.

False Creek Ferries

These little bumboats run by Granville Island Ferries and Aquabus make regular runs to points on either side of False Creek including the Vancouver Aquatic Centre, the Maritime Museum, Stamps Landing in False Creek, Science World, and of course, Granville Island. The best time to watch for them, though, is on fireworks nights. Just before the show starts, a group of 9 or 10 of them herd together at the mouth of False Creek and perform an intricate little dance, chugging around one another in a riotously intricate-looking pattern. Despite the physical awkwardness of the boats, the overall effect is decidedly elegant, rather like the dance of the hippos in *Fantasia*.

Barnston Island

Where else in the entire province does the ferry come at your command? Simply drive up to the dock at the end of 104th Street, a few kilometres east of the Port Mann Bridge in Surrey, honk your horn, and wait. Within minutes the ferry will arrive, and you'll be on your way to the quiet little enclave of Barnston Island, a combination agricultural community and nature preserve set in the midst of the Fraser River. The magic horn call works equally well on the way back.

the place for a speedboat for a fast getaway. 17 feet of fibreglass with 70 horses on the back will cost ya $32.75 an hour. The three gas tanks are enough to make it to Indian Arm and back or in the other direction, perhaps as far as the American border. That, of course, will cost you the $350 damage deposit, since you're not supposed to take the boats out any further than Bowen Island, but with the cops on your tail, that's the least of your problems.

Sailboat

For a spot on a yacht, the bulletin board at the Coal Harbour Marina is the spot you want. Failing a freebie, Westin Bayshore Yacht Charters (691-6936) rents all shapes and sizes.

M . V .   B r i t a n n i a

The ferry *Britannia*, which, from May to September, departs daily at 9:30 a.m. from the north foot of Denman Street, makes the run up Howe Sound to connect with the Royal Hudson steam train, or you can continue on to Whistler. Call Harbour Ferries at 687 9558.

Air

Floatplane

Harbour Air Seaplanes at Tradewinds Marina (west of Canada Place, 688-1277) offers float plane service to the Gulf Islands or Victoria. Cost begins at $68 one-way. You can also charter planes to other destinations.

Twin Otter Plane

You can get Vancouver-to-Victoria harbour-to-harbour service on a twin otter plane via Harbour Air (west of Canada Place, 688-9115). A half-hour trip costs $95.23 one-way.

Helicopter

Helijet International offers the same route as the float plane guys, but you get to fly on a nifty Sikorsky F-76 helicopter. Vancouver Helicopters – the tour arm of the company – will take you anywhere you want. Round trip to Victoria costs $298, or rent the Sikorsky for $2,600 an hour. Both can be found east of Canada Place, 273-1414 or 270-1484.

Balloon

Fantasy Balloon Charters Inc. *(5333-216 St., Langley, 530-1974)* offers champagne flights on a hot-air balloon for $185. And guess what? Direction and final destination are dependent entirely upon the wind.

Land

Train (Traditional)

Photo: Blaine Kyllo

There is a daily train service to Seattle via Amtrak *(Pacific Central Station, Main at Terminal, 1-800-872-7245)* that leaves everyday at 6 p.m. One-way fare is $21 US. Customs inspections are performed before boarding, so if you can make it onboard without being checked (by ducking in through that hole in the chain link fence by the warehouses on the north side, perhaps?) you're clear all the way to Seattle.

Train (Alternative)

For a more unusual, if less comfortable, train journey, wander down to the railyards by the loading dock underneath the Waterfront Centre. Freight trains often stop for hours at a time, and from the conveniently elevated staff parking lot it's just a convenient step (not even a hop) onto a waiting flat car. Snuggle in next to a container, and according to sources, if you aren't noticed by a railyard cop, you'll be in Winnipeg by Thursday.

Car

At Auto Driveaway *(3A-1583 Pemberton Ave., North Vancouver, 985-0936)*, you can fork over a $50 registration fee, a $350 damage deposit, a Polaroid photo, and three pieces of ID (preferrably consistent) and you're on your way to somewhere in someone else's car, bound by wherever it is the owner wants it transported. (Driveaway has 80 offices continent wide.) Travel limit is 600 miles per day, and you're given a set number of days to reach your destination (Whitehorse, for example, is calculated to be 12 days away).

Secrets About Skytrain

Photo: Mandelbrot

Ridership
Average weekday: 145,000
Average Saturday: 94,000
Average Sunday: 72,000

Busiest Time
07:40 - 08:40 am weekdays;
average on-board load, departing
Broadway to downtown: 7,600

Busiest Events
Symphony of Fire fireworks nights, July/August: up to 20,000 passengers carried in 2.5 hours. Approximately 20-25 percent of all crowds attending events at BC Place or GM Place use SkyTrain.

Photo: Mandelbrot

Photo: Mandelbrot

offbeat rentals

Exotic Cars & Motorcycles

Ever dream of driving a Ferrari, Jaguar, Mercedes, Viper, Prowler, BMW, Hummer or Beetle? Exotic Car & Motorcycle Rentals *(1820 Burrard St., 644-9128)* is the place. Prices range from $299 to $1,299 per day.

Photo: Blaine Kyllo

Bicycles

Spokes *(1798 West Georgia St., 688-5141)* has a huge selecion of touring bikes, mountain bikes, and tandems (as well as coffee). Bayshore Bicycle and Rollerblade Rentals *(745 Denman St., 688-2453)* has the above plus rollerblades and baby strollers. Bicycle Tours *(930-BIKE)* offers tours of the city by bike.

Photo: Blaine Kyllo

Vintage Cars

Early Motion Tours *(687-5088)* has personalized tours of the city in a 1930 Model A Ford convertible courtesy of "The Fridge" owner, Dennis Fridulin.

Gondolas

At Viaggio Gondolas *(1820 Mast Tower Rd., 688-3362)*, you can have lunch, brunch, dinner or dessert aboard a luxurious Italian gondola while touring False Creek. Tours are 1½ hours long or you can charter the boat for the day.

Photo: Blaine Kyllo

Secret trails and naughty nudist enclaves. Inside info on where to pan for gold, climb a wall, huck a disk, or commune with a homesick llama. Also, the secret significance of baby heads and chunder, the best places to seek out seriously sick mountain biking, the definitive guide on where not to seek out snowboard glory, and an answer to that eternal question: what makes plastic better than pigskin or rubber?

Halibut Surfing

Ever wonder where your food's been before you eat it? In the case of halibut – a large, flat, oval-shaped fish – and an Annacis Island fish plant, it's probably best not to ask. Showing the same working-class ingenuity that led to belt-sander racing, workers on the graveyard shift at this warehouse have invented a brand new sport: halibut surfing. To play, you need the frozen carcass of a largish halibut – four feet long or more is best – and a forklift. The rules are relatively simple: the contestant places the fish on the floor, his feet on the fish, and his hands on the back of the forklift. The forklift driver then attempts to drive around the plant floor, swerving and weaving in order to force the surfer to go flying off into a corner. Whoever hangs on the longest wins. If Vancouver gets the nod to host the Olympics in 2010, may we suggest halibut surfing as a demonstration sport?

Checkmates

Chess is not exactly a sport you think of in the great outdoors, but outdoor chess and its close cousin, outdoor speed chess, have taken off quicker than hackey sack in this town. Games are available in the summer at the foot of the Vancouver Art Gallery steps, by the

steam clock in Gastown, on Kits Beach, in Stanley Park (by Ceperly Meadows), and in the winter in the Park Royal Shopping Centre in West Vancouver. And there's always the oversize chessboard in the Denman Place Mall.

Mountain biking is a world of its own, a secret subculture replete with its own language, its own hidden hierarchies of honour and prestige and of course – in this era of increasing trail restrictions – its own territory, a vast network of secret pathways carved through the bush on Vancouver's North Shore. Some years back, a group called the Secret Trail Society began the trail building, branching its own trails off the official pathways, and marking them with notices reading "You are entering secret territory." It didn't last. As the trails grew more popular, outsiders – hikers and rangers – twigged to their existence and closed each new trail as it was uncovered. The Leather Enema trail in Pacific Spirit Park suffered this fate some years back. Recently so too did the North Shore's Hangman, Reaper, and Swollen Uvula.

In response, the bikers have gone even further underground. Signposts are a thing of the past, and most trails now are walk-ins, meaning you have to pick up your bike and lug it through the bush for a 100 metres or so to the actual trailhead. Needless to say, there are no maps of secret territory (next page). Knowledge of a trail's location comes only from the trail-builder, legendary figures with cryptic names like the Digger or Dangerous Dan. As enforcement grows, the number of people in on the secret location grows ever more restricted. Fifty people, perhaps, know the whereabouts of Sagarmatha, a trial somewhere on the slopes of Cypress. Blind Skier and the Bogeyman are better known. Nearly new is the Circus, an obstacle course of teeter totters and ramps and dangerous obstacles. And then there's Canoe, a trail with a 40-foot-long, hollowed-out cedar tree lying on a steep slope somewhere in the woods of

Photo: Blaine Kyllo

Cypress. The trick is to get your wheels in the polished wooden halfpipe, then ride it down to the bottom. As you go, you're supposed to call out "CANOUUUUUU!"

Climbing the Walls

Ever wonder what it might be like to climb a wall? Find out at these indoor rock climbing gyms:

Cliffhanger
106 W. 1st Ave., 874-2400

Edge Climbing Centre
2-1485 Welch St., North Vancouver, 984-9080

Great Wall Underground
Whistler's Climbing Centre,
604/905-7625

Rock House
520-3771 Jacombs, Richmond,
276-0012

In the sick, sweet world of hardcore mountain biking, trails flow from one spot to another as quickly as a river delta, as bureaucrats search and destroy old obstacles, while bikers themselves push on to something ever faster, sicker and more insane. Drop off the cutting edge just slightly, however, and things are a tad more stable. Indeed, in recent years trails have stabilized enough that now there's even a guide. Available at bike shops around the Lower Mainland, the *Vancouver and Area Mountain Bike Guide* has maps and trail descriptions – complete with ratings from green to double-diamond – for the North Shore, the Endowment Lands, Burnaby Mountain, Maple Ridge, Mission, and Chilliwack. Finding the trail head is just the start of course. For the neophyte looking to fit in, the next critical step is to master the lingo. And while it won't fool anyone into thinking you're an expert, the small glossary below will at least get you launched:

BABY HEADS: washed out stones the size of babies' heads

CHUNDER: to wipe out

DISCOMBOBULATOR: a series of teeter-totters linked together by strips of rubber

FLOW: to ride smoothly; to hit the line

HACK: opposite of flow; to not ride smoothly; see also chunder

HUCK: to hurl oneself over a precipitous drop

KODAK COURAGE: the willingness to hurl oneself over drops far sicker than normal because a friend or bystander has brought along a camera

LAUNCH: a wheelie-drop with speed

LINE (THE): all-important vertical pathway that will safely take you down the mountain safely and at speed; significant deviation from the line leads to chundering

SICK: suicidal, terrifying; life-threatening, but with positive connotations; see also sweet

SLIDER: trail so steep that a mostly uncontrolled slide is the best that can be hoped for; see also sick

STUNTS: man-made obstacles such as ladders, teeter-totters, and forced wheelie drops

SWEET: feeling one gets from flowing down a sick trail

WHEELIE-DROP: a drop performed by pulling up the front wheel and landing on the back wheel

HAVE OAR, WILL TRAVEL

Looking for the perfect afternoon wilderness adventure? Drive over Burrard Inlet to the North Shore, then out along the Dollarton Highway to Deep Cove. Rent a kayak at Deep Cove Canoe and Kayak (*2007 Rockcliffe Road, 929-2662*) and set out across Indian Arm. When you reach Jug Island on the far side of the arm, head for the beach on the north end of the island. Look north. The spectacular scenery could make you believe you're in Alaska, or Haida Gwaii, or somewhere on the wild mid-coast of B.C. But you're only an hour or two from home.

Photo: BC Sports Hall of Fame & Museum

Hard as it is to believe, hockey in Vancouver didn't always suck. Well, the Canucks always have, but that's a separate story. To find Vancouver's glory days of hockey, you have to go past the NHL's arrival in Vancouver in 1970, way back to the 1915 heyday of the Pacific Coast Hockey League. Formed in 1910 by brothers Lester and Frank Patrick, the PCHL had teams in Vancouver, Victoria, and Seattle. The Vancouver squad, known as the Millionaires, played out of a huge arena built in 1911 at the foot of Denman Street. In 1915, having taken the PCHL championship, the Millionaires challenged the for the Stanley Cup and won, the only time a Vancouver team has ever taken home Lord Stanley's cup. Alas, it didn't much help the team or league's finances. In 1924, the league merged with the larger Western Canadian Hockey League, which in turn merged the following year with the U.S.-bound National Hockey League. Vancouver's team folded, Victoria's team – the Cougars – were transferred to Detroit, and the founder of the league, Lester Patrick, went on to coach the New York Rangers, winning the Cup not once, not twice, but three more times.

CANUCK WORLD

In the 28 years since the Vancouver Canucks first entered the National Hockey League, the team has enjoyed a few highs and many lows. Perhaps their greatest year was the surprise appearance in the Stanley Cup finals in 1982; although they lost to the New York Islanders in four straight games, who could forget the sight of thousands of white-towel-waving fans at Pacific Coliseum? The Canucks made the finals again in 1994, but we won't talk about the wee bit o' rioting on Robson Street following the final game that made national headlines, will we?

First-ever Canucks goal: October 9, 1970 by defenceman Barry Wilkins (Canucks lost the game 3-1 to Los Angeles Kings)

Record for 1st year of play (1970-71): 24-46-8

Record for most recent year (1999-2000): 30-37-15-8* (*overtime losses)

Number of years that elapse, on average, before the Canucks' management change the design of the team jersey: 7

Number of years that elapse, on average, before management changes head coach: 2.15

Frisbee Golf

For many, the existence of the sport itself is a secret, and yet Frisbee Golf — Disc Golf to purists — has been around since the early 1970s. There's even a local society (The BC Disc Sports Society, 1-888-878-7387). The pros tote a satchel of up to 12 disks, from large heavy drivers to dense, compact putters. A round of 18 holes takes about two hours. Here are 5 local courses:

Jericho Hill, Vancouver
9 Holes, Par 27

Mundy Park, Coquitlam
9 Holes, Par 31

Pender Island Disc Golf
9 Holes, Par 36

Queen Elizabeth Park, Vancouver
9 Holes, Par 43

Robert Burnaby Park, Burnaby
9 Holes, Par 27

Who Needs Professionals?

When it comes to the performance of Vancouver's professional sports teams, there isn't much to brag about. But in the world of ultimate, Vancouver teams are tops. Ultimate, the game where teams throw and catch discs (known to many by the brand name Frisbee), is much like football without the steroids, and in the 2000 Canadian National Championships, held at UBC, Vancouver teams won each of the five categories: juniors, masters, co-ed, women's, and open. Two of the teams, open winners Furious George and the all-women squad Prime, went on to the world championships in Germany, which featured more than 70 teams from 23 countries. Furious George came home with a bronze medal, while Prime was crowned world champions. Even better: you can watch games for free. Check the Vancouver Ultimate League website for game times and locations: www.vul.bc.ca.

Photo: David Walters

Amid the sea of Tudor and Craftsman houses in West Point Grey, Dorothy Stowe's Vancouver Special doesn't quite fit in, nor does it really seem to care. In the upstairs living room the furniture is resolutely Modern, like a coffee table book West Coast style. It was much the same, says Dorothy Stowe, when her husband Irving and friends Jim Bohlen and Paul Coté first began laying plans for the little activist group that grew to become the most influential environmental organization on the planet: Greenpeace.

The Stowes – who originally hail from New England – had arrived in Vancouver in 1966 on board the passenger liner *Oriana* from Auckland. Resolute Quakers, they had originally left Rhode Island for New Zealand in 1961 to escape the Vietnam War, a plan that backfired when the Kiwis' treaty obligations with the U.S. dragged them into Indochina. The Stowes packed their bags and came north.

It was at an anti-war rally on the steps of Vancouver's courthouse that the Stowes first met fellow American refugee Jim Bohlen. It might have been in '67 or '68; Dorothy isn't sure anymore. "We were holding a Quaker banner at an anti-Vietnam protest, and Jim and Marie [Bohlen's wife] came up to us because we happened to be holding the banner, and that's how we got to know each other." When the U.S. military announced plans to begin underwater nuclear tests in the Aleutians, the Stowes, Bohlen, and Paul Coté began plans for a protest that drew upon the Quaker tradition of bearing witness. They would hire a boat and sail up to the Bering Sea to see the blast. They formed the Don't Make a Wave committee and set to work raising funds.

The focus on whales and wildlife, the phenomenal growth and corporatization of the organization, all came later. But it all began in this modest, unmarked little house just off West 10th. Even today, the only sign of anything vaguely eco-friendly about the place is a small sticker on the front door, the kind Greenpeace gives to paid-up members.

INDY BLADING

Where's the best place to rollerblade in town? For those who want to avoid hills, cars, and crowds of people, the Molson Indy track near Science World is just the place. In 2000, the Indy organizers left the race area nearly intact. As a result, long stretches of smooth new concrete became available to speed down without having to worry about obstacles in the way. On a hot and breezy day, these stretches are like cooling wind tunnels. If you miss the crowds, the seawall is just minutes away.

Slam City Jam

Want to hang with the boardheads? Every first weekend in May for the past seven years, Vancouver has been the site of the largest skateboarding event in North America, the North American Skateboard Championships, otherwise known as Slam City Jam. In addition to the competition, there are boarding demonstrations, skateboard bands, skateboard consumer madness at the Skater Marketplace, and – proving that skateboard culture is not an oxymoron – the SkateLounge, showing the latest in skateboard video and art. For more information, visit www.slamcityjam.com.

Photo: Blaine Kyllo

RUNNING WILD

Started in the 1930s by British expatriates in Malaysia, and self-described as "a drinking club with a running problem," the Hash House Harriers stage a weekly run along a cross-country course laid out with paper markers. Runs are semi-competitive, and rugby-like in the absence of rules and degree of physical contact. At the end of the race, runners find a stash of booze and proceed to get sloshed. Often, races have a particular theme, such as the Liederhausen Run, the Red Dress Run, and the Full Moon Run. They have chapters in 1,500 cities worldwide, with an international website at www.gthhh.com. Call the local hotline at 290-9443 to find out where the runs are being held.

Our Own Slam City

Slam City, held each spring at the Pacific Coliseum, is where to see some of the best skateboard professionals in North America compete for over $65,000 in prize money. And if you get the urge to watch the board rats nosegrinding a handrail or heel-flipping a ledge, check out the plaza of the AT&T Canada building on Dunsmuir Street, next to Christ Church Cathedral. Evening hours only.

Let it All Show

Everyone knows the place to doff your clothes is Wreck Beach, located down a steep cliff trail at the top end of the UBC campus. But why is it called "Wreck Beach"? Local wags might put it down to the general state of the mostly male humans moved to exhibit themselves there in the altogether. But no, there are actual shipwrecks hidden down there on the Point Grey sands. For example, in 1923 the *Trader*, a 100-foot coastal freighter weighted down with a cargo of cement bags, began sinking after it ran into the breakwater on the north arm of the Fraser River. Nearby ships managed to drag it as far as the beach, then a popular spot for derelict ships. Salvage crews took off some of the cement cargo, but as for the ship, she was finished. In subsequent years, the shifting sands of the gulf slowly buried her over. She makes the occasional reappearance however, as freak storms and extreme tides re-expose what is otherwise keep covered. The last such peek-a-boo was in the 1960s. The old boat was in sad shape — bare ribs exposed, structure slowly returning to dust – but not at all lacking for company.

Underwater Fun

For those who don't scuba dive, the realm beneath the sea must forever remain a deep, dark mystery. For those who can, and are bored of looking at fish, here are some more interesting options: a scavenger hunt, an afternoon of underwater pumpkin carving, or the ever-friendly Valentine's Day dive. Of course, for a foretaste of this wonder, you can also check www.diveandsea.com, a website where diving clubs in and around Vancouver post a schedule of upcoming events, as well as trip reports from previous expeditions. And the most popular underwater exploration? The Hornby Island shark swim.

Urban Cowboys

Where does one go to horseback ride in a major urban centre like Vancouver? Here are a few places to try that won't have you driving for hours:

Adventures on Horseback
9230 Ladner Trunk Rd., Ladner, 940-8160

Back in the Saddle Again
1036-208 St., Langley, 501-6784

JP's Golden Ears Riding Stable
13175-232 St., Maple Ridge, 463-8761

Langley 204 Riding Stables
543-204 St., Langley, 533-7978

Matsqui Trail Stables
6480 Tall Rd., Abbotsford, 604/826-0806

Ocean's Edge Riding Estates
120 N. Tsawwassen Dr., Tsawwassen, 948-2269

URBAN AERIE

Vancouver's large coyote population isn't a secret. And the hordes of ravenous skunks around Lost Lagoon in Stanley Park were long ago discovered by equally ravenous hordes of photo-hungry Germans; apparently, wildlife in Europe is such a rarity that the smelly rodents are cooed at and fed. But what of the city's bald eagles?

At the corner of 49th and Larch stands a tall, lonely cedar, home for the past four years to a pair of nesting eagles. The pair arrive each spring to rebuild the nest and remain until their young are old enough to fly.

According to the woman whose house lies beneath the urban aerie, the only problem with eagles, as opposed to, say, hummingbirds, is their tendency to toss leftover food scraps out from the nest. Gull wings often plop down on her front lawn, as does the occasional half-munched salmon. And once, the young eaglets tossed out the bloody carcass of a large brown rat.

Gone With The Wind

For the truly adventurous, the Thornton Tunnel promises adrenaline rushes by the bucket. It is a train-sized passageway that runs beneath the streets of Burnaby from the Second Narrows railway bridge all the way to the Lougheed Highway. To find the tunnel mouth, drive east on Hastings past the TransCanada and then turn north on Skeena. Follow Skeena up the hill and around the corner to a grassy verge known as Bates Park. Leave the car and scramble down the cliffside to the tracks.

Here's where the fun begins, for would-be daredevils. Stand away from the tracks but fairly near the tunnel mouth until a southbound trains comes along. After it passes, walk over next to the tracks and get sucked down into the dark black passageway by a 30-to-40 kph wind. The wind continues until the train exits the other end of the tunnel 3.2 kilometres away. It's a simple matter of physics. The shaft is only slightly larger than the trains, so as the engine chugs its way down the tunnel it pushes the entire air column in front of it out the tunnel's far end. A partial vacuum is created behind the train, which is filled by air rushing in through the tunnel's mouth, thus creating a tiny localized hurricane. The reckless can ponder Bernouilli's equation as they lean back and pretend they're on the set of *Twister*. It's almost as much fun as the PNE roller coaster. Just – and don't say we didn't warn you – infinitely more dangerous.

Fraser River Windsurfing

Photo: courtesy Jen Letham & Paul Sapk

Windsurfers in the know seeking the Vancouver equivalent of the Columbia River Gorge look to Steveston. There, with honkin' winds and an outgoing tide, one can surf the mighty Fraser's standing waves. Dust off the roof rack and head for the launch site at Garry Point Park, but only when Environment Canada's Sandhead station reports better than 12-knot winds from the west or northwest. Oh, and watch out for the barges, freighters, fishboats, logbooms, deadheads, and other commercial traffic in this active harbour mouth.

Photo: Gerry Kahrmann/The Province

Photo: Eric Sinclair

What was it that sped Whistler snowboarder Ross Rebagliati to victory in the world's first Olympic snowboard downhill? Well, it probably didn't hurt that the THC level in his bloodstream indicated he'd very recently been very much exposed to large amounts of marijuana. Unfortunately, when the B.C. bud consumption showed up in his mandatory drug test, the International Olympic Committee tried to strip away his ounce of Nagano gold. It wasn't the performance enhancing aspects of marijuana that disturbed the IOC – there aren't any. Instead, the Olympic brass felt that Rebagliati's behaviour set a bad example (bribes and sexual favours are apparently okay, so long as they're directed exclusively towards senior members of the IOC). Rebagliati denied that spliff smoking was a regular part of his training regimen. The THC, he said, must have come from second-hand smoke at one or another Whistler going-away party. It's simply part of the culture, he said. His gold medal was eventually returned after vigorous campaigning by the Canadian IOC delegation. Later, Whistler city fathers honoured Ross for his achievement, giving the name Rebagliati Park to the little oblong greenspace between Whistler and Blackcomb base camps. It's a pleasant little spot, with Fitzsimmons Creek gurgling away like a water pipe, day and night all year long. Come summer, according to sources in the Whistler law enforcement community, it's also the spot where you're most likely to see illegal outdoor consumption of a certain green weed.

NINE THINGS TO DO IN WHISTLER IF YOU DON'T SKI

Invited to Whistler in the winter but a fear of avalanches, broken legs, or wet snow make you not want to ski? Well, there's a plethora of things to do instead. Here are just a few:

1) Rent a video camera and film your friends skiing. Foto Fantastic, 604/938-9961

2) Play pool, video games, or bowl at AlpenRock House, Whistler Village Centre Square, 604/938-0082

3) Visit Expressions "You Paint It" Ceramics Studio and make your own creations. 604/932-2822

4) Go snowmobiling, snowshoeing, ice-skating, or tubing. Explore Whistler Adventures, 604/935-3445

5) Work out at the gym, go for a swim, or have a jacuzzi. Meadow Park Sports Centre, 604/938-PARK

whistler watersports

Rafting

C3 Rafting, in the Village by taxi loop, 604/905-2777 or in Le Chamois base of Blackcomb, 604/938-1821

Wedge Rafting, Carleton Lodge near Whistler Village Gondola, 932-7171

Whistler River Adventures, Whistler Village Gondola Building, 604/932-3532

Jetboating

Whistler Jet Boat Adventure Ranch, 604/932-5078

Kayaking

Alta Lake Watersports, Kayak Rentals, 604/932-SAIL
Captain Holiday's Kayak & Adventure School, 604/905-2925

6) Treat yourself to a massage. Advanced Physiotherapy and Massage, 604/932-4203 and Blue Highways Shiatsu & Massage, 604/938-0777

7) Visit a spa. Esperanza Day Spa & Esthetics, 604/905-4855 and The Spa at Chateau Whistler, 604/938-2086

8) Have a drink in one of the many pubs, such as Black's Pub, Mountain Square, 604/932-6945; Cinnamon Bear Lounge, Delta Whistler, 604/932-1982; Crystal Lounge, 4154 Village Green, 604/938-1081; Mallard Bar, Chateau Whistler Resort, 604/938 8000; and many more.

9) Visit an art gallery. Black Tusk Gallery, Summit Lodge on Main St., 604/905-5540 and Plaza Galleries, Whistler's Town Plaza, 604/938-6233

Whistler Snuff Film

Brett Carlson had been planning the jump for weeks. Friends of his had started a Whistler film production company to make extreme skiing films, and Brett was one of the stars. He had the spot – a 30-metre snow-clad cliff next to Nordic Drive. He had the gear – a ramp was in place partway down the slope, and a buddy was standing by with a camcorder waiting to record the spectacular leap for the film. About all Carlson was missing was the speed. When he launched himself into the air late in the day on January 17, 2000, it quickly became clear he wasn't going to make it. He slammed into the blacktop about ⅔ of the way across the drive; the impact killed him instantly. Standing right nearby, his friends got everything on tape. Whistler RCMP seized the recording as evidence. After reviewing it to ascertain exactly what had occurred, they returned it. The owner – reportedly – tossed it into the fire, but there must have been a second copy. The film, *Parental Advisory*, which includes footage of Brett's ill-fated jump, is now available at the Heavy Hitting Films website (www.heavyhitting.com).

At Least it Wasn't *War of the Worlds*

Mark Monahan was a little late on the morning of January 27, 1999 when he drove across the bridge to pick up his buddy Rory Manning. The two were planning to set out early to hike up the Grouse Grind and do some snowshoeing, but Monahan had a book to finish reading first. He arrived to pick up Rory around 11 am, and the two made it to the base of the Grind around noon. Halfway up, an avalanche – the first ever recorded on the Grind – came crashing down, pinning Monahan to a tree and sweeping Manning out of sight. Monahan managed to dig himself out. Manning was never seen alive again. His body wasn't recovered until May. So what was the title of the book that delayed Monahan's arrival? *Into Thin Air.*

Hollyburn Folkies

Winter evenings when the moon is full, those in the know make their way up the snowy slopes of Cypress to Hollyburn lodge. Located a kilometre hike in from the parking lot on the cross-country ski trails, the 70-year-old mountain chalet plays host once a month to Fiddle, Folk and Full Moon Dancing, a regular winter event featuring hot cider and jigs and reels played on accordions, spoons, and old-time fiddles. Admission to the lodge is free, but you have to make the 20-minute trek up to the lodge on your own power. Flashlights are a good idea in case the moon doesn't quite shine through, but the silver bullets are really not required: werewolves can't abide the sound of folk.

Photo: courtesy Cypress Mountain

Photo: courtesy Cypress Mountain

WINTER SPORTS IN SUMMER
Blackcomb Mountain offers public summer glacier skiing and snowboarding from June to August, if conditions permit. Whistler also offers a summer snowboarding camp that will provide an intimate coaching environment, small groups, close supervision, and comfortable accommodations. *604/932-3434*

Lost Canadian Traditions

Canoe rentals? How's that a secret, you ask, in a town with rollerblading, sea kayaking, river rafting, sailing, snorkeling, and diving readily available. But with all of these choices, Lotuslanders have seemed to lose their appreciation for that most quintessential of Canadian activities, canoeing. Here are three local spots to reconnect with your paddling roots:

Buntzen Lake

Nestled up in the mountains north of Port Coquitlam, this beautiful lake comes to you courtesy of BC Hydro. Canoe rentals at Anmore Grocery. *469-9928*

Pitt Lake

The largest tidewater lake in the world offers incredible bird life and a chance to look at beavers. Rentals from Ayla Canoes at Grant Narrows. *941-2822*

Alouette Lake

Hidden away in Golden Ears Park north of Maple Ridge. Rocky Mountain Boat Rentals rents canoes to aid in exploration. *856-2883*

Ski Bums

On a wall in a bar called the Londoner in Kitzbuhl, Austria there's a poster of some 30 long-haired skiers, facing the camera wearing nothing but boots and smiles. The quasi-famous shot was taken in 1973 outside a notorious sex and party ski-bum squat in Whistler named Toad Hall. Photographers Tony Spence and Chris Speedie were so impressed with their effort they formed the Naked Truth Poster Company and printed up 10,000 posters. Copies of the shot, complete with bums, breasts, and all the associated paraphernalia, made their way from Whistler round the world. One of them wound up in Austria, where it now holds court over the Londoner's bar. According to the bartender, if you can prove you were in the photo, your drinks are on the house. Showing your face is not considered acceptable evidence.

fun in the outdoors

Should you tire of walks and cycles and blades, here are a few alternative ways to spend your leisurely weekends:

Gold Panning

It's not too late to strike it rich. True, the odds are against you, but you never know until you try. Gold pans can be purchased at Capilano Rock and Gem in North Vancouver (987-5311); they cost $10-15. For best results, scorch them over an open flame to burn off oil, then douse in cold water to give the kind of blue finish that contrasts well with placer gold. As for places to try your luck, the following have some history on their side, but no guarantees:

Emory Creek Provincial Park, Hwy. 7 south of Yale on the site of the former boomtown of Emory City.

Cayoosh Creek Park, near Lytton; has a panning preserve. Call 256-4289 for information.

Anywhere along the Fraser gravel bars near Hope. Watch for fish eggs, and call 660-2672 to see if anyone else has claims.

Llama Trekking

The Incas weren't entirely in the dark when it came to getting around. Llamas, unlike donkeys or burros, are remarkably docile, and more than happy to carry your 40 kilos of camping gear while you stroll along. Their only disadvantage, apparently, is a tendency to hum while they walk. Golden Ears Llamas (467-8555) offers a fully catered three-course meal on luxury treks, or a no-frills economy package. You can also try Cloudraker Llamas in Brackendale, north of Vancouver (898-4249).

CIVIC WAR?

Ever wonder about the Vancouver Parks Board's source of power? Vancouver is the only city in Canada where a body independent of the city is elected to rule over its system of municipal parks. And given that the Parks Board and City Hall have been fighting tooth and nail since the board was first established, it's a wonder that the city hasn't at some point simply moved to abolish those pesky park folks altogether. It may well have been to prevent just such a coup that the Parks Board installed its own artillery.

Ostensibly, of course, the Nine O'Clock Gun in Stanley Park, which makes itself known every night, was erected for the benefit of ships' captains; the cannon's evening report was the signal for ships' officers to reset their chronometers. But the gun's true purpose was let slip when its first keeper, William D. Jones, explained why the artillery piece was pointed the direction that is was: he had aimed it, he said, straight at City Hall.

Twice since then the Lord Mayors have shifted the seat of municipal power, but then the gun emplacement has also twice been renovated and realigned, the latest time in 1987. One can only presume that even now the parks board has the cannon pointed in exactly the direction it thinks necessary, to keep City Hall at bay.

Hidden Boat Rides

Everyone knows about the conservatory at Queen Elizabeth Park. But few, if any, know about the park's Black Water Boat Rides. Beneath the parking lot at Little Mountain's peak there lurks a dank, dripping chamber two football fields long and 30 metres deep, holding 30 million gallons of the city's drinking water. Periodically, engineers from the Greater Vancouver Regional District don rubber boots, drag an inflatable dinghy down the manhole, and set out on a tour of inspection through the pitch black chamber. So far, every boat has come back. With increasing cutbacks, will the GVRD soon be offering boat rides as a regular tourist attraction?

A Maze-ing Place

In the prologue to the British mystery novel *Summer Days*, a cuckolded English gentleman strips his wife naked and leaves her, together with the equally naked corpse of her latest lover, in the centre of a huge and fiendishly difficult garden maze. She tries to escape, but all pathways seem to lead back to the centre, where her lover's corpse lies covered in flies, growing ever more putrid in the summer sunshine. Eventually the tormented adulteress does herself in.

That's never happened in the garden maze at the VanDusen Botanical Gardens, at least according to the Vancouver Botanical Garden Society, which has operated the 22-hectare labyrinth since its inception in 1975. That's not to say it couldn't, however. Those considering a little extramarital activity might want to check out the maze first, just in case.

High School Shooting Gallery

Secluded behind the faded yellow walls of Vancouver Technical High School lies the remains of the city's only high school shooting gallery. Students from the 1950s and 1960s still remember tramping down several flights of stairs into a long narrow sub-basement with dirt walls and an eight-foot high ceiling, where they'd spend a happy hour loading and shooting .22-calibre slugs into wooden slabs set against the far wall. It's not exactly Columbine....

parking spaces

Tired of fighting the crowds on the Stanley Park seawall? Can't afford the pec or breast implants required for an afternoon at Kits Beach? Here are three of Vancouver's least-known places to commune with nature:

Renfrew Ravine Park

The term "park" is only a recent appellation; for the longest time this unloved bit of ravine – leftover from the days when Still Creek used to flow through here out to Burnaby Lake – was thought of mostly as a convenient spot to dispose of those used refrigerators, paint cans, or stolen Chevies cluttering your backyard. Then locals discovered that the little declivity's thick hedges and trees provided a great sheltering spot for passing birds, and a needed bit of nature on Vancouver's east side. Even with the official park designation, the powers-that-be still provide no maintenance, and passersby still dump their junk, but a local citizens' group meets each year to clear out the worst of the debris. Best discovery so far? A 1950s-style Coca-Cola fridge that, when cleaned off, repaired, plugged in, and inspected by an antique dealer, was reported to be the real thing.

Charles Park

Like certain Soviet cities at the height of the Cold War, this little neighbourhood park is so secret that it doesn't appear on any of the maps given out by the city or the Parks Board. So what are they hiding? A delightful little enclave, featuring exotic shrubs with magnificent flowers, a tranquil duck pond, and towering cottonwood trees that seem to block out the noise and bustle of the busy east side. Alas for the casual visitor, trying to locate Charles Park by driving around and asking the locals is a little like wandering the Siberian countryside asking the peasants for directions to Magnetogorsk. They all know it's there, but no one's quite sure where, and anyway, why are you asking? Fortunately there's an easier way. The next time you take your car for testing at the Boundary Road Air Care station, take a moment and park by the gate. Then get out and wander around. You're there.

STREAM LINES

As befits its rainforest location, the place that would one day be Vancouver used to overflow with more than a dozen little creeks and streams. Charting these old watercourses on a current city map shows a surprising number began where there are now shopping malls or parks. (Actually, this makes sense when you figure that shopping malls and parks are built on land generally undesirable for housing, which tend to be swamps, where streams tend to begin.) One such stream used to run from Arbutus Ridge Mall down through Kitsilano to the beach past Point Grey Road; remnants of this stream can be seen in Ravine Park at Yew and 33rd. Another, in the Mountain View Cemetery, flowed down through what is now Kingsgate Mall to the banks of False Creek on Great Northern Way.

For a while these little streams did their best to adapt to the newcomers in their midst. One early Kitsilano resident recalls that around 1910 there were chum salmon in the stream that flowed past his place at Fifth Avenue and Maple. Later on in the 1920s, when that branch became a ditch running beside Third Avenue, salmon would congregate under the electric street lamps. As the settlers and developers advanced, however, most of these little streams gave up the fight, either drying up entirely or becoming pathetic little trickles like the one that flows through Tatlow Park. Still others went underground. Put your ear to the manhole cover at the corner of 38th and St. George and you'll heard the rushing of one of these little streams, carrying on until the day it's safe to return to the surface.

Everett Crowley Park

The far southeast corner of Vancouver is an intriguing little realm, seemingly exempt from the laws that govern the rest of the city. In place of the usual comforting grid of rectilinear streets, this area sports a complicated tangle of cul-de-sacs and curvilinear crescents. And in place of the standard swings and soccer pitch there's Everett Crowley Park, 13-plus hectares of thick alder woods and grassy meadows, laced here and there with the occasional dark ravine, sunny babbling brook or clifftop view of Richmond's rural bits. There are paths for strollers, joggers, and mountain bikers, with the only proviso being that Vancouver's quasi-fascist obsession with anti-smoking measures has been given a slightly stronger imperative here: beneath this wilderness playground lie several thousand still decomposing tonnes of municipal waste. The methane seepage is expected to continue for at least another half century. Final tip for trivia lovers: Everett Crowley was the founder and operator of the still-functioning Avalon Dairy *(5805 Wales St., 434-2434)*, itself well worth a visit, if only for the all-natural ice cream.

Did lawn bowling ever strike you as a mysterious kind of activity? If you're a Vancouverite, your answer is probably no. Outsiders find the sport – older people in white outfits tossing balls across a severely manicured expanse of lawn – both peculiar and compelling. A European of my acquaintance at first remarked how nice it was that our mental patients got such regular exercise. And in the images of Vancouver presented to the rest of the world, lawn bowling appears with surprising frequency, showing up in a Robert Altman film set in Vancouver *(That Cold Day in the Park)* and in the following excerpt by the American author Mark Helpirn, published in the *New Yorker*:

The second and last time he had seen her had been in Vancouver during the war … he never found out what she had been doing there, apart from bowling on the green, in a formal white suit, in the company of a lot of pretty old ladies who took the game very seriously.…

They stood in the center of the green, oblivious of a growing stream of reprimands – she because she could not hear them, and he because he was enthralled. The old ladies were incensed: not only had their game been spoiled but they had been ignored. So they returned the fire and resumed play, paying no attention to the two wickets who stood apparently insensate, staring at one another in the middle of the contest. Balls began to whiz about like shrapnel.…

TOP SECRET NURSERY

A secret research station, where nameless civil servants conduct experiments with growth hormones, chemical agents, and genetic manipulation – only in America, or even worse, *The X-Files*? Try 51st and Main, where a 30-foot-high cedar hedge and a chain-link fence cordon off 10 city acres of undisclosed biological activity. Actually, the activity is disclosed every spring, when the folks from the city-run Sunset Nursery trot out their vast collections of *Lantana*, *Tibouchina*, and *Lisanthous*, not to mention mums, daffodils, and orchids, for display in the city's many parks. According to nursery officials, the hedge and fence are there only to prevent would-be orchid thieves, and not to disguise what's going on inside.

HOOP HIGHS AND LOWS

Bet you thought this secret — the second part at least — was about our beloved Grizzlies. Wrong. It's about the city's highest and lowest courts, measured from street level. The lowest is hidden away in the loading dock piers beneath the Waterfront Centre Hotel. Employees often pass their breaks shooting hoops, though it's a tough court for beginners; missed shots end up either in a hydro transformer or on the railway tracks. The highest court locally stands atop the roof of the main Post Office building on Georgia Street. Not much use for the general public, but Canada Post night crew have a running pick up game that starts each morning around 7:00, shortly after quitting time. That's not to say there's no Grizz connection, though. If things don't improve, the Grizz could look at using one of these locations for a practice court. At least then they'd be out of sight.

Photo: Blaine Kyllo

For those looking to accept their fate as Vancouverites and take up the sport, the following clubs are possibilities:

Dunbar Lawn Bowling Club,
31st Ave. and Highbury St., 228-8428

Kerrisdale Lawn Bowling Club,
5870 Elm St., 261-1116

Pacific Indoor Lawn Bowling Club,
169 E. 19th Ave., 874-2817

Stanley Park Lawnbowling Club,
Beach Ave. & Lagoon, 683-0910

Vancouver South Lawn Bowling Club,
4850 St. Catherines St., 874-3038

West Point Grey Lawn Bowling Club,
4376 W. 6th Ave., 224-6556

In days of yore, brave exploring types were said to be most intrigued by the parts of the map where cartographers had inked in "Tygers" and names of other more outlandish beasts. Take a look at a map of Greater Vancouver and you'll see something very similar: a huge expanse of the map of Delta, lying roughly between Highways 10 and 91 and the river, where there are absolutely no distinguishing features. Here, there may not be tigers, but there are bears. And blueberries, and sphagnum moss, and deer, and stunted lodgepole pine and hardhack spireas and a great deal of highly acidic water, all combined in a unique ecological system with the disingenuously prosaic name of Burns Bog.

Developers have tried at times to fill or dredge the area, most recently in 1999 when there was talk in Delta of a massive, new Disney-style amusement park, but the outcry from environmentalists has always saved the day. Access to this uncharted wilderness can be tricky, because it is not now (and may never be) a designated park. However, for those who dare, there's a reliable entranceway at the end of 80th Street off River Road. Once in the bog, it's wise to stick to existing trails. Wandering off can damage the fragile ecosystem, and increase your chances of being swallowed up in a sinkhole of soft peat, to be found only many centuries hence – your body perfectly preserved in the acidic ooze – by a troupe of curious anthropologists.

THE SECRET OF PACIFIC SPIRIT

To locals, of course, the name "Pacific Spirit Park" is itself a mystery – true Vancouverites refuse to call the 500-odd hectares of parkland that separate UBC from the city anything but the "Endowment Lands." Locals are also likely to suggest that the only mystery you'll ever stumble across on one of the area's many small trails is a decaying human corpse or two (the area has long been a favoured spot for getting rid of inconvenient dead bodies). In recent years, however, the Seymour Demonstration Forest has claimed the prize for favoured human dumping ground, and in any case there's more lurking in the Endowment Lands than the occasional lost skull.

Stanley Park Larks

Photo: Blaine Kyllo

For example, just off Top Trail — which runs from Imperial Road to the water reservoir on Sasamat Street — are the remains of what used to be a spy station. The grown-over foundation near the alder grove is all that's left of a remote monitoring station and antenna farm used by the CBC to eavesdrop on foreign radio broadcasts from 1961 to 1971. Up by the Plains of Abraham near Belmont Avenue, the grass masks the remains of a different kind of farm. John W. Stewart ran a dairy operation on this site around 1909; the only portion remaining is the concrete foundation of his barn on the south side of the clearing. In the 1960s, a later owner tried to get permission to turn the land into a shopping mall, to which the province and local residents replied: "Over our dead bodies." The land was subsequently sold back to the province.

Stanley Park is without question one of Vancouver's most beautiful attractions, a large urban greenspace that is visited by tourists and Vancouverites alike, on foot, bike, blade, or in car. Here are a few things you probably didn't know about it:

On Swans and Squirrels

The plethora of park swans are descendants of a pair obtained from New South Wales Zoological Society in 1901. The park's grey squirrels are descended from a half-dozen pairs imported from the New York Parks Department in 1909.

Fort Siwash

Far up on a tree by the path on the sandstone cliffs above Siwash Rock is a set of weathered crossbars, the last remnants of a battery of four-inch guns installed in the park in 1914 to protect the city from the German battleship *Leipzig*, then in port in San Francisco. Authorities made use of much the same spot in World War II, this time installing a powerful searchlight battery. The remnants of this installation are still visible in the bunker/observation area looking out over Siwash Rock. The area is famous for other things as well; just after World War II, police arrested a man brewing tea in a cave near Siwash Rock. It turned out the man had been living there for 17 years. He liked it, he said, because in those pre-seawall days it was a spot much favoured by nude sunbathers.

A Place for All

Stanley Park's Ceperly Playground (between Second Beach and Lost Lagoon) is truly a place for all ages – young, old,

dead. If you examine the low granite divider separating the playground from the picnic area, you'll notice that some of the stones forming the wall appear quite regular and polished, as smooth and neatly formed as gravestones, which in fact they are. Back in 1968, the city replaced many of the stones from the 1919 section of the Mountain View Cemetery. It seemed a shame not to make use of such stones, so the city installed them here. Names and dates have been faced towards the inside, so as not to freak out the little 'uns.

Lost Road

Stand by the Aquarium in the midst of Stanley Park and let your eyes follow the double line of deciduous trees parading down through the picnic area almost to the pedestrian underpass. You're looking at the remains of the Esplanade, one of the park's first ceremonial driveways. It was long ago torn up, and the roadbed replaced with sod.

Secret Signals

Though now the exclusive abode of tourists and aggressive raccoons, the series of terraces cascading down from Prospect Point was built for neither. Originally it was part of a long staircase leading from a lighthouse at the base of the cliff up to a signal station located more or less where the restaurant is now. Back in the pre-radio days of 1909, the little flags and Morse flashes from the men on the point were the only way the harbourmaster could find out what was happening out in English Bay.

Regional Riches

Call it a poverty of riches, but when Vancouverites look for outdoor playgrounds outside of the city limits, their thoughts tend to glom on to the big three or four. There are reasons for this, of course. Whistler has its massive advertising budget, Cypress and Seymour are just there in the city's consciousness day and night, and Manning Park to the east has history on its side. What gets overlooked are some of the quieter, quirkier, more secretive outdoor spots in close proximity to the city.

Minnekhada Park

Enough with the mountains already. This park offers a now-rare chance to experience that other landform that makes B.C. so special, the riverine marsh. A series of marked trails lead to spots to view the incredible quantities of birdlife. Most impressive, perhaps, is the spot overlooking the nearby Addington Wildlife Management Area, a massive marsh adjoining the Pitt River that is entirely off-limits to humans. Also worth a visit is the Scottish-style hunting lodge, now a visitors' centre. Access is via Coast Meridian Road, off the Lougheed Highway in Port Coquitlam.

Redwood Park

Although Stanley Park's collection of great cedars is impressive, and the trees around the lighthouse at Point Atkinson are sublime, nowhere in the Pacific Northwest can you get a better view of that western beauty, the Giant Redwood, than at Redwood Park, where an early settler and his sons collected 32 species of this western tree, including the mighty redwood. Walking trails let you wander amidst the tree trunks, and you can also clamber about the treehouse, where the family had their home until 1958. The park is near the intersection of 176th St. and 20th Ave. in Surrey.

Cypress Falls Park

In addition to providing views of a lovely series of waterfalls, the short walk through this park offers the chance to see some of the finest groves of Douglas Fir and Red Cedar still standing in the Lower Mainland. Access is via Woodgreen Place, off of Woodgreen Drive in West Vancouver. Take Exit #4 from the Upper Levels Highway.

Remembering a Disaster

Canada has been called a nation of beautiful losers, which is perhaps why there are so many monuments to disaster, such as the Chehalis monument, set in a fringe of trees on the land side of Stanley Park Road, just before the Brockton Point cut-off. The flared column topped by a cross commemorates a 1906 disaster in which the Union Steamship tug *Chehalis* collided with the CPR liner *Princess of Victoria*. Nine of 15 people on the *Chehalis* died, including the captain and his bride of just a few weeks. Neither the bodies nor the tug were ever recovered.

Animals and Activists

Anyone watching the ongoing struggle between the Aquarium and animal rights activists could be forgiven for thinking it's the kind of issue that carries on forever. They'd be more right than they knew. The park's first permanent structure, built in 1894, was a bear pit, dug to house the zookeeper's captive black bear. Before that, the bear had been chained to a stump near the park's Georgia Street entrance. He spent the days snoozing away his captivity, watched over by curious but cautious passers-by. That is, until a visiting Methodist minister's wife, possibly hoping to convince the brute to give up his slothful ways and make himself respectable, took it upon herself to poke the sleeping bruin repeatedly in the side with the tip of her umbrella. The bear put up with the first few pokes, then swiped at her with enough force to relieve his erstwhile instructor of her umbrella, her skirt, and her petticoat. In the ensuing uproar, a pit was deemed necessary, if only to protect the bear. (Eight years later, the Parks Board received its first complaint letter about the bear pit, asking "what can be done to remedy the evil." The pit was closed two years later.)

Dining

Of the many secrets to dining out in Vancouver, the greatest secret is the city itself. Vancouver has become a sort of culinary paradox: at once paid lip service by visiting food journalists and toasted by visitors for our innovative and distinctive local cuisine, but still somewhat undiscovered, certainly when compared to other Pacific Rim culinary destinations such as San Francisco and Sydney.

That's good news for you and me, but the gastronomic landscape is changing, and quickly. Fuelled by articles in food magazines and our burgeoning cruise and ski industries, the word is spreading fast. It has everything to do with our diverse palate of cuisines and the extraordinary quality and value that Vancouver's restaurateurs are able to put to the plate. Consider this: dining out here is at least one-third less than in major American cities, and about half that of Europe. And for Brits, of course, it might as well be free. So our advice is straightforward: plunge in – as unafraid as the cooking you will find in this city – and eat it up.

In the pages that follow, we let slip the ultimate insiders' secrets to the city's dining scene, including the newest of the new, prime spots for power lunches, and romantic spaces. We give you some free advice on how to navigate a power room. We even deal you some restaurants with bars where your server can't get lost.

When Bad Things Happen to Good Diners

Scoping a dining room is easy. Look at the menu, often posted outside, taking special note of typos, misspellings, and (the number-one reason to flee) any hint that a copywriter was involved. Also glance at the reviews posted alongside. If there are typos and misspellings in them, or if the reviewer is too obviously related to the proprietor, move quickly along. (A complete absence of reviews is not necessarily a bad sign, suggesting, at the very least, confidence.) Let us dissuade you from two popular misconceptions: lineups and semi-trailers in the parking lot are not reliable indicators. We've seen lineups for methadone clinics, and semi-trailers outside establishments where the waitresses were savoury but the food decidedly less so.

Inside the door, mentally time how long it takes someone to notice you – if it's more than half a minute or so, keep your guard up. If the greeting, when it does come, reflects a nasty attitude problem, suggest that "Gosh, we really do hope you're feeling better soon," and show your heels. And if you are kept waiting longer than 20 minutes (much more likely to occur for the second "turn," i.e., after 8 pm) you are completely within your rights to leave – but of course, you'd better have backup.

Restaurant Navigation

While the days of intimidating proprietors and imperious headwaiters are history, there are some common sense approaches to make your evening more enjoyable, and maybe even memorable.

The best thing to do on a first date or for an important business dinner? Visit the restaurant ahead of time, get to know the room (and pick your table), examine the menu, spend a moment with the wine list, and get to know your new best friend – the maître d'. At the very least, introduce yourself over the phone, exchange pleasantries, and have a copy of the menu faxed over. Consider pre-ordering a platter of starters (perhaps a platter of fresh seafood or antipasti) and an iced bottle of wine (bubbles can be helpful) to get the evening rolling right along the moment you sit down.

Finally, a word about wine. Don't be shy about telling the server what your tastes run to. And certainly don't be shy about saying what your wallet can manage. If you are already seated, point to the section on the wine list that suits your budget, and repeat after me: "We're going to be ordering the roasted chicken and the ahi. What do you think about this Quivering Pines pinot gris?" This is restaurant code for your price point. The server is then honour-bound to confirm that choice as suitable, or to suggest something else, plus or minus about $5 to $10.

And your side of the contract? Well that's easy, too. First, never be a "No Show." If you can't make your reservation, absolutely, positively let the restaurant know. Second, tip well – 15 percent of the bill (net of tax) for standard service, 20 percent for exemplary; and a little more if the barkeep drives you home.

ROMANTIC DEUCES

Okay, so you've met Mr. Right, he cooks, you think you can train him to do windows, and he adores your Jack Russell. Where to go for that closing date?

- Table 45 in the rear corner at **Bacchus Ristorante** (845 Hornby St., 689-7777) or, in the lounge, Table 15 beside the fireplace.

- Table 20, in one of the side alcoves at **Il Giardino** (1382 Hornby St., 669-2422), or Table B20 – a raised deuce – on the patio.

- Table 1, around the corner from the sideboard at **Piccolo Mondo** (850 Thurlow St., 688-1633).

the quintessential Vancouver

Vancouver's burgeoning regional cuisine is underwritten by restaurateurs and chefs with a heady passion for sourcing the very best of local ingredients. To find these distinct flavours and the comfortable rooms that speak loudest to this city's perch on the Pacific at the edge of the rainforest, go here:

BEST ROMANCE-ON-A BUDGET (Outdoors)

Vera's Hamburger Shack
No better place than Vera's Hamburger Shack, in West Vancouver's Dundarave Park (across the street from the Beach House at Dundarave Pier). Dundarave is an improbably beautiful beachside park pointed towards Point Grey. Proprietor Gerald Tritt looks like everyone's image of the jolly restaurateur, and is. His reasonably priced, fresh-grilled hamburgers are legendary — try "Vic's Special," billed as "double patties, onions, tomatoes, and bypass." Quality drinks, desserts, and snacks. Open April through October. Cash only, no liquor license.

Photo: Blaine Kyllo

Bishop's

Proprietor John Bishop (who has taken a strong leadership role in sourcing fresh, local ingredients in the season) works shoulder to shoulder with chef Dennis Green to present an uncomplicated but intense approach to local cooking. The small dining room is a charm, with a rotation of canvases by local artists and a stunning wine cellar. *2183 W. 4th Ave., 738-2025*

C

Proprietor Harry Kambolis's passion for all things local (see Raincity Grill, next page) shines through chef Rob Clark's unfettered approach to modern fish cookery. It's tough to make a misstep here (but do listen to the nightly specials), and the restaurant's oceanside location on the north shore of False Creek doesn't hurt, either. Clark's octopus bacon is extraordinary and his combinations of scallops and *foie gras* a suave pleasure. The wine list is beautifully paired to the menu, the service assured. Locals flock for the lunchtime seafood dim sum which is reasonably priced and delicious.
1600 Howe St., 681-1164

Chartwell

Executive chef Douglas Anderson has pushed this lovely, cosseting room even further into a local palate: extraordinary fish preps and an attention to vegetables and the subtle saucing of a savant. The regular Producer's Dinners celebrate the provender of the province and alternate with the quarterly wine dinners that are the city's best. The service is calibrated *à la minute*; the wine list lusty and far-reaching.
Four Seasons Hotel, 791 W. Georgia St., 689-9333

Diva at the Met

Under executive chef Michael Noble's direction, Diva continues to evolve in its role as progenitor of our cooking dialect, but now with a greater emphasis on sauces. Diva restaurant chef Andrew Springett is a talented and disciplined young master in delivering locality onto the plate – you know you are eating *here*. The Diva tasting menus are unique, contrapuntal displays of taste and texture. The wine list is beautifully

BEST HOTEL DINING

900 West

It seems a little absurd to call the Hotel Vancouver's 900 West a "secret." Yet this is a restaurant that will often yield a choice table on nights when lesser restaurants are booked up, which is difficult to understand. We think it's one of the city's nicest rooms, and the contemporary North American cooking, under the direction of executive chef Robert Le Crom, is superlative.
900 W. Georgia St., 669-9378

Manhattan

Manhattan is hidden away on the second floor of the Delta Suites Hotel and locals haven't discovered it yet, making it the perfect place for an illicit meeting. Even if your motives are completely pure, we recommend chef David Griffith's expressive and just plain beautiful creations, very reasonably priced for downtown power-fare. Weekend brunches are also first-rate.
550 W. Hastings St., 689-8188

More Great Tables

For Closing an Important Deal
Tables 233 or 243, the cozy fours in front of the fireplace, at **Chartwell**.
791 W. Georgia St., 844-6715

For parties of eight
Table 1, a large round, at **Il Giardino**. 1382 Hornby St., 669-2422

For taking out-of-towners
On the window at the **Five Sails** in the Pan Pacific.
300-999 Canada Place Way, 662-8111

organized, with a long section of hard-to-find VQA bottles. The service is utterly professional.
Metropolitan Hotel, 645 Howe St., 681-1164

Lumière

Celebrated chef Rob Feenie has outgrown his wunderkind status (Lumière has won *Vancouver Magazine*'s Restaurant of the Year Award five years running). What shows up on the plate now is a less constructed, more nuanced take on local with just the barest innuendo of Feenie's French training. The tasting menus — vegetarian and carnivorous and of varying lengths — are why you are here. It's one sitting, spend the evening, and eat it up. This is consistently one of the best restaurants on the continent; the wine list and service match.
2551 W. Broadway, 739-8185

Raincity Grill

Another Harry Kambolis treat of a room, this time slightly more casually-styled, but with the same assertive reach for local ingredients and flavours. Consulting chef Scott Kidd's menu starts with sturdy delicacies such as Pearl Bay Oyster "Japafellers," a Pacific Rim take on Oysters Rockefeller served Motoyaki style. The grilled Prince George leg of lamb is served with local rainbow chard and chanterelles in a fig-port jus. The wine list is legendary, not least for pioneering the "edutainment" of local and Cascadian wines by the glass.
1193 Denman St., 685-7337

best restaurants with bars

Not penal institutions, although some bad-mannered diners would qualify. Bar dining can actually offer many comforts, not the least being that your server can't get lost.

Bacchus Lounge

Superb bar menu (or dine from the full restaurant card) in one of the city's premier lounges. This is a warm and inviting place where drinks are made properly, deals get done, and even far-fetched romances are launched.
Wedgewood Hotel, 845 Hornby St., 608-5319

Blue Water Café & Raw Bar

Three bars, actually: a raw bar, a bar bar, and a vodka and sake bar with a surface of ice (bring your own Zamboni). Very consistent, innovative seafood preparations from the accomplished hand of chef James Walt, and a well-constructed wine list. Experts take a *plateaux de mer* – heaps of fresh seafood – at the raw bar.
1095 Hamilton St., 688-8078

Cioppino's Enoteca

A happy new arrival, Enoteca (literally "wine library") is a pretty feat of tall blonde design, comprising a bar, an elegant private dining room, and a granite sushi bar, behind which the incomparable Yoshi Tabo lets loose torrents of the city's Japanese cuts of fresh fish with exemplary presentation.
1129 Hamilton St., 685-8462

Circolo

Umberto Menghi – never one to rest on his laurels – has doubled the space formerly occupied by Mangiamo and, in a gutsy makeover, recast the space completely. The look is a jambalay of Umberto's greatest hits: scads of rich wooden millwork, gold highlights in the picture frames and trims, and chubby plaster cornucopia suspended over modern banquettes. In a departure for Umberto, Circolo pulls in the cuisines of America (husky steaks and chops),

BEST ELEGANT CHINESE

Imperial Seafood

The view from this soaring Art Deco room in the historic Marine Building is but one reason we keep returning to Imperial. The service is smart and highly professional, and conducive to entertaining out-of-town guests. But it's the food that really draws us back: high-end Cantonese, very well-prepared, and amongst the best dim sum in the city.
355 Burrard St., 688-8191

Kirin Seafood

This City Square veteran has settled into a long run, serving up platters of Cantonese and Szechuan seafood to round tables of appreciative business groups and families. If business takes you to City Hall (immediately across Cambie Street), book Kirin, then return for the weekend dim sum.
555 W. 12th Ave., 879-8038

Oriental Tea Garden

Offering "exquisite dim sum" in the opinion of one of our Chinese-Canadian friends, the Oriental is both a destination restaurant, and a great place to eat pre-boarding. The smile of contentment on your face (as your fellow passengers chow down on an Air Canada steak tougher than Pat Carney) will say it all.
Vancouver International Airport, International Terminal, 303-3238

Italy (well-made pastas and a superb, if expensive, beet and *bufala* mozzarella salad), and France (very good fish soup). Circolo means gathering or meeting place in Italian – but be assured of one thing: this ain't Rotary.
1116 Mainland St., 687-1116

Pastis

Skillful, forward bistro cooking from the pans of the accomplished Frank Pabst. Co-proprietor John Blakeley is one of the best (and most charming) front guys in town. Pay attention to the specials. Pabst is one of those young but old-school guys who does his shopping every day. Order a roasted chicken at the bar with a glass or two from the wisely chosen wine list.
2153 W. 4th Ave., 731-5020

The Sandbar

Brent Davies' (Teahouse, Cardero's) renovation of the historic Mulvaney's on Granville Island uncovered a lot of memories and not a few petrified Cajuns. The Teredo Lounge offers well-made drinks and the well made-up; when you get hungry, order the squid with chilis, the best item on the menu.
1535 Johnston St., 669-9030

Smoking Dog Bar & Grill

The city's best steak *frites* (a generous filet *au poivre*) and duck, and, funnily enough for a French-styled bistro, some of the best pastas. The patio, facing the intersection of 1st and Cypress, is ground zero for watching the tightly clad and nearly had strolling to nearby fitness academies and condos.
1889 W. 1st Ave., 732-8811

Pink Pearl

The Pink Pearl moved from strength to strength recently, as superchef Lam Kam Shing moved from the Grand King to head up the Pink Pearl's wok line. His presence was felt at a recent banquet featuring Monk Jump over the Wall soup and diabolically good peppered ostrich. The restaurant continues its reputation for sophisticated, inventive cooking; the dim sum is also superior.
1132 E. Hastings St., 253-4316

Sun Sui Wah

Consistent, reliable, noisy, huge, crowded, and chaotic: all of these describe Sun Sui Wah. It may not be the best place to take a new romance, but it's marvelous family entertainment and the cooking lively and intelligent. The squab is a signature dish not to be missed; the dim sum is high calibre, too.
3888 Main St., 872-8882

best Japanese

Cioppino's Enoteca

I want to have a cut-man in my corner like Yoshi Tabo. I like everything about him, including his fastidious cleanliness, his use of only prime ingredients, and his delicate presentations. But most of all I like his food – captured in the nuanced style of Kyoto, his rolls are innuendoes of layered flavours, brought forward with contrapuntal textures. Yoshi is now ensconced at the coolest sushi bar in town, and he himself is the genuine article – his knives are old and beautiful. His maguro gomae is a gently spiced take on tuna belly cubes and crispy scallions. The more adventurous sit at the bar, and point.

But there's more at Cioppino's Enoteca. Much more, in fact – rotisseried chickens, braised beef short ribs in Marsala and red wine, classic pastas (such as the best spaghetti Bolognese in town – a steal at $13.95), very well made soups (try the lobster bisque to kiss off the chill of January), and seafood antipasti. Bonus round: the crafty wine pairings with the sushi, from local pinot gris to iced sake. This may be the best pre-event venue in town.
1129 Hamilton St., 685-8462

BEST CHEAP AND CHEERFUL CHINESE

Bo Kong Vegetarian

You certainly don't have to be vegetarian to enjoy Bo Kong's fresh cooking. The prices are hardly discouraging, either, with a lot of creative dishes that you may want to replicate at home, even if you decide to leave the rather spare décor at the door. *3068 Main St., 876-3088*

Daimo Noodle House

A quick noodle fix on the way home? The east side location is open until 2 am, the better to soak up the evening's excesses with noodles galore and very good won tons. *3163 Main St., 876-8520; Daimo Noodle Express, 8185 Granville St., 264-7873*

Kam Gok Yuen

Homey Cantonese selections but insiders go for the barbecued pork and duck. Very good value. *142 E. Pender St., 683-3822*

Victoria Chinese Restaurant

Food writer Stephen Wong, a former chef, is the authority on Chinese cooking in Vancouver. He counsels that if you like dim sum and want to venture beyond the ordinary this should be your next stop. Among his recommendations: ostrich and ginseng and, at dinner, a lettuce wrap with minced squab.

1055 W. Georgia St., 669-8383

Wing Wah

Ask James Barber, urban peasant and *Vancouver Magazine* columnist, to suggest a place for lunch and this little family-run Szechuan spot may well be his answer. In season, order their asparagus version of the classic Szechuanese fried green-beans dish.

260 E. Broadway, 879-9168

Sun Wong Kee

This is that elusive entity: a cheap, everyday Chinese restaurant with food to match much more expensive spots. It's best to order from the specials scribbled on a board by the kitchen; look especially for live crab, rock cod, and lobsters, and trust that however they're cooked, they'll be wonderful.

4136 Main St., 879-7231

Misaki

Everyone in Vancouver has their favourite Japanese spot, whether it's pricey-but-exquisite Tojo's or a hole-in-the-wall down the block like Shiro's at Cambie and 15th. Few would name Misaki, hidden away in the bowels of the five-star Pan Pacific Hotel, largely as a service to the hotel's large Japanese clientele. But the truth is, this is some of the most interesting Japanese food in town, especially notable for its subtle incorporation of flavours and ingredients from around the Pacific Rim.
300-999 Canada Place Way, 891-2893

Sushi Q/Modern Club

Japanese restaurants in Vancouver tend to follow a formula. Don't get me wrong, it's not a bad formula. In fact, visitors from Hong Kong, the US, and yes, even Japan, are consistently amazed at the quality and bargain prices of our sushi. Still, there's no mistaking most of them as Vancouver-style Japanese restaurants. Two spots that break the mold are located, oddly enough, in Dunbar, a pleasant neighbourhood not normally known for much of anything and certainly not its restaurants. Sushi Q specializes in seldom-seen soups, stews, and noodle dishes, available for eat-in or takeout, while Modern Club is noted for, among other things, its Japanese pizza, which uses no pastry, cheese or tomatoes. (Glad you asked: shredded cabbage, among other things.) Both are interesting, inexpensive, and quick.
Sushi Q, 4385 Dunbar St., 221-7874; Modern Club, 3446 Dunbar St., 739-0170

Best South Asian (and beyond)

Vij's is one of the best-known and most-acclaimed Vancouver restaurants – so acclaimed that Vikram Vij was invited to cook his North American/South Asian fusion cuisine at a James Beard Foundation dinner in New York; so well-known that getting in can mean a half-hour wait in the attractive bar (decorated like a very stylish, slightly retro rumpus room), as reservations aren't accepted. *1480 W. 11th Ave., 736-6664*

Can't wait? Well, one solution is a short spin, or even a walk, to one of three nearby restaurants that serve cooking that's in the same Indian/North American fusion vein and, while perhaps not quite as ambitious, is priced substantially lower.

One of these, in fact, is Vikram Vij's original, much smaller, and more modestly turned-out space at 1453 West Broadway *(736-3312)*, now operating as **Velvet Café**, which, despite its current ownership by a woman named Yoo Choi, still serves a menu reminiscent of Vij's early days and is also open for lunch weekdays.

Another is **Sami's**, which was opened in 1998 by Sami Lalji, who like Vij, cut his restaurant teeth working at local fine-dining standard-bearer Bishop's. Lalji went on to open the much-lauded Star Anise before moving on to launch Sami's, unprepossessingly located in a strip mall at the high-traffic corner at Broadway and Oak. Here, as at Vij's, the emphasis is on beautifully presented meat, fish, and vegetarian dishes that employ South Asian spicing and techniques in contemporary North American fashion. Unlike Vij's, every dish is a mere $10 ($9 at lunch), and every bottle of wine a barely marked-up $20. Servings aren't large, but sometimes (as with a chicken in pastry dish offered as a daily special recently) verge on the exquisite. *986 W. Broadway, 736-8330*

The third is **Major Chutney**, which opened in the summer of 1998. Here the cooking is more classic but, if possible, even a better value. A huge dinner – say, parathas stuffed with caramelized onions, spiced potatoes, and fresh cilantro, followed by Bengal-spiced curried chicken served with basmati rice, vegetable subji, a raita, a salsa, and naan bread – will run all of $12 or $13. And we think the cooking ranks with the very best of Vancouver's more traditional South Asian restaurants, few of which can match it in atmosphere. *3432 Cambie St., 875-9533*

BEST FORGOTTEN BISTRO

Beetnix

In the past couple of years, Vancouver has experienced an explosion of bistros serving quick, high-quality, $15-range entrees that take their influences from French, Asian, and local cuisines. Predating most of them but somehow lost in the shuffle is Beetnix, a pretty little spot across from City Hall, where chef Adrienne Woolfries does a nice job serving bistro favourites displaying subtle Asian influences. *2549 Cambie St., 874-7133*

BEST BARBECUE

Dix Barbecue & Brewery

Mark James' most recent entry, and many would say, at least from a food standpoint, his best. Southern, slow-cooked barbecue and micro-brewed beers – the smell of smoke welcomes diners, especially before and after sporting events. Best in show: the pulled pork shoulder (try it on its own, or in the reasonably priced sandwich), back ribs, and Kentucky-style smoked lamb. This is good food, fairly priced, in an attractive Yaletown room. Service is you-all friendly, especially from the barmen, one of whom is an off-duty BC Lion. *871 Beatty St., 682-2739*

BEST POWER BUSINESS LUNCHES

Susan Minton's supremely gracious service at **Chartwell** in the Four Seasons Hotel *(791 W. Georgia St., 689-9333)*. Or sample David Griffith's stellar cooking at the quietly contemporary **Manhattan** in the Delta Suites Hotel *(550 W. Hastings St., 689-8188)*.

BEST BUDGET BUSINESS DINNERS

Favorito

A pleasantly proper little Italian trat, where beautifully made pastas run less than $10 at lunch and wines such as the Taurino Salice Salentino receive only a modest mark-up. *552 W. Broadway, 876-3534*

Phnom Penh

If they're cool enough to handle the hot and sour soup, garlic prawns, fried squid in lemon pepper, and Chinese greens, take them to the Chinatown location of Phnom Penh. Inexplicably, this award-winning Cambodian/Vietnamese room still remains a secret, especially amongst occidents waiting to happen. *244 East Georgia St., 682-5777*

Zinfandels Grill & Seafood Bistro

Especially if your clients (or bankers) appreciate good cooking and your economical approach to life. *1355 Hornby St., 681-4444*

When it's not raining, Vancouverites love to eat in the great outdoors. Many restaurants offer al fresco dining; here are a few of them:

Jericho Galley

This food at this café on the second floor of the Jericho Sailing Centre is fairly standard pub fare – the equivalent of a Milestones. The view, however, is outstanding – an unobstructed vista of English Bay, Howe Sound, and the glaciers of the Tantalus Range in the distance. *1300 Discovery, 224-4177*

Il Giardino

Photo: Blaine Kyllo

Hidden behind a little yellow house not far from downtown, the flower-decked patio is a favoured haunt of Vancouver's movers and shakers. Not surprisingly, the cuisine is Tuscan. *1382 Hornby St., 669-2422*

CinCin

This nearly waterproof second-floor patio boasts overhead heaters and fine Mediterranean cuisine, both designed to battle the winter chill. *1154 Robson St., 688-7338*

Mona's Fine Lebanese Cuisine

Courtyard surrounded by high-rises features fountain, smoking lounge, and belly dancers Thursday to Saturday. The fare is Middle Eastern. *1328 Hornby St., 689-4050*

Joe Fortes Seafood & Chop House

First-rate shellfish bar downstairs, but on fine evenings go to the outdoor rooftop patio to find the bold, the beautiful, and the bivalves. *777 Thurlow St., 669-1940*

Photo: Blaine Kyllo

Cioppino's in Yaletown has a large open dining room, composed of timber posts and beams looking into the backlights of the kitchen: deceptively simple. It's a fitting arena for chef (and proprietor) Pino Posteraro's deceptively simple and brilliantly clean cooking. The much-abused descriptor of Mediterranean cuisine truly applies here – Posteraro draws on both his Italian lineage and his extensive resumé built in southern France – on any given night this is one of the city's top restaurants. The results are often most astounding in classic dishes: a *casarecce* with duck ragout and oranges that just goes on and on; a perfectly cooked Dover sole served off the bone; an understated spaghetti Bolognese. The crowd is liberally sprinkled with local and visiting celebrities, the long bar a gauntlet of young people with the bones of a German airport. The private dining room seats up to 24 and offers the best catered meals in the city. The wine list is very extensive but can get pricey quickly. Mâitre d's Massimo Piscopo and Celistino Posteraro choreograph the room professionally. Long Friday lunches at Cioppino's are becoming a welcome Vancouver salon of good food and conversation.
1133 Hamilton St., 688-7466

BEST USE OF $20 WE KNOW

Tangerine

For the price of bribing your way into a disreputable nightclub, you could eat a very good meal here, albeit with water. Start with chef Trevor LaValley's sesame and honey roasted eggplant, served on baby spinach with jasmine rice ($8), then follow with his grilled ponzu kingfish, served on an udon miso salad with green chili tempura ($12). There – you've just eaten a meal that is complex and remarkably satisfying and in a room that is attractively sleek and modern, as is the service. Tangerine is the best place to eat on the two-block outdoor mall of mini-gastrodomes, located at the north foot of Yew Street just above the beach—explore a few of the other spots if you have something else on your mind.
1685 Yew St., 739-4677

carnivores live here

Vancouverites, it seems, are not unlike other urbanites who are increasingly scoffing at healthful eating and going gung-ho on red meat and martinis. What else can explain the booming popularity of retro, high-end steakhouses, appealing to those with limitless expense accounts? Here are a couple of prime choices for your carnivorous pleasure:

Photo: Elaine Kyllo

Gotham Steakhouse & Cocktail Bar

Best beef: 23 oz. Porterhouse, $48.75
615 Seymour St., 605-8282

Morton's of Chicago

Best beef: 24 oz. Porterhouse: $45.95 (or 48 oz. Porterhouse for two for $91.90)
Sinclair Centre, 750 W. Cordova St., 915-5105

Best Place to Get Healthy

In the village of cafés (and fitness academies) that now hugs West 1st between Cypress and Chestnut, **Raw** offers roughage in such a variety and profusion that the tasty organic salads, smoothies, and sandwiches are a powerful draw. But the other draws are the artful little place itself, with window boxes that remind more of Saltspring Island than Kits, and the proprietors, the fabulous Savereux triplets. Sunny summer afternoons, this strip is centre ice.
1849 W. 1st Ave., 737-0420

BEST AIRPLANE REPLACEMENT FOOD

Globe @ YVR

Concept: an in-terminal (thus: YVR) restaurant, bar, and lounge (filled with plump furniture for weary travellers) that serves very good food and drinks in a calming and beautifully decorated room. In short, Globe is like a first-class lounge for the price of a beer. The food is innovative and often as international as the livery of the taxiing aircraft beneath: long braises, well-ramped curries, local fish heightened with lightly acidulated sauces, and very good vegetable preps. Like all Fairmont hotels, Globe has a daunting list of draft beers, and an extensive wine list featuring a range of VQA selections. Cool your jets.
Fairmont Vancouver Hotel, International Terminal, Vancouver International Airport, 248-3281

In Quest of the Perfect Espresso

Arise, ye self-medicating espresso fetishists: the best two-shot in town is at **Artigiano** *(1101 Pender St., 685-5333)*. Operated by Vince Piccolo, former owner of Villa del Lupo, Artigiano offers extraordinary grinds that remind one of Italy – and of a time before those ubiquitous green coffee shops swiped all our best intersections. Suave soups and first-rate pannini inform the lunch hour. Closed dinners and Sunday.

Internationally renowned television personality Steve Burgess recommends **Turk's Coffee Exchange** *(3-1276 Commercial Dr., 255-5805)*, **Lugz Coffee Lounge** *(2525 Main St., 873-6766)*, and **Bean Around the World** *(2977 Granville St., 730-9555)*.

In the heart of downtown Kitsilano, at the corner of First and Cypress lies the **Epicurean Deli** *(1898 W. 1st Ave., 731-5370)*. Various bikers (from ten-speed teams to Harleys) collide with cashmere twin sets, all for terrific coffees, pastries, and gelato. Lunchtime brings the town's best casual sling of carbonara, meatballs the size of softballs, and great bread; local experts take home the hot pickled eggplant, the Italian equivalent of a bar snack.

Best of the Broadway Strip

At **Vertical**, successor to Moomba and Orestes, the young but experienced owners have re-styled the room in warm taupe walls, cool blue lighting, and a pretty bar. Chef Christine Irvine has styled the menu to attract the core crew that eats up and down Broadway. So what's her secret? Well, everything – food, service, and décor all mesh, something you can't always say about the neighbourhood competition. In fact, it all works – fetching cooking, especially at night when the card steps into bistroland with long-braised lamb shanks, a risotto- and walnut-stuffed game hen, and several sharing platters, with a long suit in seafood.
3116 W. Broadway, 737-2181

BEST DAILY BREAD

Boleto at Ecco il Pane

Pamela Brown's keen eye for maximizing small spaces steered Boleto at Ecco il Pane in the right direction – she's warmed it up, quieted its hard edges, and made for a more convivial room. Partner Chris Brown has warmed the menu as well. With chef Rebecca Olfert, the food has become more serious: a sautéed rabbit starter is served on spring greens; follow it with a generous chump of pan-roasted lamb. You can tell the kitchen is paying attention – the vegetables are beautifully selected and prepared, and generously served. The wine list is very well laid out, with helpful descriptions and sound pairing suggestions from the wait staff.
2563 W. Broadway, 739-1314

casually French

Cyrano

Chef Pascal Dagome looks too skinny to do the French thing, but trust me, the food is an unctuous and multi-leveled departure into striking Gallic flavours. We like the *foie gras* and apples, the salmon in *fleur de sel* and wine, and just about anything with one of his signature morel reductions. The *table d'hote* menu is reasonably priced. *1459 W. Broadway, 609-7760*

Café Salade de Fruits

"How do they do that?" you might well ask about this culinary version Le Cirque de Soleil. Three guys work without a net in this tiny room, adroitly making way for each other as *côtes de boeuf* are juggled with *carpe diem* – fish of the day. There's a sense of humour about this place, which spills out onto its sidewalk patio. But there's also a sense of honour – for this is more than French Club, allophone cooking. The prices are more than reasonable; the generous three-course *prix fixe* seemingly priced in old francs at a mere $19.95. Wines are available in two styles: one is red, the other white. The beer is cold, and the décor, which is reminiscent of a French travel agency, circa Alain Delon, is delightful unfussed. *1551 W. 7th Ave., 714-5987*

and a near neighbour ...

Le Petit Geneve

Très gentile and dependable Kerrisdale charmer captures locals with laudable standards: lobster bisque and oyster stew starters, a wealthy tasting crab and *crème fraiche* Napoleon, grilled duckling breast in cherry sauce with Savoyarde potatoes. Warm, "you're one of the family" service—even if you've been experimenting with being the black sheep. Commendable desserts and nicely turned wine list. Entrées very reasonably priced. All that's missing is the fountain in the lake. *2106 W. 41st Ave., 266-9611*

BEST PLACE TO SPOT IKE AND MAMIE

Hy's Encore

Hy's Encore, Hy Aisenstat's place of legend and myth, still turns out the city's best steak — AAA Canada beef, grilled in front of a diverse crowd, some of whom take their steak with nostalgia, others with irony. The colour scheme runs to black and red, and so do the reasons you've come here — the main event steaks are expertly trimmed and grilled. While the 22 oz. T-Bone may be a model of understatement, the Caesar salads, prepared tableside by formally dressed but unpretentious waiters, are pungent and deep. The vegetables (order the creamed spinach to keep your cholesterol up around your ears) and desserts are largely an afterthought. But that's not why you're here. The service is faultless, the drinks sturdy and well-priced, and the wine list runs deep to American and French reds. Try to ignore the baronial-looking, gilt-framed portraits on the walls — the proprietor insists they are deceased waiters. *637 Hornby St., 683-7671*

the sopranos
ate here

Il Ducato

If John Wayne had starred in spaghetti westerns, he could have been the namesake for this Kitsilano restaurant. Vestigially decorated in the style of Topo Gigio, many of its patrons enjoy the romantic mood of its languorous atmosphere and service. The delicious meat-stuffed cannelloni and other pastas offer value for money. The wine list is long on mid-priced Italian reds. *2042 W. 4th Ave., 739-7675*

Nick's Spaghetti House

Even if we didn't like the food, it's highly unlikely you would read about it here. Nick's is one of the last of the dependable, red-checkered, and raffia-bottomed *boîtes* left in town and enjoys many regular customers. Many other people — overdosed on arugula, 25-year-old balsamic, and over-priced double veal chops — also come here for a fix. And when the fix is in, well, it's very satisfying. There's just nothing like the "crisp" salad to prove that water-retention is in fact a virtue, and there's great meat action in the meatballs that are almost the size of hailstones. Attach a useful tavola wine from the hearty list, and listen in to the regulars handicapping everything from horse races at the nearby track to former business associates. *631 Commercial Dr., 254-5633*

THE BEST PLACES TO DO IT IN PRIVATE

Private dining rooms — the latest rage in public dining — are more than a passing fancy: perfect for a birthday party, wine dinner or corporate bonding. We like two new ones especially: the wine room at **Cioppino's** *(1133 Hamilton St., 688-7466)* accommodates up to two dozen with extremely good cooking and wonderful wine pairings. Also attractive is the wine room at **Villa del Lupo** *(869 Hamilton St., 688-7436)*, a handsome room suitable for up to 20, or upstairs for groups of up to 28 (although two dozen is more comfortable). The wine cellar at **Blue Water Café and Raw Bar** *(1095 Hamilton St., 688-8078)* accommodates 18 around a beautiful

Vancouver's dining scene plunged into a five-decade-long period of gloom just before World War I. The provincial government, acceding to the powerful hotel lobby, passed legislation limiting the public consumption of alcohol to hotels. Not surprisingly, without wine and liquor revenues, independent restaurants vanished within several years. Dining out became a split decision: greasy spoons or hotel dining rooms with imperious headwaiters and gloppy sauces.

And that was a shame, because Vancouver had a thriving restaurant scene at the turn of the century. There were numerous oyster bars, bistros, and even a vegetarian restaurant called the Pure Food Café. Although the bawdiness of the saloons dried up, so did what we eat, and it wasn't until 1952 that the legislation was repealed and stand-alone restaurants began to reappear.

wooden table, and the wine cellar at the redecorated **Borgo Antico** *(321 Water St., 683-8376)* will take up to 22. For slightly larger groups, try the **Connaught Room** at the Metropolitan Hotel *(645 Howe St., 602-7788)*, which is catered by Diva at the Met. The Pan Pacific Hotel *(300-999 Canada Place Way, 662-8111)* has three excellent rooms: a small private room at the **Five Sails**, which holds a dozen; the 22nd-floor **Canada Suite**, which will overwhelm your party of up to 40 with its lofty views over the harbour; and the **Governor General's Room**, an excellent venue to marry well in front of 250 of your closest friends.

Best Fish and Chips

"He has a very even disposition – a chip on both shoulders."

The best fish and chips in town almost aren't – the peripheral location of **King's Fare** in a small strip mall in Marpole make it a sought-out, on-the-way-to-the-airport kind of destination. The King's Fare is a sign incarnate that great fish and chips are not created by man alone: the near-religious zeal for fresh cod and halibut is evident on the platter.
1320 W. 73rd Ave., 266-3474

young and urban

Where do the hip kids go to nosh and be stylin'?

Photo: Mandelbrot

Alibi Room

Funky Gastown eatery whose owners include Gillian Anderson and Jason Priestley. Eat at optional communal tables and peruse copies of various movie scripts lining the wall.
157 Alexander St., 623-3383

Bin 941

A tiny hole-in-the-wall that serves inspired tapas dishes. Lineups most nights. Older brother to Bin 942 in Kitsilano.
941 Davie St., 683-1246

Brickhouse Late Night Bistro

If you can get over the not-great neighbourhood you'll find excellent Pacific Northwest fare.
730 Main St., 689-8645

Sandwich Heaven

A good sandwich is hard to find. Here's where you can find some excellent ones:

Photo: Blaine Kyllo

Arbutus Market
Just a block off Kits' main drag is this quaint ol' house, which operates as a market and a neighbourhood deli, offering tasty soups and hearty sandwiches. On a nice day sit outside at one of the picnic tables in the yard. *2200 Arbutus St., 736-5644*

Big Dog Deli
Start at the grilled pannini or salad selection, and as you get further down the menu, you'll realize just how many options you have.
523 Seymour St., 684-9987

Ecco il Pane Bakery
A great selection of breads and sandwiches. Ecco il Pane also runs the restaurant Boleto at the Broadway location.
238 W. 5th Ave., 873-6888;
2563 W. Broadway, 739-1314

Photo: Blaine Kyllo

Terra Breads

One of the city's best places for bread; pick up a fabulous roasted-veggie sandwich while surveying the offerings.
2380 W. 4th Ave., 736-1838; Granville Island, 685-3102

Tomato to Go

The take-out counter of the Tomato Café, owned by chef-about-town Diane Clement; huge sandwiches that will fill you up.
530 W. 17th Ave., 873-4697

Tony's Neighbourhood Deli

Commercial Drive's favourite sandwich-maker, with plenty to choose from in their glass display case.
1046 Commercial Dr., 253-7422

Yaletown Market

Grilled panini and soup to go for Yaletownies.
1002 Mainland St., 685-9929

Photo: Blaine Kyllo

Crime Lab

Constructed in what used to be the Vancouver Police Department's crime lab, this hangout has two-levels: upstairs are booths for dining, while downstairs is a small bar where you can enjoy your favourite cocktail served in a beaker or test tube.
1280 W. Pender St., 732-7463

Monsoon

Located in the newly-chic SoMo (South main) district, fusion dishes for carnivores and vegetarians alike.
2526 Main St., 879-4001

Section (3)

Owner Salli Pateman got into trouble over this bistro's former name DeNiro's (see Notoriety). The word "nerd" over the bar was supposed to spell "DeNiro," but she didn't get that far. Plush, oversize booths; order a retro cocktail from their pages-long bar menu.
1039 Mainland St., 684-2777

Photo: Blaine Kyllo

Subeez Café

Yaletown gathering place run by the owners of Commercial Drive gathering place Wazubee's. Goth candelabras and great fries.
891 Homer St., 687-6107

shop with the pros

Where do leading chefs source their prime ingredients? The very best utilize up to 30 fresh suppliers for their meats, fish, produce, and other supplies. Here are some of the best:

Albion Fisheries

The great white of seafood wholesalers and the largest in western Canada. In addition to more conventional items, stun your guests with skate wing, Australian blue bass, and tombo, or actually alarm them with barracuda and moonfish.
1077 Great Northern Way, 875-9411

Gourmet Warehouse

The retail side of a specialty wholesaler, this store stocks very high quality ingredients at low prices. The freezer reveals specialty cuts (the chicken drumettes are useful during football season), and you'll find a large selection of estate olive oils, truffle paste, sea salts, and French copper cookware.
1856 Pandora St. (lane entrance), 253-3022

Hi-To Fisheries

Primarily an exporter, Hi-To's retail division supplies local sushi bars with delicacies such as albacore, sea urchin, pine mushrooms, and geoduck.
1575 Vernon Dr., 253-5111

Hills Foods

Organic meats, specialty poultry, and game. There's no showroom, but they're helpful in batching retail orders (minimum $50) the next day. How about some peppered ostrich?
109-3650 Bonneville Pl., Burnaby, 421-3100

BEST DESSERTS TO GO

Lesley Stowe Fine Foods
Absolutely top drawer desserts, cookies, frozen canapés, oils, spices, and cheeses and a broad range of prepared foods.
1780 W. 3rd Ave., 731-3663

Notte's Bon Ton Pastry
The best traditional patisserie in town featuring diplomat and orange cakes, a plethora of pastries, chocolates, and candies. A quaint tea room in the back offers tea cup readings in the afternoon and is a welcome respite from the maddening crowds of the Granville mall, but hurry: it will be vacating the premises soon.
874 Granville St., 681-3058

BEST BRUNCH

Hotel brunch buffets are for amateurs, and for the life of me I can't figure those line-ups on West 4th Avenue, especially when you can breeze into one of these rooms and be treated like a visiting potentate.

Tangerine

Casual but stylish in design and patrons. Excellent breakfasts and unusually gracious service.
1685 Yew St., 739-4677

Diva at the Met

Write yourself back into Grandma's will by taking her here — the lovely Frette linen, silver, and china show off artful morning cooking. This is Vancouver's best brunch: order chef Michael Noble's revelatory smoked cod hash, topped with poached eggs, and thank me.
Metropolitan Hotel, 645 Howe St., 602-7788

Sienna

Very reasonable eggs every way to Sunday, great breakfast drinks, lively crowd. Stay on for the sporty Sundays over a pitcher of bloody Marys; in the evening, Sienna serves a sprightly menu of tapas, several of the best pizzas in town and a short menu of bistro classics.
1809 W. 1st Ave., 738-2727

Marche Transatlantic

Warehouse specializing in fine foods from Quebec and France. Among the highlights: cheeses (including a whole family of Munsters), escargots, smoked Nova Scotia eel, beluga and flying fish caviar, and aged red wine vinegar with truffles.
138 W. 43rd Ave., 322-7172

Menu Setters

Huge, well-managed selection of global cheeses, including a dependable supply of prime *bufala* mozzarella and moist gorgonzola.
3655 W. 10th Ave, 732-4218

Sing Lobster

Fabian Bates' family plies the waters off Cape Breton. Air Canada takes care of the rest. Call *631-7697* if you're planning a lobster roast.

Windsor Meats

Specializes in exotic cuts of buffalo, Moroccan lamb, ostrich, and free-range Nicola Valley beef — but there are lots of conventional, well-aged examples of prime beef, excellent poultry products, and well-sourced lamb and bacon.
1820 Marine Dr., W. Vancouver, 926-1440

in the neighbourhood

Each of these moderately-priced rooms, all located outside of the downtown core, offer excellent value on the plate, skilled cooking, and an inviting atmosphere. In fact, they're where we go with people we know well, our mothers, or simply when we want to decompress on our nights off!

Cyrano's

Chef proprietor Pascal Dagome cooks from a palate of country-styled French: duck terrines with cornichons, *foie gras,* and apples in puff pastry, seared filet in an unctuous sauce of port and morels. The daily *table d'hote* is very reasonably priced, the service warm and welcoming.
1459 W. Broadway, 609-7760

The Pear Tree

Chef Scott Jaeger's aggressive local sourcing of prime ingredients assures comfortable and reasonably priced cooking, especially on his *table d'hote* card. Consider his pre-theatre menu, which kicks off at 5:30 each evening. The room is cosy, the food unfussed, and the service, choreographed by wife Stephanie, is gracious and informed.
4120 East Hastings St., Burnaby, 299-2772

Provence

This cozy room in the university district welcomes a disparate group of UBC profs, celebrating students, and happy locals – in short, it's a Saab story. Go for the well-made Provencal and Med-basin cooking and a wine list that is particularly kind (lots of half bottles and by-the-glass entries) to couples. Pay special attention to the specials sheet-this kitchen shops fresh. The weekend brunch is particularly good value.
4473 W. 10th Ave., 222-1980

BEST EXCUSE FOR TAKING AUNTIE FOR A SPIN

Cloud 9

As the patented Savardian spinnerama move was to hockey, so is the revolving Cloud 9 to dining downtown – the view changes every hour. The bar portion of the circular restaurant is popular on view days; try one of the well-selected B.C. wines. Although the service can be a little starchy (hmmm – where did that table go?), management has being trying to elevate the menu above its continental beginnings. While the result may be hardly revolutionary, the 42-storey view still qualifies. Our advice: drink well, eat lightly, and don't counter-rotate.
1400 Robson St., 662-8328

Photo: Blaine Kyllo

BEST SOUP

The best soups are aromatic, flavoursome, and punch up your senses while not stealing your appetite. Chef Stephan Meyer's fish soup at **Piccolo Mondo** *(850 Thurlow St., 688-1633)* — made from proprietor Michele Geris' family recipe — and his raviolini in *brodo ricco* (goat cheese and gorgonzola stuffed raviolini in chicken consommé with a dash of truffle oil) are the best in town.

The **Soup Doctor** *(Royal Centre Mall, 1055 W. Georgia St., 682-7687)* serves up to half a dozen flavoursome meals-in-a-bowl, rotated seasonally. The recipes, developed for them by a leading chef, are gutsy, delicious, and travel well in special insulated mugs.

Quattro on Fourth

The Corsi family know how to treat their neighbours, offering well-priced pastas (the Spaghetti Quattro, billed "for Italians only," is a spicy treat) but also pulling cross-town traffic for carefully made fish, poultry, and game entrées. The service is incredibly friendly and the wine list particularly strong in thoughtfully chosen Italians. The bar is where the neighbours hang out, and the barman, Jason, is one of the cheeriest in town.
2611 W. 4th Ave., 734-4444

Photo: Blaine Kyllo

Zev's

New Yorker Zev Beck brings his version of moderately-priced global cuisine (or as he says, "just good food") to this charming room in the former Delilah's space. The cocktails at the front bar kick up the gold ceiling and leopard skin carpets, the brigade of chefs thrum in the exhibition kitchen. The wine list is long on half bottles and a great by-the-glass roster. Zev's oozes cool, friendliness, and tight cooking — go!
1906 Haro St., 408-4783

Photo: Blaine Kyllo

The secret life of the literati exposed, for all to see. Not to mention the straight story on readings, auctions, and openings. And don't forget the best in theatre, dance, galleries, and magazine stores. It's all ahead, if you can just read between the lines.

Cyberspace: The Bagel Connection

Benny's Bagels is a Kitsilano original. So is William Gibson. It was while living in Kits that the American-born author introduced the world to his vision of a gritty post-industrial future, where the only escape is to a realm of intertwined computer networks that Gibson labelled "cyberspace." And it was from Kits that Benny's introduced Vancouverites to the idea that a bagel wasn't just a hard, funny-shaped bun. Both were wildly successful; Benny's expanded to include shops all over town, while Gibson moved to Shaughnessy. The only question that remains is, where exactly did Gibson develop his singular vision of a dystopic future? One clue may come from the following bit from Gibson's 1993 novel *Virtual Light*:

"Now they were walking past this bagel place that had a kind of iron cage outside, welded out of junk, where you could sit in there at little tables and have coffee and eat bagels, and the smell of the morning's baking about made her faint from hunger."

Literary scholars might want to check out the Benny's on Broadway (2505 W. Broadway). For those just looking for a bagel, the other Benny's are just as good.

See Dick Run

 Incessant rain, Asian faces, glaring neon, and piles of uncollected trash. Despite the obvious similarities to Vancouver's downtown eastside, it has always been assumed that Los Angeles was the template for the 1982 sci-fi film classic *Blade Runner*. What few know is that in the early 1970s Philip K. Dick, the author of the book on which *Blade Runner* was based, spent several formative months living amongst the downtrodden in Vancouver's downtown.

Dick arrived in February of 1972 for a two-day science fiction conference at UBC, and fell so in love with the city that he plunked himself down for a permanent stay. Two months later, depressed by the rain, the shallow materialism of Vancouverites, and his own lack of success in seducing the dark-haired wife of a *Province* newspaper reporter, he deliberately overdosed on 700 milligrams of the amphetamine potassium bromide. Ambulance drivers came and, in Dick's own words, "scooped up the puddle of ooze on the floor of my apartment that was me." They took him to a downtown group home for heroin addicts called X-Kalay, where he spent the better part of the next two months living the life of a wrung-out ex-junkie. Shortly after his discharge from X-Kalay, Dick abandoned Vancouver and returned to his writing desk in sunny California, taking with him nothing but memories of advanced urban decay and incessant rain.

The Ghost in the Gallery

Fairacres Mansion in Century Park is currently home to the Burnaby Arts Council Gallery, but the huge Tudor building has seen a lot of strange goings-on in the 90-odd years since it was built. It's no wonder it harbours a ghost. Built in 1909 as a country home for retired real estate baron Henry Ceperly and his wife, the house fell on hard times after Mrs. Ceperly died in 1919. According to her will, the house was supposed to have been sold and the proceeds used for a children's playground in Stanley Park. Her husband sold the half-timbered chateau all right, but pocketed the proceeds himself.

The mansion became, in turn, a sanitarium for TB victims, a Benedictine monastery, and in 1954, the home of a religious cult, the Temple of the More Abundant Life. The cult's leader, the self-styled Archbishop John I, was actually an American named William Wolsely, wanted in several U.S. states on charges of extortion and wife-beating. Despite this, the cult carried on – complete with live-in school and rumours of ritual sex and Satanic worship – until 1964, when the Archbishop packed up his belongings and fled south to the States.

Following a brief stint as a student dorm, Fairacres became the Burnaby Art Gallery in 1967. And that was when the hauntings began. A nightwatchman reported seeing the translucent figure of a woman in an old-fashioned dress flowing along the hallways upstairs. Others began hearing footsteps padding across the upstairs floors. Gallery management brought in a psychic to investigate, followed by a pair of newspaper reporters who asked to do the same. Their prognoses were very similar. All reported sensing something, but none could state exactly what it was besides a very definite presence. Odds-on betting, however, is on the ghost being the spirit of Grace Ceperly, still waiting for someone to build her playground.

SOME ARTSY TYPES

Vancouver has a rich history of artists living and working here, many of whom have achieved international reputations. Here are some of them:

Stan Douglas

Douglas uses film, video, and photography to explore themes such as colonialism, urban development, and historical memory. A big art star in Europe, he has been the subject of a retrospective book published by Phaidon, the British art publisher.

Gathie Falk

Falk is an acclaimed painter and sculptor whose work is concerned with defining women's spaces. While her work now appears comfortably in collections of Canadian masters, she has been largely unappreciated in the larger scheme of Canadian artists, even though her work was the subject of a major retrospective at the VAG in 1999.

Richard Attila Lukacs

While studying painting at Vancouver's Emily Carr School of Art and Design, Lukacs honed his ample capacity for rendering opulent, decorative (and often controversial) oil paintings of male skinheads, monkeys, and military cadets, among other subjects. Madonna and Elton John are among those who have purchased his work. While no longer living in Vancouver, he is still considered a local boy; his work has been featured at UBC's Belkin Gallery and the Diane Farris Gallery.

Jeff Wall

Wall, who used to teach at UBC but recently moved to Europe, is considered a big star in the international art scene. His huge, backlit Cibachrome prints are collected by some of the most prestigious and influential art institutions in the world, and like Douglas, was the subject of a Phaidon retrospective book. His work can be seen locally at the Vancouver Art Gallery.

Gu Xiong

Gu Xiong is a multimedia artist originally from Chongqing, China who taught traditional woodcut printmaking at the Sichuan Fine Arts Institute. He came to Canada following the Tiananmen Square massacre. He now lives in Vancouver, where his charcoal paintings (such as the self portrait shown here) and prints speak to his immigrant experience. His work has been exhibited at the Diane Farris Gallery and he frequently exhibits at other art spaces around town.

Lawrence Paul Yuxweluptun

One of Vancouver's new breed, his paintings of imaginary landscapes incorporate Native west coast mythic iconography while effectively commenting on contemporary environmental and Native issues. His last name is Salish for "man of many masks." His paintings are often on view at the Vancouver Art Gallery.

Vogue Theatre Phantom

Photo: Blaine Kyllo

Beneath the stage of the Vogue Theatre on Granville Street is a long, narrow corridor with dressing rooms and workshops on either side that have been the site of many a strange occurrence. On several different occasions, theatre staff walking down the corridor have felt a cold presence, as if someone just brushed by behind them, then turned around to see nothing but an eerie shadow that quickly vanished from sight.

Reports of these occurrences were kept quiet during the Vogue's 46-year run as a movie house, but in 1991, when the Art Deco classic returned to a role for which it was built – as a venue for live music and theatre – the ghosts came back with a vengeance. One night in November 1995, a spectre even appeared to watch the show.

It happened during a performance of the stage show "Unforgettable: The Music of Nat King Cole." Dancer Shane MacPherson was tapping up a storm when he looked out over the audience and saw the apparition of a man in a cream-coloured dinner jacket suddenly appear by the wall of a side aisle, stared at him just long enough to make eye contact, and then abruptly vanish from sight. His rhythm completely broken, MacPherson scrabbled about on the stage for a minute or so more before ending the number in confusion.

The ghost's next appearance came in response to a comment from then-radio host Vicki Gabereau, in the Vogue taping her farewell show on CBC Radio, about how the Vogue was haunted. Shortly thereafter, a wild, eerie wail echoed out through the theatre's audio system. Whether the cry was one of joy or lamentation, however, is still not clear.

Bill Reid's Most Explosive Sculpture

It's no secret that Bill Reid's massive yellow cedar carving *The Raven and the First Men* is a masterpiece. The statue depicts a creation myth from Haida mythology, in which Raven, the Trickster, coaxes a reluctant humanity from its womb inside a clam shell. Tourists and locals who view the piece, on display at the UBC Museum of Anthropology, always come away impressed. What they may not come away knowing is that this beautiful symbol of creation sits smack atop a concrete engine of destruction. The museum occupies the site of a former artillery battery, set up during World War II to protect Point Grey from invasion. When it came time to design the museum, architect Arthur Erickson realized he'd never be able to move the massive 15-foot concrete gun turrets, so he designed them into the building: using one to form the base of the west wall, and another – the central one – as the pedestal holding up what is arguably master carver Bill Reid's finest creation.

A Great Garage Sale

The best garage sale in the city is the one held every fall at the Vancouver Art Gallery. Old picture frames, banners, props, and a lot of other art-associated materials are put up for grabs at bargain prices. Big, funky picture frames can be had for as little as $5.

For gallery staff, the garage sale is a mixed blessing. On the one hand, there's the extra revenue, and a lot less stuff in the way. On the other, they have to go down into the gallery's vaults and catacombs – the dark, spooky rooms with rough-hewn walls and five-foot ceilings that sit beneath the gallery's old courthouse site – and bring the stuff up. Word at the gallery is that you're not really a full-fledged employee until you've been sent into the vaults on an errand and had the maintenance guys turn off the lights. If you heart doesn't stop, you're in the club.

Offbeat Galleries

Vancouver has tons of art galleries, some great, some cheesy. Here are some that are worth checking out:

Art Beatus
Vancouver outlet of a Hong Kong gallery, showcasing contemporary Chinese and international art.
1M-888 Nelson St., 688-2633

Artspeak Gallery
A small but respected Gastown gallery for emerging artists.
233 Carrall St., 688-0051

Aunt Leah's Gallery
Sells art and craft work by over 80 B.C. artists and craftspeople in a urban-rustic setting. Run by a non-profit society, all proceeds go to help youth in need.
221 Abbott St., 266-7783

Morris and Helen Belkin Gallery
This large gallery space at the University of British Columbia has had many celebrated shows recently, including ones by art badboy Richard Attila Lukacs and French master Theodore Gericault.
1825 Main Mall, UBC, 822-2759

Photo: Blaine Kyllo

The Brickhouse

Fred Varley was once tossed out of the National Gallery because he refused to put out his cigarette. That wouldn't be a problem at the Brickhouse. Not only can you smoke (cigarettes and cigars), but you can drink (lots of draught and some very fine whiskey), toss darts, play pool, or even wander around admiring the artwork, some of which is worth collecting, and very reasonably priced.
730 Main St., 689-8645

Contemporary Art Gallery

Downtown gallery featuring regional and international exhibitions; scheduled to relocate to the corner of Richards and Nelson in 2001.
555 Hamilton St., 681-2700

Exposure Gallery

Specializing in photography, this non-profit gallery aims to promote B.C. photographic artists and to promote photography as a fine art.
851 Beatty St., 688-6853

How to become head curator of a major Canadian art gallery? Well, you could study for years, develop a fine appreciation of art both ancient and contemporary, then apprentice yourself to gallery after gallery, expanding your knowledge of the Canadian artistic scene as you work your way up through to the top. Or you could do it Joe McHugh's way. An entrepreneur from Chicago, McHugh made his money as a turn-around artist – taking control of and quickly turning around failing companies, then pocketing a bonus and heading out again – before moving to Vancouver in 1987. Once in town, McHugh discovered a love for the cultural world, taking, in turns, a Masters in Fine Arts, effective control of the Vancouver Opera, and total control of the Vancouver Art Gallery. The latter came after the VAG director resigned rather than accede to a deal in which a collection of photos by Bryan Adams to be hung in the gallery lobby in exchange for a very large cheque. McHugh happily stepped in to fill the job, in spite of the objections of some 50 local artistic luminaries – among them Doris Shadbolt and Arthur Erickson – who signed a petition asking him to step down and hire someone else as full-time director. The VAG ignored this unsolicited advice, and for many weeks it looked as if McHugh's appointment would become permanent, the culmination of a picture-perfect *coup d'etat*. Alas, for all plotters everywhere, under intense pressure from artists and their funder-friends, the VAG eventually announced a hiring committee for a new director. At last report, McHugh was casting about for something else to turn around.

Raymond Chandler needs no introduction. The author of dozens of novels, short stories, and screenplays, among them *Double Indemnity* and *The Big Sleep*, Chandler created an unforgettable literary character in hard-bitten detective Philip Marlowe, at the same time originating an entire new movie genre, the American film noir. What isn't so well known is Chandler's connection to Vancouver. Ineligible for service in the U.S. armed forces (then closed to immigrants), Chandler came north in 1917 and enlisted in the Canadian army instead. After service in France he was discharged on February 20, 1919, in the city of Vancouver.

He left almost immediately for L.A., but our city clearly must have remained in his imagination. When in 1947 he negotiated the richest deal ever to that point for a screenwriter – unlimited creative freedom and $4,000 a week until completion – Chandler chose to set his master *oeuvre* in Vancouver. $250,000 later, the result was a screenplay called *Playback*. The studio hated it. Not only did Universal refuse to produce it, but like the Avro Arrow they attempted to destroy all available copies. They got all but one. Nearly 40 years later in 1985, a researcher stumbled across a copy hidden away in Universal's archives.

In hindsight, it's easy to see why it was so despised by American execs. The hero is a Canadian – a detective named Killaine. The bad guy is a corrupt American playboy. The cops all speak with Scottish accents. Most amusing for Vancouver readers, however, is Chandler's spotty recollection of the city's geography. The heroine – Betty Mayfield – stays in the Vancouver Royal Hotel – "a massive brick and sandstone building, set in beautiful gardens which slope down towards Puget Sound." It is here that we see early signs of a budding romance between Mayfield and detective Killaine as they meet by

> A WALL AT THE FOOT OF THE HOTEL GARDENS BETTY AND KILLAINE are leaning on it, looking out over Puget Sound.
>
> KILLAINE
>
> Down below's Stanley Park. On the other side of the trees, there's a beach. You can't see it. (points over to left) Steveston's over there. Coast Guard station. (points to right) There's the Yacht Club, and beyond it, the docks. Then over on the other side

Gallery Gachet

This artist-run co-operative showcases the paintings, installation work, sculpture, ceramics, and performance art of its members.

88 E. Cordova St., 687-2468

Photo: Mandelbrot

grunt gallery

A veteran artist-run centre on the east side.

116-350 E. 2nd Ave., 875-9516

Havana Gallery

This gallery is located within the popular restaurant of the same name, a favourite haunt of Commercial Drive types. If you're there to look but not eat, just head past the bar and you're in the gallery. The rotating shows feature exhibitions of painting and photography.

1212 Commercial Dr., 253-9119

Or Gallery

A venerable and respected artist-run centre located just outside Yaletown.

103-480 Smithe St., 683-7395

Presentation House Gallery

The only public photography and media arts gallery on the west coast, featuring contemporary and historical work.

333 Chesterfield Ave.,
North Vancouver, 986-1351

Charles H. Scott Gallery

The on-site gallery of the Emily Carr Institute of Art and Design, one of Canada's most prestigious art schools, located a few steps from the Granville Island Public Market.

1399 Johnston St., 844-3809

The Western Front

The Front is Vancouver's oldest artist-run centre, with a colourful history. In addition to art exhibits, there are numerous events featuring dance, music, and performance art. See their bimonthly magazine *Front* for details.

303 E. 8th Ave., 876-9343

of the inlet, there's Grouse Mountain. It's about 4000 feet high. There's a restaurant on top of it. Very nice restaurant.

(he turns to Betty)

I'm sorry we couldn't have met in pleasanter circumstances, Miss Mayfield.

BETTY

We wouldn't have met at all.

KILLAINE

True. I was a bit irritable last night. I apologize.

BETTY

You were a Galahad, compared to some cops I've known.... but you have a job to do. I'm a girl who's in a jam, and it's your job to keep me there. Don't go considerate on me, I might start to bawl.

(Their eyes meet in a long look)

Later on, in a scene that takes place before Vancouver's parliament buildings, Killaine will declare his undying passion for Miss Mayfield – in a polite, repressed, Canadian kind of way, of course.

Touched by Greatness

The best way to win a Nobel Prize, 'tis said, is to study with someone who has one. Much the same could be said of the Governor General's Award for Literature, at least as It applies to Vancouver writers. Governor General Award winner Emily Carr (see photo), for example, began and ended her career as a painter, making ends meet giving lessons on a little studio on Burrard Street. One of her students was a young society girl named Ethel Malkin (niece of the mayor who gave his name to the bowl) who 20 years later, as Ethel Wilson, would reign over Vancouver's small literary world as the city's first – and ergo finest – successful novelist. One of the women who attended Wilson's regular teas was a shy North Van housewife, only recently arrived in the city. Her name? Margaret Laurence.

Kip Can't Flip

Rudyard Kipling, famed Victorian literary figure, was a regular visitor to Vancouver. He even tried to make a little money dabbling in the local real estate market. On his first visit to the city in 1889, Kipling paid cold hard cash for what he though was a double lot in Mount Pleasant. For the next twenty odd years he faithfully paid his taxes, waiting for the day when the land would be ripe for flipping. Alas, when Kipling finally tried to realize a profit on his real estate, he discovered he'd been swindled. The real estate agent had sold the same lot several times over, always to out-of-towners. Worse, the lot wasn't even his to sell. This little episode may have been in Rudyard's head when he wrote his poem "The White Man's Burden," a slightly modified version of which is included below.

> Take up that mortgage burden
> pay faithfully what you owe
> and whether or no a killing you'll make
> is not for you to know
> Take up that mortgage burden
> send forth near all ye earn
> and pray like a banshee to the devil himself
> the market don't crash and burn

Vancouver's First Novelist

Vancouver's first native-born novelist, Alfred Batson, led a life of adventure surpassing any of his own works of fiction. Born in 1900, Batson lied about his age to get into the Canadian Army during world War I. He then fought as a captain with rebel forces in Nicaragua before being forced by invading U.S. Marines to flee overland to Mexico. His first and only novel, *African Intrigue* (1933), tells of the rivalry between France and Germany in interwar Africa. It's believed to be based on personal experience, although no one knows for sure: Batson's whereabouts and fate remain unknown.

THE WRITER, VANCOUVER STYLE

There are writers in Vancouver who achieve success elsewhere, and come to Vancouver to vegetate. And there are writers who have also achieved success elsewhere, and are then claimed by Vancouver on the basis of the most tenuous of connections (i.e., Malcolm Lowry). But Vancouver-born scribes are as rare as Vancouver-born salmon: what few exist are exceptionally tough. What follows is a brief, idiosyncratic, wholly unrepresentative sampling of this city's collection of scribblers. And what's so secret about it? Well, being a writer is an almost certain guarantee of obscurity. The secret is why anyone would want to do it for a living. For the answer to this question, you may want to talk to some of these folks:

Bill Bissett

Most Recent Book:
B leev abul char ak trs
Best Known Book:
Seagull on Yonge Street
Secret Fact: Ran away from home to join the circus

Lynn Coady

Most Recent Book:
Play the Monster Blind
Best Known Book: Strange Heaven
Secret Fact: was once so broke, her phone was disconnected at the same time she was on it, being notified of her Governor General's Award nomination

Stanley Coren

Most Recent Book: How to Speak Dog

Best Known Book:
The Intelligence of Dogs

Secret Fact: Once worked in a laundromat; shares his bed with two dogs and a cat

Douglas Coupland

Most Recent Book: City of Glass

Best Known Book: Generation X

Secret Fact: designs furniture on the side

Wade Davis

Most Recent Book:
The Clouded Leopard

Best Known Book: One River

Secrect Fact: Ethnobiologist has published nearly 50 different ways of getting stoned, the latest involving a hallucinogenic desert toad

Terry Glavin

Most Recent Book:
The Last Great Sea

Best Known Book: This Ragged Place

Secret Fact: Has never ridden PNE rollercoaster because of his fear of heights

Reel and Real Drama

When architect Arthur Erickson redesigned the old Vancouver courthouse for its new role as the new Vancouver Art Gallery, he left the courtroom of former Chief Justice Allan McEachern intact – not out of any fondness for the judge, but as a sop to heritage buffs who wanted to preserve the intricately carved wooden judge's bench. It turned out to have been a fortuitous move. Room 360 has since become a popular shooting location for U.S. film crews; filming fees provide the gallery with an excellent source of extra revenue. But of all the films shot inside the gallery's walls – among them Jodie Foster's Oscar-winning turn in *The Accused* – none have come close to matching the drama and soap opera intrigue surrounding the death of the buildings original architect, F.M. Rattenbury. The most successful B.C. architect of his day – he also designed Victoria's legislature building – Rattenbury left these shores late in life for a quiet, and as it turns out, very brief retirement in England. In 1935, he was murdered by his wife and her teenaged lover, who until then had been the family chauffeur.

Mapper's Delight

Going to the ends of the Earth? Odds are, your journey will begin in a obscure little upstairs office in the far off reaches of Broadway and Main. That's where Jack Joyce, map-maker extraordinaire and proprietor of International Travel Maps, designs and manufactures maps of places so remote and obscure that other map makers just don't bother: think Azerbaijan, Bujumbura, Tashkent, and Tierra del Fuego. J.J.'s maps sell well, in part thanks to his artistry, and in part because Joyce is a stickler for accuracy, sending real people out to verify that the things he's drawn actually do exist. Of course, that requires people willing to go the dangerous and obscure places depicted in International Travel's maps. Which may be why, in 20 years' existence, ITM has never yet done a map of Surrey.

specialty bookstores

British Columbians read more books per year than any other Canadians, so it's no surprise that Vancouver has no shortage of great bookstores. In addition to various Chapters locations around the city, there are a number that cater to specific tastes and clientele. Here are some of them:

ABC Book and Comic Emporium

Everything the name suggests plus – and this is close to our heart – the city's best selection of magazine back-issues.
1247 Granville St., 682-3019

Banyen Books & Sound

Here you'll find the city's largest selection of New Age books, both fiction and non-fiction, as well as all of the accoutrements necessary for a new age lifestyle. A special attraction are the works of David Icke: how shape-shifting Martian lizards took control of humanity and re-invented misery – it's a B'nai Brith favourite.
2671 W. Broadway, 732-7912

Barbara-jo's Books to Cooks

Chef Barbara-jo McIntosh's own menu for a cookbook store. Features in-store cooking demos and classes.
1128 Mainland St., 688-6755.

Biz Books

Walk in to audition their film bios and screenplays, while friendly staff direct you to "how to make it in the industry" books and more.
136 E. Cordova St., 669-6431

Black Sheep Books

This Kitsilano independent features weekly readings by local and visiting writers.
2742 W. 4th Ave., 732-5087

Laurence Gough
Most Recent Book: Shutterbug
Best Known Book: Killers
Secret Fact: Detective novelist was caught stealing ballpoint pens from Sears at age 13

W.P. Kinsella
Most Recent Book: Magic Time
Best Known Book: Shoeless Joe
Secret Fact: Has said he wishes he could write like Judith Krantz or Danielle Steel

Evelyn Lau
Most Recent Book:
Choose Me: Stories
Best Known Book:
Runaway: Diary of a Street Kid
Secret Fact: Has said she'd like to work at Holt-Renfrew

Blackberry Books

A bookstore on Granville Island, in the Netloft building opposite the market.
1663 Duranleau St., 685-6188

Book Warehouse

Great remainders and discounted new titles.
632 W. Broadway, 873-0661, plus 4 other locations

Dead Write Books

As the name implies, Dead Write specializes in crime and mystery.
4374 W. 10th Ave., 228-8223

Duthie Books

So what's secret about Duthie's? That they've been able to buck the trend and thwart bankruptcy court. Once boasting ten stores, Duthie Books has scaled down to one, in Kitsilano.
2239 W. 4th Ave., 732-5344

Granville Book Company

This small, central store features great alternative literature, science fiction, and tons of computer books. Open seven days a week until midnight; great for book-browsing before catching a movie at the nearby cineplex.
850 Granville St., 687-2213

Shani Mootoo

Most Recent Book:
Cereus Blooms at Night
Best Known Book:
Cereus Blooms at Night
Secret Fact: Giller-nominated novelist started out as acclaimed visual artist

Eden Robinson

Most Recent Book: Monkey Beach
Best Known Book: Traplines
Secret Fact: while enduring writer's block, spends hours playing Tetris

Michael Turner

Most Recent Book:
The Pornographer's Poem
Best Known Book: Hard Core Logo
Secret Fact: has not missed an episode of *Coronation Street* since October 12, 1989

Photo: Rosalee Hiebert

Photo: Mandelbrot

Health Sciences Book Shop

An offshoot of the UBC Bookstore, this store carries over 7,000 titles in the medical and allied health fields (nursing, chiropractice, herbal, alternative, etc.).
2750 Heather St., 875-5588

Little Sister's Book & Art Emporium

Quick! Drop by this much-harassed gay and lesbian bookstore, the only one in B.C., before Customs seizes its books – again.
1238 Davie St., 669-1753

MacLeod's Books

Arguably the best antiquarian bookstore in the city, full of great finds for would-be collectors.
455 W. Pender St., 681-7654

Oscar's Art Books

Art books on all the arts.
1533 W. Broadway, 731-0553

People's Co-op Bookstore

This socialist-minded bookstore also features a great general section.
1391 Commercial Dr., 253-6442

Photo: Robert Ballantyne

Secret Readings

Evenings of the spoken word are always a gamble. On occasion, you're rewarded with a stunning new use of language. And sometimes you're subjected to a poet from the Frou-Frou the Talking Cat school of poetry (i.e., "black emptiness ... black, black emptiness....") We've tried to present some of the best of local readings but you don't know until you give them a try. As Ginsburg probably said, the experience is half the experience. In addition to these, various bookstores around town regularly host readings, including Black Sheep Books, Women in Print, Little Sister's, and various Chapters locations.

Poetry at the Shadbolt
Starting at 7:30 on the last Friday of every month, the Centre, an ultramodern building on the edge of Burnaby's Deer Lake, is the best place in the region to hear an eclectic mixture of new and established poets. Now in its third year (which makes it ancient by poetry standards), "Poetry at the Shadbolt" begins with a reading from an established poet – including

the likes of Robert Kroetsch and George Bowering. After about an hour, the stage opens up and local poets get to strut their stuff. Call 291-6864 for more details or to sign up to perform.
The Shadbolt Centre, 6450 Deer Lake Rd., Burnaby

Vancouver Public Library
Poets, novelists, journalists, and winners of the Pulitzer, the Booker, the Seal, the Giller, the Webster, and the Herman have all read at the Vancouver Public Library. The only real mystery, considering how poorly they're advertised, is why they're so well-attended. It could be because they're free. Readings are held in the rooms below the atrium, and the only reliable way to know what's happening is to visit a branch and check the posters on the noticeboards. The seasonal "City Poets" series happens every Monday night. Call 684-8266 for information.
350 W. Georgia St.

Photo: Mandelbrot

Sophia Books

Vant a French veedeo? How about a little Swedish book, eh? Since merging with Manhattan Books, Sophia Books has expanded from a primarily Asian selection to include fiction, non-fiction, art books, magazines, and comics in languages from around the world, especially Japanese, French, Spanish, German, and Italian.
492 W. Hastings St., 684-0484

Photo: Blaine Kyllo

32 Books

The North Shore's only independent bookstore; hosts regular book club gatherings.
3018 Edgemont Blvd., North Vancouver, 980-9032

Spartacus Books

Out of the way on the second-floor in a run-down office building is this bookstore catering to alternative art and political readers.
311 W. Hastings St., 688-6138

UBC Bookstore

More than just UBC courseware, this bookstore has a very large computer book and children's reading section.
6200 University Blvd., 822-2665

Vancouver Art Gallery Gift Shop

The VAG giftshop carries a large selection of art books, with a strong emphasis on Canadian artists. They are also known for their selection in the area of theory and criticism. And if you want to find an exhibition catalogue from a Canadian show, chances are you'll find it here.
750 Hornby St., 662-4706

Vancouver Kidsbooks

Carries the largest and most varied selection of children's books in Vancouver. Also carries other-language children's books, as well as a parents' resource section.
3083 W. Broadway, 738-5335; 3040 Edgemont Blvd., 986-6190 (North Vancouver)

Photo: Blaine Kyllo

White Dwarf Books

Experts in science fiction and fantasy since 1978.
4368 W. 10th Ave., 228-8223

Women in Print

Palatable neighbourhood shop offers regular readings, launches, and popular books by women with a literary emphasis.
3566 W. 4th Ave., 732-4128

Kootenay School of Writing

A pair of poets every week is the norm for this non-profit writing school. Readings are usually on Sundays, and usually in the evening, but can also be offered on other days at other times in other locations. Call 688-6001 for details.
201 - 505 Hamilton St.

The Java Joint

Check out their poetry nights held every Tuesday.
10727 King George Hwy., Surrey, 588-JAVA

Other Open Mikes

There are other venues in which to get your words into the air, or just get things off your chest. They include "Coffee Nights" at the Gallery Gachet *(88 E. Cordova St.)* on the last Friday of every month, "Tales of Ordinary Madness" at Bukowski's Bar and Bistro *(1447 Commercial Dr.)* on Tuesdays, "Slam-Bam-Jam-a-Rama" at the BC Marine Club *(573 Homer St.)* every Wednesday, and "Bolts of Fiction" at El Cocal *(1037 Commercial Dr.)* on the second Monday of every month.

Stay as you are.

by Brad Yung

Issue 6 $ 2.00

Warning! May contain traces of squirrels.

Seal in the City

Is there an underground river running between False Creek and Deer Lake in Burnaby? In her book *Legends of Vancouver*, Mohawk writer and long-time Vancouverite Tekahionwake (otherwise known as Pauline Johnson) relates a tale told to her by Chief Joe Capilano, about a time he was out hunting on False Creek and saw an enormous seal. He paddled close, took up his prized elk-bone spear – inherited from his grandfather's father – and hurled it with all his strength. It hit the animal square in the side, and with a great cry the seal swam off. Capilano's line of braided cedar fibre paid out, and the chief hung on as the seal pulled him along the creek. Then somewhere around where Main Street is now, the seal dove straight down below the surface. The rope jerked out of Capilano's hand and disappeared, together with the seal and the chief's elk-bone spear. And though he searched for months, Capilano found nary a trace of seal nor spear.

One evening the next spring, when Capilano was again out hunting, he saw a red light in the eastern sky and went to investigate. A fire was raging around Deer Lake, and all the animals were fleeing. When the chief got to the water, he found the great seal lying dead by the shore, Capilano's spear imbedded in its side. In gratitude for its return, he stayed the night singing songs of great power, while around him the fire raged. And though he searched the rest of his life for the river that had brought the seal to the lake, he never succeeded in finding it.

Words Found on the Street

Imbedded in the concrete of the sidewalk on the northern side of Pacific Boulevard between Drake and Homer Streets are a series of seemingly random words: "born" appears, as does "shining," "grids," and "trees." (So also do "whoa!" and "rough 'n' tumble," but these appear to be later additions intended for skateboarders.) It's only by walking along the pavement and noting every word that sense emerges: "Born from the glares come the freakish form of tugs ... towing shining grids of the trees stricken." and so on. If you don't recognize, it, blame your CanLit teacher. It's from the poem "November Walk Near False Creek Mouth," written in 1961 by the city's best-known poet, Earle Birney.

Photo: Lincoln Clarke/Ruby Slippers

Poor old Bertholt Brecht. The avowed socialist playwright was best loved by the bourgeoisie he despised; when the Nazis came to power, Brecht – in a bit of karmic justice – was forced to seek exile in Southern California. Aside from all that, of course, he was a talented playwright – the best produced by pre-war Germany. Every two years in August, Ruby Slippers Production Society, in conjunction with Touchstone Theatre Company and Vancouver Moving Theatre, puts on "Brecht in the Park", a free outdoor staging of one Bertholt's plays, held at various greenspaces around town, among them Nelson Park, Victoria Park, Douglas Park, and McLean Park on the edge of the downtown eastside. Upholding the spirit of the left-leaning playwright, producers try to bring the theatre experience to "the people" (whatever that is in a town without a recognizable proletariat), both those who already enjoy theatre and those who wouldn't usually go. These spectacular productions are made up of a mix of professional actors and lighting, stage, and costume designers, coupled with amateur celebration artists such as fire dancers, stilt walkers, puppeteers, and musical ensembles. And when it gets dark, the entire event is lit solely by fire torches. The result is a highly visceral experience for both performer and audience. Pictured above is actor Linda Quibell. *602-0585*

Free Shakespeare, Anyone?

For two weeks every August, Carousel Theatre Company presents "Shakespeare Under the Stars," a festival of free outdoor Shakespeare performances at the Performance Works outdoor stage on Granville Island. Each year one play is performed by a group of theatre students whose levels of experience range from very little to nearly graduated. *669-3410*

Shall They Dance?

Ballet B.C. is Vancouver's largest and best-known dance company, but there are other companies putting on dynamic dance shows at any given time of the year. Also watch for "Dancing on the Edge," a festival of alternative dance held every July.

Dance Arts Vancouver Society
402-873 Beatty St., 606-6425

EDAM Performing Arts Society
303 E. 8th Ave., 876-9559

Karen Jamieson Dance Company
706-207 W. Hastings St., 685-5699

Kinesis Dance
803-207 W. Hastings St., 684-7844

Kokoro Dance
1201-207 W. Hastings St., 662-7441

Mascall Dance
1130 Jervis St., 689-9339

Lola McLaughlin
204-873 Beatty St., 683-6552

Mortal Coil Performance Society
200-275 E. 8th Ave., 874-6153

Yasel Dancesport
770 S.W. Marine Dr., 323-1221

Play Time

Vancouver Playhouse and the Arts Club Theatre are the city's two largest live-theatre companies, but Vancouver is also home to a number of tiny companies that produce some of the city's most daring and innovative shows. Check local listings for current productions.

Axis Theatre Company
1398 Cartwright St., 669-0631

Carousel Theatre Company
1411 Cartwright St., 669 3410

Pacific Theatre
1440 W.12th Ave., 731-5483

Prospectus Theatre Group
127-345 E. Broadway, 623-2010

Ruby Slippers Production Society
1405 Anderson St., 602-0585

Rumble Productions
315-207 W. Hastings St., 662-3395

Theatre la Seizieme
226-1555 W. 7th Ave., 736-2616

Touchstone Theatre Company
399 W. 5th Ave., 709-9973

Theatre for the Young Mind and Soul

Vancouver's unique Green Thumb Theatre for Young People develops and stages original plays for young audiences. Their productions, which strive for entertainment, education, and enlightenment, deal with contemporary issues like substance abuse, the environment, racism, native culture, AIDS awareness, and more. For 25 years, their original productions have been staged by 200 theatre companies worldwide and translated into seven other languages. To date, they have performed over 10,000 times to 3.2 million people around the world. *254-4055*

The Rainforest Train

Want to teach your kids about the rainforests while having fun? Then check out the Rainforest Train in Stanley Park. Produced by the Mortal Coil Performance Society, this July-August family event combines music, theatre, and science. As the train winds through scenic Stanley Park, passengers encounter such spectacles as a gigantic mosquito about to devour its prey, an enormous dragonfly hovering over its pond, a massive mushroom patch, percussionist woodpeckers "pecking" to the beat of an imaginative drum solo, giant frogs doing the samba, stilt-walking herons, and much more. *257-8531*

Photo: courtesy Mortal Coil

Photo: Mandelbrot

It's hardly a secret that conspicuous consumption is a popular Vancouver pastime. How could it be, with the landscape dotted left, right, and underground with miles and miles of shopping malls, among them Pacific Centre (700 W. Georgia St., 688-7236), Burnaby's Metrotown Centre (4800 Kingsway, 438-2444) and Lougheed Mall (9855 Austin Rd., 421-2882), and that elder statesman of consumption parks (the first covered mall in western Canada), Park Royal Shopping Centre in West Vancouver (2002 Park Royal South, 925-9576). For those who prefer to practice the habit in the midst of the madding crowd, there are shopping streets full to brimming with shops in areas such as South Granville, West 4th Avenue, Main Street, Commercial Drive, and Robson Street.

That said, the critical question becomes, where do I find that all-important fake birthmark, crystal ball, used bustier or vintage chowchilla?
Read on....

Here's Looking at You, Kid

The custom-made eyeglasses from **Granville Eyeland** (188-0909) have attracted luminaries such as Elton John and Robin Williams. One local forest industry executive – who wants to stay out of the public eye – commissioned a set of 18-kt gold frames for $17,000. Recently opened is a **Granville Eyeland Just for Kids** in the Kids Only Market (682-KIDS).

Just Jack's Junk

Looking for a cherry-red toilet? How about a clawfoot tub? Not into home renovation? Then how about the last door from Oakalla prison, or one of eight over-the-top Modern chandeliers salvaged from the ballroom of the Bayshore Hotel? These and stacks and piles of other junk (er, salvage) are (or were) available at the acre-sized salvage yard of **Jack's Used Building Materials**. Located at 4912 Still Creek Avenue in Burnaby (299-2967), Jack's has been the place for pre-owned everything since 1948. Bring a camera (used, of course) and you may get a shot of Bryan Adams, searching for yet another cast-iron tub in which to put his houseplants.

Photo: Robert Ballantyne

Each year, the Vancouver Film Festival sponsors a contest for the best storefront window display celebrating the festival. Entrants include big names such as Club Monaco, Birks, and Le Chateau, but no one ever beats **Urban Empire**, a quirky little gift and novelty shop on Commercial Drive. What's their secret? Owner Paticia Salmond seems to put just the right amount of audacity into her creations. Her 1998 display – which contained bits and pieces that visiting filmmakers could conceivably have left behind – featured a bloodied and dismembered ear, left over perhaps from Robert Altman's Van Gogh epic *Vincent & Theo*. Elsewhere in the window was a can-can line of crucified Christs kicking it up around a pile of leftover aluminum beverage containers, a reference to the Denys Arcand film *Jesus of Montreal*. And then there was Farrah Fawcett. The former *Angel*-turned-serious-actress had been doing her best to recreate her bimbo image by doing the interview circuit more than slightly sloshed. Urban Empire responded with a disembodied Fawcett head – much battered à la *Extremities* – and a caption reading, "Farrah: you've left your mind behind; come get it."

In order to encourage other entrants to show some of the same *savoir-faire* in their *mise-en-scène*, the Film Festival office has issued memos challenging contestants to be more like Salmond. That way, they explained, someone else might claim the prize. So far no luck. She won again in 2000. The Empire remains unrepentant, and unvanquished. *1108 Commercial Dr., 254-4700*

Odd Fun

Oddball is one of those eclectic, hard-to-describe novelty stores, full of curios, novelties, collectibles, candy, and the best stuffed elephant this side of a Republican convention.
439 W. Hastings St., 632-0090

Paper Goods

You want ordinary stationery, go to Staples. You want specialty stuff, find it here.

Paper-Ya

A great source of creative paper products, many hand-made, from writing-oriented material to gifts.
*9-1666 Johnston St.,
Granville Island, 684-2531*

Paperhaus

Everything is functional at Paperhaus, which specializes in contemporary portfolio and presentation material with a Modernist bent. Clients include functional graphic designers and even more functional architects, though Paperhaus also sells functional desk accessories and paper products to non-industry people who simply want to function better.
3057 Granville St., 737-2225

Urban Source

Home to a smorgasbord of art materials gathered from local industry, including paper, rubber, foam, fabric, and other goodies.
3126 Main St., 875-1611

Flower Power

Garlands
Judy doesn't work here. Never did. Instead, Garlands offers "European style" bouquets, in this case arranged by a pair of real Europeans.
2955 W. Broadway, 739-6688

Giverny
An elegant source of fresh-cut flowers, arrangements, and unique accessories.
2404 Marine Dr., 926-8272

Metropolis Flori
Premium arrangements at the edge of Yaletown.
493 Davie St., 688-2222

Hillary Miles Flowers
Well known for their pricey yet artistic arrangements.
1-1854 W. 1st Ave., 737-2782

Scentrepiece Flower Market
When the richest man in the world wanted flowers for his sweetie on her (and his) wedding day, this is where he came. For those who don't own Microsoft and much of the known world besides, there are still a few affordable arrangements to choose from.
2112 W. 41st Ave., 263-2121

Plans for Plants

Plant lovers in need of a bargain know that every spring just as the swallows return to Capistrano, so the UBC plant sale returns to the **Botanical Garden** on the campus of the University of British Columbia. Started 22 years ago as a way of encouraging students to spend more time with greenery – not to mention make a little money for the Botanical Garden – the sale has grown to be the largest of its kind in the world. It's also among the cheapest places to pick up a plant in town, with the smallest of green living things starting in at $3. Call the UBC Botanical Garden (822-9666) for exact dates.

Petals for some Metal

Need some emergency flowers to make up for a missed anniversary? Why not buy in bulk? Early in the morning, three days a week, hundred of buyers gather at the S.W. Marine Drive site of the Auction (or the **United Flower Growers Co-operative Association**, to give it its full name) to stare intently at a dial as it sweeps towards zero. The first person to stop the dial buys the lot at that price. And what's for sale? Everything. Growers from around the Fraser Valley bring in hundreds of potted plants and cut blooms of every shape, colour, and variety. Nearly 12,000 transactions are completed everyday, making it the largest flower auction in North America. The only catch for would-be repentant husbands? The sale starts at 6 a.m.

Tasty Tools

The works at **Chocolate Arts** *(2037 W. Fourth Ave., 739-0475)* are of such exquisite craftsmanship, they're sometimes a wrench to eat (occasionally also a hammer or nail – they make little chocolate toolboxes filled with tiny chocolate tools). The Native masks of thick dark chocolate are also worth a look. But best of all are the window dioramas – little scenes with characters made entirely of chocolate. Past creations have included water-skiing chocolate eggs (a summer creation), an all-chocolate cruise ship (when *Titanic* came out), and a little chocolate barnyard full of milk-chocolate cows and white-chocolate chickens. After a month or so in the window, these toothsome works of art are sent to the Children's Hospital, where they are fully – and finally – appreciated.

Supplier of Stinky Stuff to the Stars

Upscale soap outlet **Lush** *(1025 Robson St., 687-5874, plus other locations)* has made quite a splash since appearing on the scene several years back. The boutique that sells soap shaped like bread and cheese and luscious bright deserts has even popped up in award-winning bits of fiction such as Zsuzsi Gartner's *All the Anxious Girls on Earth*. Even more intriguingly, this fragrant little shop has been surreptitiously selling bits of soap to the stars, among them Sarah Jessica Parker, Ally Sheedy, and looks-(and now smells)-like-a-woman Leonardo DiCaprio. Best celebrity seller so far? The "Kiss Me Klimt" bath bomb, sold to First-Lady-turned-Senator Hillary Clinton.

Cheap Skates
(and Inexpensive Gear)

Looking for rollerblades, but don't want to pay full price? Here's a place or two to try:

Cheapskates Consignment Stores
3644 W. 16th Ave., 222-1125
3496 Dunbar St., 734-1160
3228 Dunbar St., 734-1191

Ride on Sports
2255 W. Broadway, 738-7734

Sport Buy & Sell
872 E. Hastings St., 251-2262

The Sports Exchange
2151 Burrard St., 739-8990

Sports Junkies Consignors
600 W. 6th Ave., 879-0666
Prices drop weekly, Dutch auction style. The secret is knowing when that cool mountain bike drops to the magic price you want to pay.

Vintage Comics

ABC Book & Comic Emporium

1247 Granville St., 682-3019;

3347 Kingsway St., 430-3003

AC Card & Comics

1792 Renfrew St., 255-1158

Comic Land

3831 Rupert St., 437-4545

The Comicshop

2089 W. 4th Ave., 738-8122

Golden Age Collectibles

830 Granville St., 683-2819

Tazmanian Comic Connection

4702 Hastings St., 298-6208

U.N.I Comics

6942 Victoria Dr., 323-2821

TV, or Not TV?

Dreaming of Jeannie? Get a life-size Barbara Eden cut-out for your den at **Couch Potatoes**, a store which sells nothing but knick-knacks and novelty items from the land of TV. If you're not into Jeannie there's *Star Trek*'s Worf, Xena, *Gilligan's Island*'s Skipper, and all three original *Charlie's Angels*. Serious root vegetables can even host a couch potato home party.
1976 W. 4th Ave., 737-2900

Photo: Blaine Kyllo

Signature Store

Everything for his nibs. Or her nibs. Or anyone's nibs, really, for the **Vancouver Pen Shop** (*512 W. Hastings St., 681-1612*) has perhaps the city's sharpest selection of pens, including that take-everywhere $30,000 Mont Blanc.

joeys and bettys were here

Not a shop, but a phenomenon. In the past few years, the corner of West 4th Avenue and Burrard Street has become the spot for high-quality snow/skate/surf board gear, and *the* spot to see top-level boarders and their groupies hanging out. Also the place to pick up stuff for the board Betty or Joey in your life: **Pacific Boarder**, 1793 W. 4th Ave., 734-7245; **Thriller**, 1710 W. 4th Ave., 736-5651; **Boardroom Snowboard Shop**, 1745 W. 4th Ave., 734-7669; and **West Beach**, 1766 W. 4th Ave., 731-6449, which sometimes hosts pro-skate demos on the half-pipe at the back of the store.

OTHER SHOPS AROUND TOWN INCLUDE:

Exposure
Carries the hottest boarding fashions.
900 Granville St., 683-6031

Level Board & Fashion
1025 Robson St., 683-8200
25 Alexander St., 681-9098

Northshore Ski & Board
1625 Lonsdale Ave., North Vancouver, 987-7245

Pacific Boarder
1793 W. 4th Ave., 734-7245

Second Wave Surf & Snowboard Shop
139 Lonsdale Ave., North Vancouver, 986-9283

Westbeach Snowboard, Skateboard & Surf Shop
119-4350 Lorimer Rd., Whistler, 932-2526

Photo: Blaine Kyllo

Westside Sports & Ski
2625 W. 4th Ave., 739-7547
232 W. Broadway, 872-6860

Glitter Kids

What with all the street kids, trash, and neon, the eastside of Granville Street between Robson and Drake often looks like a set for *Escape from New York or Road Warrior*. But nestled among the pizza-slice dispensers, pawn shops, and purveyors of top-notch, low-grade porn are some of the funkiest urban-wear shops the city has to offer. Whether it's fangs or genitalwear (what's a man without a Prince Albert?), general bits of piercewear and body metal, body paint, bondagewear or just temporary tattoos, glitter, jewellery, and wigs for the serious urban wannabe, you'll find down here somewhere.

Cabbages and Kinx
So it's not on Granville. It should be. Leather fetish and bondage wear/accessories, clothing, jewellery, and accessories. Everything you need, in fact, for your next rave or fetish party. Also a great used clothing selection.
315 W. Hastings St., 669-4238

record deals

Vancouver enjoys some of the best prices in the world for CDs and tapes, not to mention vinyl. Look to the following for music not to be found in the Top 40:

Bassix
A large offering of danceable music, as well as the equipment to mix/spin it on.
217 W. Hastings St., 689-7734

Black Swan Records
Collectors will find those hard-to-locate vinyl and imports from many different musical genres.
3209 W. Broadway, 734-2828

D & G Collectors Records
A wide selection of vintage and used records from the 1930s to present. *3580 E. Hastings St., 294-5737*

Highlife Records and Music
A lively spot on the Drive, specializing in jazz and worldbeat. *1317 Commercial Dr., 251-6964*

La Bamba Records
Vancouver's Latin music source. *937 Commercial Dr., 606-0677*

Magic Flute Record Shop
Mostly classical and jazz, as well as some other genres. *2203 W. 4th Ave., 736-2727*

Scratch Records
Purveyors of independent music and electronica. *726 Richards St., 687-6355*

Sikora's Classical Records
Specializes in classical, so you're sure to find what you're looking for here.
432 W. Hastings St., 685-0625

Zulu Records
Focuses on alternative and indie-rock, but you'll also find jazz and a second-hand section.
1972 W. 4th Ave., 738-3232

Cheap Thrills
Odd jewellery, accessories, and knickknacks. Also has clothing.
852 Granville St., 682-7250

Futuristic Flavour
Clothing, mixed tapes, and DJ gear.
1020 Granville St., 681-1766

Pharsyde
Clothing and accessories.
860 Granville St., 683-5620;
2100 W. 4th Ave., 739-6630

The Underground
Specializes in clothing, jewellery, and accessories.
848 Granville St., 681-8732

bud's no spud

BC bud is where it's at, as famous as P.E.I. potatoes and infinitely more lucrative. Those with a taste for – or just a healthy curiosity about – the local herb might want to drop in at one of the following spots for information, accessories or just some agreeable smoking companions.

Blunt Brothers: A Respectable Joint

This café is a little taste of Amsterdam: tasty food and drink, live music, nifty paraphernalia, a special daytime smoking room, and an after-6 pm policy of smoke 'em if you got 'em. Note: if you ain't got 'em when you get there, you ain't gonna get 'em inside. Not only is buying and selling *strictly* prohibited, it's decidedly uncool. On the other hand, the Brothers are located on the edge on the downtown eastside. If you can't score there, it's time to head back to Iowa.
317 W. Hastings St., 682-5868

Asia West

Never been to Hong Kong? At this new commercial area at the junction of No. 3 Road and Cambie Road in Richmond, it looks as if six full malls – the Yaohan Centre, President Plaza, Aberdeen Centre, and Parker Place – were airlifted in from Kowloon especially to cater to Vancouver's newly arrived Asian community. On offer is a rich array of Chinese, Japanese, Korean, Malaysian, and Thai products, services, and restaurants, all within walking distance from each other. Oh and remember, if the prices seem a bit high, a simple inquiry is often enough to bring them plummeting down as much as 80 percent.

Photo: Blaine Kyllo

Grass Roots

Doubles as a community centre for the hemphead scene. Check out the billboard in the back for clippings on pot-related events in and around the city. Start a conversation on decriminalization and spend the rest of your natural existence listening to vaguely spaced-out conspiracy theories centering on William Randolph Hearst (psst: Rosebud was his sled).
2048 Commercial Dr., 253-4146

Rasta Wares

Besides the usual smoking gear, you'll also find gorgeous hemp and summery cotton clothing as well as jewellery and drums. Tune in and turn on. They also take Visa.
1505 Commercial Dr., 255-3600

Happy Cannabis Day

The stairs of the Vancouver Art Gallery are the yearly site of the Cannabis Day celebration, held on the same day as Canada Day. The stairs also serve as a gathering place for various marijuana protests and gatherings year round. Bring your own bud!
750 Hornby St. (Robson side)

Aberdeen Centre
4151 Hazelbridge Way, Richmond,
270-1234

Central Square
4231 Hazelbridge Way, Richmond,
278-9399

Fairchild Square
4400 Hazelbridge Way, Richmond,
273-1234

Parker Place
4380 No. 3 Rd., Richmond,
273-0276

President Plaza
8181 Cambie Rd., Richmond,
299-9000 (ext. 8181)

Yaohan Centre
3700 No. 3 Rd., Richmond,
299-9000 (ext. 8282)

Rubber Haute-Couture

Everything for the cock of the walk, the **Rubber Rainbow Condom Company** (*953 Denman St., 683-3423*) has ribbed, rib-less, and riblets; banana, grape, and cherry; and purple, green, pink, and a lovely little Neapolitan number, all in sizes ranging from Texas Small to South Chicago Superhumongous. Look especially for the Spankie – invented by a lonely lad from Kitsilano – a washable cotton sock tailor made for catching errant sperm (more info at www.spankie.com). As one would expect, Rubber Rainbow itself is run by two mature and demure sisters, one of whom has grandchildren.

designing women

Vancouver is blessed with top fashion talent. Below are a few whose couture get snatched up by those in the know.

Yumi Eto

Sold through ultimately upscale Holt Renfrew (633 Granville St., 681-3121) – where even a scarf will cost a new mortgage –, Eto's designs are favoured by the likes of Calista Flockhart and Sarah McLachlan.

Patricia Fieldwalker

Noted maker of women's unmentionables has seen her creations displayed on the bods of *Fatal Attraction's* Glenn Close and Julia Roberts in *Pretty Woman*. Available at Diane's Lingerie (2950 Granville St, 738-5121).

Teresa Findlay Studio

Accessory designer has flogged more than one purse and hat to femme fatale Sharon Stone. Failed to sell her on the extra lingerie. *689-9831*

Nancy Lord

Fabulous leathers, as well as linen and microfibre wear. *4-1665 Johnston St., Granville Island, 689-3972*

Vintage Furniture

Metropolitan Home
Worth visiting just to look, this store is filled with beautiful current and vintage modernist furniture from the '50s, '60s, and '70s at reasonable prices.
450 W. Hastings St., 681-2313

Panther Decor
Filled to the brim with furniture and houseware items from the '50s, '60s, and '70s, all well priced. For real deals, wander all the way to the back, then around the corner into the dusty semi-accessible space where Panther stores its fixer-upper gems.
2924 W. 4th Ave., 733-5665

Populuxe
Carries a large selection tables, dishes, restored appliances, and kitsch from the '40s, '50s, and '60s.
1505 W. 2nd Ave., 730-9588

Photo: Mandelbrot

vintage duds

Barbie Dolls Vintage Clothes

The latest Carl Hiassen novel, *Sick Puppy*, features an ex-drug dealer turned land developer who's so sexually obsessed by Barbie (the result of having had six older sisters) that he convinces of pair of high class East European whores to allow a plastic surgeon to slowly transform them into identical living Barbie dolls, complete with 15-inch waists and 40-inch bosoms. Clothing for the two would not have been available at Barbie Dolls (and was unnecessary, in any case). However, Barbie Dolls does have great vintage clothes at good prices, as well as clothing and accessories made from bits and pieces of vintage apparel. They also have genuine Barbie dolls and associated miscellany, as well as other pop culture curios. Their selection of used Japanese pop culture magazines is worth the trip alone. *436 Homer St.*

Burcu's Angels Funky Clothing Etc.

Semi-divine shop on oh-so-funky Main is no secret to the film industry, which often rents items for use in various film shoots. Burcu, the charismatic owner, makes sure that even regular shoppers have fun "playing" with different fabrics, colours, and time periods. If you're lucky, you might even get fresh baked goodies while you're there. Also, check out the "tree box" that she puts out in front of the store daily. *2535 Main St., 874-9773*

Deluxe Junk Co.

Carries a large selection of high-end consignment which is made up of the nearly new and the lovingly preserved. The great thing about this store is that the prices are reduced regularly according to how long they have been on display. *310 W. Cordova St., 685-4871*

Legends Retro-Fashion

Famous among vintage aficionados for its one-of-a-kind treasures. *4366 Main St., 875-0621*

IT'S A PUZZLE

Actually, it's lots of puzzles. **Puzzlemania Fancy Gift Shop** sells nothing but puzzles. I know because their sign says, "We sell nothing but jigsaw puzzles." That bit of declarative prose, however, doesn't quite do justice to what's on offer at Puzzlemania's two shops (*2nd Floor Yaohan Centre, Richmond, 207-0198; Level 3, Metrotown, Burnaby, 437-0998*). There are 12-piece kiddie puzzles, Snoopy puzzles, Vincent Van Gogh and Leonardo Da Vinci puzzles. Most are top-quality, precision-cut imports. And for the serious puzzle freak, there are puzzles that are one-colour with round edges and almost all pieces cut to look identical. Sounds like fun.

True Value Vintage

Boasts "Vancouver's largest selection of cool vintage clothing." Here you can buy, sell, trade, or rent great vintage items. Also, bring in your used Levis and they'll give you cash for them. Don't be afraid to haggle: rumour has it that visitors pay big bucks for some, particularly the 501s. *710 Robson St., 437-7734*

Virgin Mary's

Great selection of vintage from the '50s to the '80s. But don't let the name fool you: the selection is hot! *430 Homer St., 844-7848*

discount daze

Though Vancouver was largely settled by the English (whinging pommy bastards, as they're affectionately known), there's enough of Scotland in the local culture for Vancouverites to appreciate a bargain. The following discount clearance outlets are good spots to start:

Aldo Shoes

Shoe freaks and the seriously cheap achieve Nirvana in this shop. Prices vary from $9.95 to about $49.95, with a few higher priced items such as boots and jackets. The trick to this store is to pop in now and again, drool discreetly over the leather boots you've been eyeing, and wait for the moment the clerk comes by to knock the price down. Once you make a great purchase, keep the tag on the bottom of your shoe for that special dungeon date when you can step on your special friend's face and show him how little you paid. *810 Granville St., 605-8939; 777 Dunsmuir St., 683-4151*

Aritzia

Has excellent bi-annual warehouse sales, but just to keep it fun, the warehouse locations are always changing. Keep an eye on the newspaper ads as end-of-season rolls around. *251-3132*

Consignment Clothing

Dragon & Phoenix Designer Consignments
Current fashions in good shape from Gap to Armani. *6248 East Blvd. (women's), 261-1317; 6260 East Blvd. (men's), 261-9693*

Ex Toggery
Conservative women's consignment clothing, with some sample and wholesale pieces as well. *6055 West Blvd., 266-6744*

Happy Three Clothing
Carries designer and non-designer clothing and accessories "that have been cleaned or dry cleaned." *3629 W. 4th Ave., 730-9638; 2824 Granville St., 733-2982*

Au Coton

The Lansdowne Park Shopping Centre location
also doubles as the factory outlet for this colourful
cottonwear retailer.
5300 No. 3 Rd., Richmond, 270-8068

Boboli

Boboli's outlet at the Aberdeen Centre in Richmond
offers last season's women's and men's clothing at 50
to 80 percent off. Included are names like Armani,
Blumarine, MaxMara, Yohji Yamamoto, V2 by Versace,
and Alberta Ferretti. And though sizes favour the folks
outside size 6 to 9, the designs themselves tend towards
the bold, and sometimes outrageous. But at least the
price won't be.
4151 Hazelbridge Way, Richmond, 207-1636

Create

Carries designer labels like Neto, French Laundry,
and Ron & Normand at great prices.
1022 Mainland St., 915-9592

Esprit

You'll find the clearance outlet for this pricey label on
the first floor of Pacific Centre.
700 W. Georgia St., 684-8152

Jax

Need to have that executive look but don't make
executive wages? Then check out one of the following
JAX Showcase stores where you'll find great deals on
high-end suit samples and fabrics.
316 W. Cordova St., 684-7004;
Brentwood Mall, 4567 Lougheed Hwy., 291-6369;
942 W. 16th Ave., 990-5293;
Aberdeen Centre, 4400 Hazelbridge Way, Richmond,
276-8222

Wear Else?

High-end casual and office wear normally costs the
same as an office computer. Unless you hit this outlet.
78 E. 2nd Ave., 879-6162

Shoe Time

Funny shoes with fancy prices. Platforms made from real steel struts. Sandals of one-piece, day-glo lucite. The sort of thing tailor-made for the rube with too much loot. Undoubtedly why **John Fluevog Shoes** appeal to the Hollywood types, carpetbagging their way through town on yet another B-flick shoot. Now in its 30th year of business, and with stores in most major cities in Canada and the U.S., Vancouverite John Fluevog's outlet is patronized by the likes of Robin Williams, Paula Abdul, Madonna, Sarah McLachlan, and the Red Hot Chili Peppers, not to mention the sort of wide-eyed tourist desperate to get a sniff of some Hollywood toe jam. *837 Granville St., 688-2828*

How Much Wood Would a Woodchuck Chuck?

If the blonde bland sameness of Ikea is giving you thoughts of tossing Sven in the wood chipper, take heart. There's a new small gallery on the edge of Commercial Drive just stuffed with original, high-quality and, best of all, local furniture designs, nearly all of them made with B.C. wood. **The WoodWorks Gallery** *(1723 Grant St., 251-4100)* is the brainchild of former Knowledge Network producer Greg Wheeler, who was looking for a way to showcase value-added wood products — items that do a bit more with B.C.'s forest resources than the usual telephone books and toilet paper. While the collection varies as pieces come in, get purchased, and go out again, the line-up often includes works of such B.C. designers as John Bird, William Forrester, and Sunshine Coast designer Steve Webber, who often disguises compartments or drawers as hand-carved apples or pears.

HOT COMMODITIES

Got money to burn? If not, there's plenty to be purchased (in $1million denominations issued from the Bank of Hell) at **Buddha Supplies Centre**. At Chinese funerals, people burn joss — paper replicas of earthly belongings — to make awaiting judgement in the netherworld more comfortable for the deceased. Here, there are more than 500 combustible objects to choose from. For sophisticated types raised in Hong Kong and Taiwan, the traditional Chinese replicas of a horse and cart or pagoda are simply too pedestrian, and are passed over for luxury items — such as a paper penthouse complete with Mercedes in the carport, a craft paper cellular phone, cardboard CD player or fax machine. *4158 Main St., 873-8169*

Puttin' on the Glitz

Got a lot of money and a taste for designer clothing? Here's where to go:

Bebe
1000 Robson St., 681-1819

Boboli
2776 Granville St., 257-2300

Boys' Co Men's Wear
1044 Robson St., 684-5656
+ 3 other locations

Chanel
900 W. Hastings St., 682-0522

Hills of Kerrisdale
2125 W. 41st Ave., 266-9177

Holt Renfrew & Co.
633 Granville St., 681-3121

L'uomo Men's Wear
2037-88 W. Pender St., 681-0998

Leone
757 Hastings St., 683-1133

Plaza Escada
757 W. Hastings St., 688-8558

Versus Boutique
1008 W. Georgia St., 688-8938

Wear Else?
2360 W. 4th Ave., 732-3521

Mind If We Call Ya Bruce?

Bruce is the place for *Wallpaper** readers to go and pretend they're in Soho. Named after one of owner Campbell McDougall's previous incarnations (when he was a philosopher at the University of Western Australia?) and located in a glass-fronted warehouse just a block from the Robson retail strip, Bruce offers all the clothing, furniture, jewellery, dishes, and decorative art you'll need to instantly look the part of today's global-minded urban citizen; full lobotomy extra.
1038 Alberni St., 688-8802

Photo: Blaine Kyllo

Sample Sales

Why do retail when you can make like an explorer and head for the source? If you can fit into sample sizes — generally 6 to 8-ish, or small to medium for any males out there unused to the secret code employed by women's clothiers — then sample sales by clothing manufacturers' agents and wholesalers can be a great way to score deals. Simply stroll down to Yaletown and check out Mainland and Hamilton between Nelson and Davie. Fashion labels such as **Diesel** *(1079 Mainland St.)*, **Hollywood Jeans** *(1020 Hamilton St.)*, and **Poorboy** *(1092 Hamilton St.)*, and manufacturers' agents like **Tension Clothing** *(1020 Mainland St.)*, will occasionally have sandwich board signs outside their offices that advertise sample sales. Some companies, including the **Dakota Group** *(215 - 1013 Mainland St.)*, will hold yearly sales on a "call-list" basis, which means that officially you have to register your number on a list and be notified by phone. If you find out via other means, however, it's possible to just walk on in. **Tommy Hilfiger** *(1168 Hamilton St.)*, however, is a tougher nut to crack; you'll need to some connection no matter how tenuous with someone working there. Ingenuity is allowed.

designer housewares

Bacci's at Home

Imaginative housewares shop. Having escaped from the telephone hygienists in Ark B, now-famous towel designer Stephen Senini got his start here.
2788 Granville St., 737-0368

Marthy Sturdy Originals

You'll find Sturdy's well-known and popular housewares at a discount, sometimes as much as half what you would pay elsewhere.
3939 Granville St., 737-0037

funky furniture

Bonaparte

Offbeat, often tongue-in-cheek furniture and housewares.
1010 Homer St., 688-8555

Chintz & Company

Everything you could possibly need to furnish and accessorize your home with style.
950 Homer St., 689-2022

Inform Interiors

A Gastown fixture for 22 years, this is the largest showroom in Vancouver for high-end architectural and design furniture, lighting, accessories, and books.
97 Water St., 682-3868

Liberty Design

Specializes in elegant furniture and accessories with a goth feel.
1295 Seymour St., 682-7499

Thrift Shops

Lady Madonna Thrift Shop
Funky clothes and great prices. Talk to the owner while you're there and she'll tell you about how her and hubby Vincent fought City Hall tooth-and-nail back in 1986 to establish American Backpackers Hostel, the first independent backpackers hostel in the city. Still there, the hostel is located just up the stairs from the shop and still offers accommodation for $10 a night, including free beer on Saturdays. Also worth noting upstairs is a wall display of hand-painted signs gleaned from the couple's extensive travels.
432 Homer St.

Photo: Mandelbrot

Montauk

Contemporary yet conservative furniture with a 24-year guarantee.
1062 Homer St., 331-2363

Rieva and Reine

Stylish and affordable furniture and linens. A refreshing alternative to Ikea.
2851 Granville St., 737-1790

Sofas à la Carte

Design your own furniture by matching various designs with a wide selection of fabrics.
909 W. Broadway, 731-9020

UpCountry

Showcases mostly high-end local and nationally designed housewares.
2210 Cambie St., 875-9004

Junior League Thrift Shop

335 East Broadway, 876-4921

**Mennonite Central
Committee B.C.**

5914 Fraser St., 325-1612

Salvation Army Thrift Shops

1900 W. 4th Ave., 737-2444

261 E. 12th Ave., 874-4721

2714 W. Broadway, 734-1821

9952 Lougheed Hwy., 444-2100

SPCA Thrift Store

3626 W. Broadway, 736-4136

Wildlife Rescue Thrift Store

1925 Granville St., 682-0381

Back Room Deals

Photo: Blaine Kyllo

Ten years ago, Jerry Wolfman, collector of west-coast Native art and the owner of **3 Vets**, started a modern-day trading post almost by accident when members of the Squamish Nation came to his store to purchase camping equipment and happened to have some carvings with them. A trade was made, and business exploded when word got out that prices are some of the best around. Now this legendary Native-art room is kept under lock and key, but Wolfman will be glad to open it upon request. Selection ranges from $12 letter openers to massive $7,000 wallhangings and engraved silver jewellery. Recently Wolfman has sold his goods to art dealers from L.A., New York, the Smithsonian, as well as several visiting Hollywood types.
2200 Yukon St., 872-5475

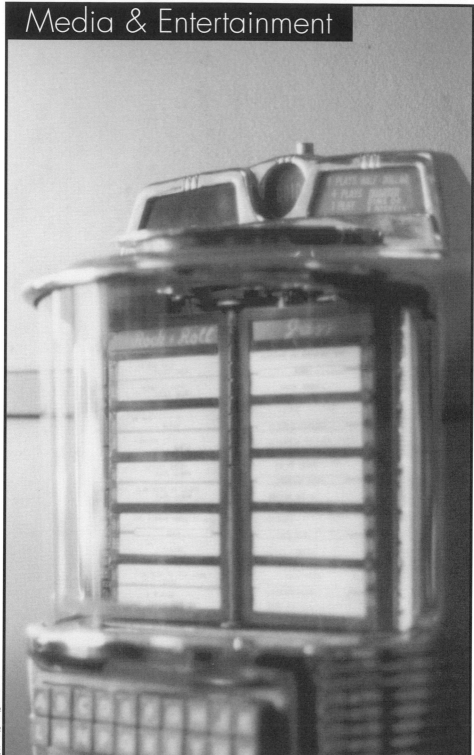

Thanks to a healthy dollop of creative talent in music, movies, and multi-media, Vancouver is blessed with more than its share of those most important of civic attributes: rumour, gossip, innuendo, and deep, dark, salacious secrets. Read on to find out how a Bunny came to be and how a game show hostess ceased to be. Discover how an ancient warrior learned to slash and jiggle. Find out about Vancouver's stars – those that were, are, and wannabe. Best of all, learn how to get in on the fun yourself.

Secret Source of the Dark Side

Word is out from Hollywood: the new Darth Vader to be is a Vancouverite, 19-year-old Hayden Christensen. Wouldn't it figure. Anakin Skywalker is, after all, the ultimate goody-goody, a law-abiding straight-arrow fond of outdoor sports (sabre duelling, fighter flying) and into mystic spirituality (Trust your feelings, Chris). And the minute he's offered a life of avarice, lust, and general corruption he's off like a shot, much like a Vancouver actor offered any chance at all of making it in L.A.

An Actor's Life for Me

Ah the life of an actor. Your name in lights, your image venerated by millions. Small wonder that so many set out on the path to fame, beginning often with a course of acting lessons. Equally unsurprising, given Vancouver's growing reputation as Hollywood North, that at least one of those schools for future superstars should choose to locate here. Open since 1989 on the corner of Hornby and Davie, the William Davis Centre for Actors' Study – owned and operated by *The X-Files'* own Cancer Man – offers aspiring thespians

intensive training in the all aspects of the craft, taught by professionals from the Vancouver film and TV world. Given the relentlessly B-movie nature of that world, of course, it's perhaps not surprising that Cancer Man has yet to launch anyone to the stratospheric heights of Harrison Ford or Gwyneth Paltrow. Davis' most successful graduate to date has been Lucy Lawless (left), the buxom, buckler-clad star of the sword-and-cleavage series *Xena: Warrior Princess*. Ah, the life of a Vancouver-trained actress: your hooters encased in leather body armour, your mug splayed out across the centrefold of *Maxim*.

Photo: Courtesy Fox

Everyone in this city, and fans worldwide, know that while the truth was out there, the TV show *The X-Files* was decidedly here, having been filmed in Vancouver for five years.

And not only was the city home to the actors for the length of the shooting season, but various locations in the city served as "homes" for the series' fictional characters. Simon Fraser University's Burnaby campus became FBI headquarters. Agent Mulder's upscale apartment in Alexandria, Maryland was represented by the Wellington building at 2630 York Avenue in Kitsilano. Agent Dana Scully's more modest abode in Annapolis, Maryland was in real life the apartment building at 1419 Pendrell Street in the West End.

Even more interesting, however, was the way the city itself began to work its way subliminally into the fictional world of the series. For example, when writers needed a name for a new FBI agent, they grabbed one off a street sign, and thus was born Agent Comox. Later, when Comox – actor Paul McGillion – was unavailable for further shooting, the script doctors simply picked the West End street one block over, and *voilà* – Brendan Beiser became Agent Pendrell, who took a bullet in the chest during the 1997 season.

NEWS ANCHORS: THE BEAUTY QUEEN CONNECTION

So what's it take to be a hotshot on the TV news in Vancouver? Brains, integrity, a nose for a story? Maybe, but a beauty queen background doesn't hurt, as the following resumé snippets show:

Gloria Macarenko
1978: 17-year-old wins
Miss PNE pageant
1989: CBC Vancouver news anchor
Now CBC National weekend anchor and
CBC Vancouver nightly co-anchor

Pamela Martin
1968: crowned Miss Teen Great Lakes;
2nd Runner-Up, Miss Teen International
1986: Hired as BCTV reporter
Now BCTV co-anchor

Carole Goss (now Carole Taylor)
1963: 16-year-old wins title
Miss Toronto
1973: Becomes host of *W5*
1986: Becomes Vancouver
city councillor
Now chair of Vancouver Port
Corporation; once touted as potential
B.C. Liberal leader

Joni Mar
1980: crowned Miss Vancouver
1984: Hired as CBC news reporter

SECRET SOURCE OF STARDOM

Even if they were nothing special when they lived here, and have been gone for years, whenever a hometown son or daughter becomes a star, Vancouverites get all worked up. Michael J. Fox and Jason Priestley are prime examples. So is Gil Bellows, born and raised in Vancouver, who was an afterthought in *The Shawshank Redemption*, but got noticed when he landed a role as Billy, the true-love interest to *Ally McBeal*. Although killed off in a dramatic courtroom collapse at the end of the 1999-2000 season, in Vancouver Bellows' name is spoken with fondness.

But that's nothing compared to the response the name Carrie-Anne Moss will get you. Raised in Burnaby, Moss moved to Toronto, then to Europe, then to L.A. She modelled, then acted, and even combined both careers for a while with a starring role on the ill-fated TV series *Models Inc.* When Moss kicked big screen ass in *The Matrix*, however, she left the land of TV far behind. Her strong performance as Trinity, opposite Keano Reeves, catapulted her into the realm of action movie star, a coveted role held by few women.

So what's the secret? Well, Bellows and Moss have more in common than the Vancouver air they breathed. Before leaving their fair home town, both attended Kerrisdale's Magee Secondary.

Save it for a Rainy Episode

Photo: Courtesy Fox

When *X-Files* star David Duchovny announced that he wanted the show moved to Los Angeles so that he could be closer to his wife and away from a city where, he said, "It rains, like, 400 inches a day," it generated more than the proverbial teapot's worth of localized tempest. Media dogged Duchovny for days looking for a comment. Callers to phone-in shows raged against his seemingly snot-nosed ingratitude. Only the most attentive of fans caught the way *The X-Files* picked up on the kerfuffle and spun it back into the show on the episode entitled "Schizogeny." For those who missed it, a truncated synopsis follows:

In Coats Grove, Michigan, Bobby Rich, a 16-year old boy is berated by his stepfather, Phil, for not finishing his work outside the house. Bobby picks up a shovel and instructs his stepfather to keep his distance. As the dispute escalates, Bobby drops the shovel and runs into a nearby orchard. Phil gives chase. Suddenly, Phil's feet are knocked out from underneath him. A short time later, Phil's wife Patti makes her way through the orchard. She discovers Phil's body buried in mud up to his shoulders, with mud seeping from his nose and mouth. Kneeling beside Phil is Bobby, his eyes wide with terror.

Scully proceeds to performs an autopsy on Phil's corpse, while Mulder looks on. She discovers over 12 pounds of mud in his stomach, leading her to believe that the man's "head was held forcibly down in the mud just a little too long." She thinks the act was likely carried out by the stepson. Mulder isn't so confident, though, reminding Scully that the body was found "buried completely in a standing vertical position."

Scully suggests that the stepson may have dug a hole and that "a recent rainstorm may have turned it into a muddy trap."

To which Mulder replies: "That's some rainstorm."

Scully: "They say it rained 400 inches a day."

Mulder: "Now that sounds like an exaggeration, don't you think?"

Maybe. Of course, it could also be taken as an apology.

1650 West 2nd Avenue: this non-descript building in a non-descript neighbourhood – across the street from a car dealership and two doors down from a discount Persian rug outlet – is nonetheless the control centre of the largest music festival touring in North America, Lilith Fair. It's also the management headquarters for both the Barenaked Ladies and Lilith Fair's creator, Sarah McLachlan.

And if you ask Terry McBride, founding president of Nettwerk Productions and Management – parent company to Nettwerk Management, Publishing, Soundtracks, Multimedia, not to mention Records – he'll tell you the 2nd Avenue address is a step up from Nettwerk's original location, his own West End apartment. The stable of performers has also improved from the days when the label existed solely for McBride's own synth-pop band Moev, and later for industrial-punk group Skinny Puppy.

Riding the success of Lilith, McLachlan's sweet-and-sexy visage has now appeared on the covers of *Rolling Stone*, *Time*, *Maclean's*, and *Entertainment Weekly*. Her *Surfacing* album has sold over 9.5 million copies to date. And while the Lilith Fair festival may be finished, it, and its creator, will live on in the frames of a documentary, directed by Lynne Stopkewich.

A ROCKIN' PHANTOM

Mushroom Studios, at 1234 West 6th Avenue, has been the site for several hit recordings, among them Sarah McLachlan's album *Solace*, Loverboy's *Get Lucky*, and Heart's smash album *Dreamboat Annie*. It's also been the site of at least one haunting. According to both artists and technicians, the phantom is never seen but often heard, humming and singing along in the background during recording sessions. For a time there was speculation that the ghost was the spirit of Shelley Siegel, the Mushroom Studios' president who died suddenly of a stroke in Los Angeles at the age of 34. However, according to one Mushroom executive, who wished to remain nameless, the ghost is far too laid-back to be Siegel.

Inconsolable because the Backstreet Boys concert sold out in seconds flat (okay, days, but whatever)? Don't give up the ghost right away: the booking computer may yield paydirt closer to showtime. Concert promoters hold back "sight-kills" on the wings, beside the stage, or near the sound board in case the sightlines become obscured by stage equipment. Many of these seats are later released as the stage plan is clarified, closer to the show date. *Bonus tip:* The Orpheum's sight kills are among the best seats in the house.

The Rattling Life

Before the knighthood, before LiveAid, before even the years of relative obscurity as the lead singer with a raunchy-but-never-really-that-successful Boomtown Rats, Bob Geldof held the venerated and much sought after position of entertainment editor of the alternative Vancouver newspaper the *Georgia Straight*. As recorded in the *Straight's* 30th-anniversary book *What the Hell Happened?*, Geldof, writing under the name of Rob, was responsible for distinguished bits of journalism such as the following bit about an Ike and Tina Turner concert. " ... Tina Turner employs the almost theatrical art of sexual overkill – subtle she is not. Tina does, however, embody a whole unisexual family of fantasies. She is the lusting available housewife/whore, nymphoid of a billion male dreams, and she is possibly the personification of an equal quantity of female alter egos."

By all accounts, Geldof liked his job as a music critic. Indeed, had it not been for Immigration Canada's eventual insistence on a work permit, Geldof, who began in 1974 and held the position for the better part of two years, might well be writing there still. That's not to say he wasn't even then thinking of other things. In a review of John Denver's album *Back Home Again*, Geldof wrote: "He's charming, has that ultra-bright smile, wholesome features, and the all-important boy-next-door quality, but if that's all it takes, why ain't I a star? I'd love to be a star. I think I'd be an excellent star."

Hidden Talents

Jimmy Pattison has never made a secret of his love of making a buck. The hustling kid from East Van took a talent for selling cars and turned it into an international business empire. But he had other talents as a child. In the late 1930s, little Jimmy Pattison was a trumpet player, and a helpmate to his evangelical dad. Evenings, in those years, if you had wandered past the Apostolic Pentecostal Mission on East Hastings street in Vancouver's Skid Row, you'd have heard little nine-year-old Jimmy Pattison blasting out evangelical tunes on his trumpet, doing his damnedest to save your soul.

Vancouver Bunny Catcher

Photo: Wayne Leidenfrost/The Province

Vancouver is blessed with beautiful women. Or to be more accurate, Vancouver is blessed with the kind of blonde, big-chested female favoured by the readers and photographers of *Playboy*. Of the 32 women featured in the magazine's 1980 "Girls of Canada" issue, 11 came from Vancouver. Even more impressively, the city has supplied more than a dozen *Playboy* Playmates (i.e., of the centrefold variety) over the years, starting with Pamela Ann Gordon in 1962. This fact must be due in part to the weather, but a good deal of credit must also go to Ken Honey, *Playboy*'s resident talent scout in Vancouver. A small, grey man with thinning hair and a penchant for brown raincoats, Honey discovered Pamela Anderson sitting in the stands at a BC Lions football game. A bit of surgery and a centrefold later, and Anderson was pulling down $100K an episode jiggling on the beach on *Baywatch*. Other Honey discoveries include Dorothy Stratten (photo above) (Playmate, April 1, 1980; discovered serving double scoops at a Vancouver Dairy Queen) and West Vancouver's Kimberly Conrad (Playmate of the Year, 1989), who later became Mrs. Hugh Hefner. And what has Honey learned from his years of looking for beautiful women, in the streets and cafés and Dairy Queens of Vancouver? "Beautiful women are like buses," he says. "Wait five minutes and another's sure to come along."

CALLING ALL VOYEURS

If, like *Being There*'s butler Chancey, you just like to look, then Vancouver is also the film town for you. Log on to www.bcfilmcommission.com and select "What's new?" and you'll find info on all the flicks currently being filmed in town. Call the contact number and ask to attend some of the filming. Many are happy to give permission, and will even allow you to take pictures. And for those that don't, thanks to the website, you know where to find them.

Death In the Sun

Sir Harry Oakes was a mining giant. The gold mine he discovered in Kirkland Lake produced millions of tons of the yellow stuff, making him one of the richest men on Earth. And the most bitter. Though rich as Croesus, none of the quality in his erstwhile home of Toronto wanted much to do with the spitting, swearing ex-prospector. He went to London and bought himself a peerage, but even as Sir Harry he never made the A-list parties. Even worse, back in Canada the *goddamngovernment* (Sir Harry used the words as one) was planning to make him pay taxes. So he moved to Bermuda – a warm sunny tax-free Atlantic haven. Once there, he made friends with another exile, Britain's Edward VIII, and his divorced American wife Wallis Simpson. The three went for walks and played cards together. They were among his better friends. They were also among the prime suspects when Sir Harry was found murdered in his palatial Bermuda home. Certainly, Edward and the Governor of Bermuda went to great lengths to delay, stall, and derail the investigation. No killer was ever found. *Eureka*, the 1981 shot-in-Vancouver film version of the mystery offered one plausible explanation of who killed Sir Harry (in this case, Gene Hackman), but to find out, you'll have to rent the flick.

Secret Fate of Quiz Show Stars

For a time in the '80s, Vanna White was hot. She'd preen and pose for the studio audience, clap her perfect hands, smile her perfect smile, turn her little letters, and rake in lots of dough. Wealth without talent or labour – the perfect '80s gig. Then the *Wheel of Fortune* faded somewhat, supplanted in the public eye by newcomers like *Survivor* and Regis Philbin's *Millionaire* show. Vanna was forced to pick up extra work primping for the people at Spring Air mattresses. And thus it was that an 18-foot image of Vanna, complete with little black dress and oversize jewels, showed up on the wall of Bob Wilson's Mr. Mattress outlet at 1815 Venables. Poor Vanna. Those she's still on display on the east side, even this gig won't last long. Spring Air now has a big, burly grizzly for a mascot, while Wilson's friends are lining up to pick up Vanna's pieces once he takes her down.

First Silver Screen

The first full-time movie cinema in the young Canadian commonwealth opened in 1902 on Cordova Street. Named the Edison Electric, it was the pet project of one John Schulberg, an early film pioneer who is also responsible for the first ever film screening in Vancouver four years earlier in 1898. That event consisted ostensibly of newsreels of the then-ongoing Spanish American War. Later, it was found out that instead of actually sending cameramen to cover the war, the Edison company had faked the footage on its own New Jersey lot.

Family Viewing

Who hasn't got old 8mm and Super 8 family films boxed up in a closet? Thanks to film buff Alex Mackenzie, who has a penchant for odd, archival footage, your memories can be shown on screen. As proprietor of The Blinding Light!! (he used to run the Edison Electric), Mackenzie sees BYO8, which usually happens one Thursday a month, as an opportunity for people to view forgotten family films, found footage, failed student films, and works in progress. Most nights attract about 20 or so submissions. Most memorable for Mackenzie? Home movies, especially if they haven't been viewed in years, if ever. He tells of one woman who brought in three films which featured her recently-deceased father. She had never seen them before and had no way of screening them herself. Films should be under ten minutes long, and VHS, 16mm, and 8mm formats are acceptable. The Blinding Light!!, *36 Powell St., 878-3366, www.blindinglight.com*

CLUB ON TOP

Look up. Look waaaay up. The city's most exclusive private screening room is hidden away on the top floor of an Alberni Street parkade, in the middle of, get this, a racquet club. Called the Club on Top, the little space, which features squash and racquetball courts, pool tables, and a bar, also has a room with a big video screen and surround sound. The screening room is used most nights to show sports events (they have a Monday Night Football package) and movies, but is also available for private viewings. And what's been seen? Commercials, short films, and other independent productions. Not surprisingly, admission to the private screenings is by invitation only. *5th Floor, 1114 Alberni St., 684-0544*

Film
Competitions

Crazy8s

Just as Vancouver's Alibi Room owes itself to Seattle, so does Crazy8s, which is sponsored in part by the local eatery and the Director's Guild of Canada. Filmmakers are provided with $800 and eight days. Originally, they were also given 800 feet of film, but with the proliferation of digital video, who needs developing solution? Participants have seen their films shortlisted for Cannes, nominated for some awards, while winning others. Get the lowdown at www.crazy-eights.com.

Reel Fast 48-Hour Movie Making Competition

Produced by the people who bring you the Cold Reading Series, the object is to write, shoot, and post a (maximum) 10-minute film within 48 hours. The (maximum) 10-member teams are provided with an "inspiration package" which includes five items to be used in the production of the film: a location, a sound bite, a photograph, a surprise, and a craft services donation (a food item). The items also serve to keep everyone honest. For more information, email reelfastvancouver@hotmail.com.

film festival fever

Everyone knows about the annual Vancouver International Film Festival. But how many of the following film events are you privy to?

Asian Film Festival

From feature length dramas to comedic short films, the annual Vancouver Asian Film Festival proves that great Asian films don't have to come from Asia. *www.vaff.org*

The Celluloid Social Club

Best possible way to schmooze with the local indie film scene. Held the third Thursday of every month at the ANZA Club, the Celluloid Social Club presents the work of independent filmmakers, followed by music, dancing, and endless opportunities to moan about funding shortfalls. *3 W. 8th Ave., 730-8090 or 876-7128*

Jewish Film Festival

Films about the Jewish experience. Usually held in late May, the Jewish Film Festival screens its flicks at Pacific Cinémathèque and at the Norman Rothstein Theatre in the Jewish Community Centre at 950 W. 41st Ave. *266-0245*

Out on Screen

For two weeks every August, six different Vancouver venues light up with films by, for or about lesbians, gays, bisexuals, and transgendereds. Also occasional screenings and fundraisers throughout the year. *www.outonscreeen.com*

movie moguls: the next generation

Shum, Pozer, Sweeney, Stopkewich. The list of Vancouver independent filmmakers who have established themselves over the years is impressive, but our city is still home to more Hollywood and movie-of-the-week productions than indigenous ones. Some believe that, with the growing acceptance of digital video as a film medium, Vancouver's new crop of independent filmmakers are poised to initiate a revolution. But that doesn't mean we'll be seeing the next *Blair Witch Project* being filmed in Stanley Park. As Ken Hegan so eloquently told us: "There's a million ways to screw up a film." Here, then, is our list of the ones to watch.

Alter Entertainment

As "convergence" (the buzz phrase of the theory that television and the Internet will one day become a single entity) becomes a reality, more web-based media are wanting unique video content for their purposes. The talents of Paul Armstrong and Jeanne Harco went into the formation of Alter Entertainment, a company dedicated to giving the online world exactly what they want. Their first major project, for Vancouver web company Blast Radius, was a series of web videos for Blast client Nintendo *(www.radiozelda.com)*. Armstrong and Harco, also the founders of the Celluloid Social Club, are looking to continue making forays into this new world of production.

Luke Carroll

A native of London, England, Carroll cut his teeth working on commercials and music videos in the U.K. before landing a job with MTV's *The Real World*. He moved to Vancouver in 1996 and went to the Vancouver Film School for a year, where he wrote and directed *Feathers*, an award-winning short film that has screened at more than 30 international festivals and has been sold for television. His next film, *Drop*, was shot in Vancouver in 1998. It has shown at numerous festivals around the world and can be viewed at www.reelshort.com. Having directed an episode of

DECADE: 1910s

BEST FILM:
In the Land of the War Canoes (1914)

DIRECTOR: Edward S. Curtis

STARS: The Kwakiutl People
COMMENTS:
Native man sets out on a vision quest. Filmed with Kwakiutl stars on Vancouver Island

WORST FILM:
The Cowpuncher's Glove (1910)

DIRECTOR: J. Searle Dawley

STARS: Not available

COMMENTS:
Two cowboys fall for the same girl and resolve to settle it on the Capilano Suspension Bridge

DECADE: 1920s

BEST FILM:
The Wilderness Patrol (1928)

DIRECTOR: J.P. McGowan

STARS: Bill Cody

COMMENTS:
Future Hollywood cowboy star Bill Cody leads a patrol through the wilds of North Vancouver

WORST FILM:
The Eternal Struggle (1923)

DIRECTOR: Reginald Barker

STARS: Renee Adoree, Earle Williams

COMMENTS:
Young woman escapes would-be seducer and flees to North Van for refuge

Transformers for Vancouver's Mainframe Entertainment, Carroll has been working for the Sony series *Heavy Gear*, also being produced at Mainframe. *The Lives of Riley*, a feature film, is next.

Ken Hegan

Despite being one of the most successful independent producer/director/filmmakers in Vancouver, Hegan recently took a job writing for a new media company, in part to pay back some of the debts he's incurred since he started making films six years ago. Of his short films, *Farley Mowat Ate My Brother* has aired widely, and *William Shatner Lent Me His Hairpiece* has been broadcast on four networks, shown at over 50 festivals, and is now available for viewing at www.microcinema.com. "That's a lot of entry fees," says Hegan. "I don't have a car, RSPs, or children, like my friends. I have film festival programs and clippings of reviews." His next filmmaking step is a feature, but Hegan is keeping details secret.

Harry Killas

Killas was born and raised in Vancouver, but after two degrees from Stanford, attended New York University's Graduate Institute of Film and Television. His first two short dramatic films, *Triangle Below Canal* and *Fortunate Son* won him awards and he went on to produce *Halloweenie*, a documentary short that won him an invitation to the Actor's Studio's directors/playwrights unit, led by Arthur Penn. Upon moving back to Canada, Killas stayed with the documentary form until 1999's award-winning *Babette's Feet*. A local film contest led to *untitled*, which was preselected for screening at Cannes. Killas has *Life is Elsewhere* and *The Evil Eye*, two feature dramas, in development.

Corren Mayrs

A casting director (for such productions as *The X-Files* and *Dark Angel*) by day, West Vancouver native Mayrs decided she really wanted to direct, and took it upon herself to write, too. *A Feeling Called Glory* was the result, and it won her writing and directing awards from Women in Film. Mayrs again impressed audiences with her second short film, 1999's *The Rememberer*. The film went on to win Best Short Film and Best Screenplay at the 2000 Leo Awards, and was nominated for a Director's Guild of America award. Her feature length directorial debut will be the adaptation of Vancouver writer Caroline Adderson's *A History of Forgetting*.

Blaine Thurier

At Toronto's 2000 International Film Festival, Blaine Thurier, known to Vancouverites as a comic artist, was being touted as the one to watch, based on the success of his ultra-low-budget (around $8,000) *Low Self Esteem Girl*, which he wrote, directed, and produced. His secret of success at the Toronto schmooze? The self-produced comics he handed out to promote the film.

Time for a new Set

Is Tony Parsons God? Millions hearken to him nightly on the BCTV evening news, and his every pronouncement is taken as the very voice of Truth. The beginnings of this vast exercise in mind control can be found deep in the bowels of New Westminster, where the first TV ever seen in the Lower Mainland still resides. It was built from a kit in 1948 by hobbyist and proto-couch potato Ed Mullins, for a cost of $248 (at the time, the cost of a good used car). Three years back, Ed donated the set to New Westminster Museum *(302 Royal Ave.)*, where it still flickers happily away. Parsons presumably, has other plans for retirement.

DECADE: 1930s

BEST FILM:
Across the Border (1937)
(filmed in Victoria)

DIRECTOR: Leon Barsha

STARS: Rita Hayworth

COMMENTS:
Customs officer falls for damsel-in-distress Hayworth, landing him in trouble with bunch of fur thieves

WORST FILM:
Rose Marie (1936)

DIRECTOR: W.S. Van Dyke II

STARS: Jeannette MacDonald,
Nelson Eddy,
James Stewart

COMMENTS:
An opera singer who slums in a tavern to support her ex-con brother (a very young Jimmy Stewart) who in turn is pursued by Mountie

DECADE: 1940s

BEST FILM:
Canadian Pacific (1949)

DIRECTOR: Edwin L Martin

STARS: Randolph Scott,
Jane Wyatt

COMMENTS:
American surveyor fights off mutinous coolies to build the CPR

WORST FILM:
Son of Lassie (1945)

DIRECTOR: Sylvan Simon

STARS: Peter Lawford,
June Lockhart

COMMENTS:
Fly-boy Lawford sends Lassie's son Laddie for help when his plane gets shot down, but the stupid mutt brings back two Nazis instead

DECADE: 1950s

A bad decade for Vancouver films — not much happening

DECADE: 1960s

BEST FILM:
That Cold Day in the Park (1969)
DIRECTOR: Robert Altman
STARS: Sandy Dennis,
Michael Burns
COMMENTS:
Repressed upper-class woman invites young hippie in out of Vancouver rain

WORST FILM:
The Sweet and the Bitter (1962)
DIRECTOR: James Clavell
STARS: Yoko Tani,
Paul Richards
COMMENTS:
The dutiful daughter of an interned Japanese fisherman returns to the west coast after the war looking for revenge on Scottish business man who took her father's boats. At least Steveston looks nice.

The truly informed among the info-geek tribe know that Scott Adams comic strip *Dilbert* is seriously antiquated. For up-to-date laughs, the code jockey crowd clicks onto *www.userfriendly.org*, the New Westminster home of the net's hottest geek strip, *User Friendly*. Published — at least at the moment — exclusively on the web, *User Friendly* features a coterie of typically maladjusted coders, tapping their way to infinite wealth from the safety of an office veal-fattening pen. For the hi-tech crowd, the appeal is enormous. Not only does the site feature the entire strip archive, there's also a fully-threaded on-line forum where real geeks — with names like codesamurai, sumo_penguin, Marxist hacker, and disposable — debate critical topics such as the real appearance of true geek's desk (loads of paper, notes, zip disks, CDs, stacks of books by O'Reilly, and the occasional magic eight ball or jar of death, since you ask). Advertisers are not immune to the attractions of a captive info-geek audience. According to User Friendly president Barry Carlson, the site brings in $40,000 a month in the form of banner ads and sponsorships from the likes of Symantec and Nortel Networks. By the beginning of 2001, he expects to have that figure up closer to $500,000 a month. Even in the info-geek world, folks'll pay anything for a laugh.

New Yorker readers pride themselves on the intelligence of the mag's film reviews, but they've got nothing on readers of Vancouver's *Georgia Straight*. Regular *Straight* film reviewer Mark Harris not only has a Ph.D. in film studies, but his graduate thesis won the Governor-General's gold medal for the best thesis in his year. The topic? America as seen in the cinema of Italy and France, from 1919 to 1929. The secret? Where exactly did he find all those 70-year-old foreign flicks?

Rambo: The Tour

"When some people think of *Rambo*, they often think of Hope." With the advent of Hollywood North, communities up and down the Fraser Valley have played host to American film crews of one sort or another. Most have gotten over it. Not Hope. Following are real excerpts from *Daytripper's Paradise*, a visitor's guide and map published by the Hope and District Chamber of Commerce:

"*First Blood*, starring Sylvester Stallone as Rambo, was filmed at Hope in 1981. Sites denoted by numbers can be found downtown, while sites denoted by letters are on the edge of town.

1. Sheriff Teasle drops Rambo off at Water Avenue, near Gardner Chev-Olds.

3. With the police in hot pursuit, Rambo drives along Hudson Bay Street, passing Hope's H-tree at the corner of Fifth Avenue.

6. Rambo rode his stolen motorcycle down the sidewalk in front of Cheyenne's Sports and the Alpenhaus Restaurant, on the north side of Wallace Street.

D. Heading towards Othello Tunnels, known as Chapman Gorge in the movie. Here the police officer falls out of the helicopter and is killed. Observers can see where Rambo clung for his life as he hung precariously on the rock walls of the gorge high above the waters of the Coquihalla River."

Murder, Lust, and Lawn Bowling

Of all the hundreds of American-financed films that have been shot in Vancouver, only one has ever resisted the temptation to disguise us as New York or Seattle and shown us as we really are. *That Cold Day in the Park*, by director Robert Altman, begins with a long slow-tracking shot, as the camera follows an attractive woman in an orange-plaid coat (it was 1970, after all) making her way through Kitsilano's Tatlow Park. And though much of the rest of the film takes place in the woman's apartment, where we observe her growing sexual obsession with a young hippie, the film does take time to document some of Vancouver's then salient features: prostitutes and sleazy taverns on lower Granville, a vibrant drug culture, and a very popular but strange Vancouver activity known as lawn bowling.

DECADE: 1970s

BEST FILM:
Russian Roulette (1975)
DIRECTOR: Lou Lombardo
STARS: George Segal
COMMENTS:
RCMP foil plot to assassinate visiting Soviet premier. Stunning climax on roof of Hotel Van

WORST FILM:
Sexcula (1973)
DIRECTOR: John Holbrook
STARS: All pseudonyms
COMMENTS:
A sex-crazed female scientist builds a monster to service her needs but, discovering it's impotent, asks her cousin Sexcula to see if she can't arouse some interest

DECADE: 1980s

BEST FILM:
The Grey Fox (1982)
DIRECTOR: Philip Borsos
STARS: Richard Farnsworth
COMMENTS:
Canadian stage coach robber Bill Miner is released after thirty years in jail. Takes up robbing trains

WORST FILM:
Dead Wrong (1981)
DIRECTOR: Len Kowalewich
STARS: Britt Ekland
COMMENTS:
Produced by BCTV's Tony Parsons — female undercover agent tracks bumbling smugglers

DECADE: 1990s

BEST FILM:
Kissed (1996)

DIRECTOR: Lynne Stopkewich

STARS: Molly Parker

COMMENTS:
Pretty girl-next-door develops sexual attraction for the dead

WORST FILM:
Mr. Magoo (1997)

DIRECTOR: Stanley Tong

STARS: Leslie Nielsen

COMMENTS:
A live-action version of the eyesight-challenged cartoon character. The Vancouver Public Library doubles for a natural history museum

There's no hard and fast rule that when Vancouver celebrities are connected to a film it has to be a bad film. MuchMusic host Terry David Mulligan showed up in *McCabe and Mrs Miller*, and BCTV news anchor Pamela Martin appeared as a reporter in *The Accused*. Meanwhile, veteran film and TV executive Daryl Duke directed a film called *Payday* starring Rip Torn that, although obscure today, predated Robert Altman's thematically similar *Nashville* and ended up on many critics' 10-Best lists back in 1972.

So it's not absolutely mandatory that the films be dismal — merely normal. Take CFUN radio host and would-be Canadian Alliance candidate Pia Shandel's first foray into film stardom, 1968's *The Plastic Mile*, which was granted half a star in a 1978 review. Even Shandel minces no words in describing how bad it was, though she notes that it did attract considerable notoriety when the provincial censor banned it from appearing at a precursor to the Vancouver International Film Festival. Why was it banned, Pia? "There was a scene in which I had an orgasm, and apparently it was fairly enthusiastic."

Or consider *Dead Wrong*, which was produced in 1981 by BCTV news anchor and editorial director Tony Parsons, who is pained to even think of the movie today.

Then there's Vince Murdocco. The kick-boxing champ isn't exactly a celeb per se, but his dad Frank owns Café Calabria on Commercial, the oldest serious coffee outlet in the city. That, and his athlete's physique, landed him a starring role in that classic piece of soft-porn schlock, *Flesh Gordon Meets the Cosmic Cheerleaders*.

And what about *High Stakes*, the thriller co-starring local journalistic legend Jack Webster? In 1992 it was included on a list of the worst movies ever made in Vancouver.

Interestingly, local actor Jackson Davies, Constable John Constable in *The Beachcombers*, has a connection to all the above except the *Flesh Gordon* flick. He wasn't around for *The Plastic Mile*, but swears he once did a nude scene with Shandel — he just can't remember where.

mad for mags

Looking for a magazine about grommets, or nude Namibian mercenary amazons? With the way the market has both fragmented and exploded, chances are there are two or more just for you, but only if you know where to look. Here's a guide to the city's magazine-only shops:

Fleet Street

A small, literate refuge hidden amongst the Native crafts and knick-knack shops in the tourist-central regions of Gastown.
375 Water St., 685-8831

Global News

Europhile title list reflects the West Van location – the place to see a photo spread of the inside of a Scottish castle.
Park Royal South, West Vancouver

The Great Canadian News Co.

Perhaps the last place on Robson where the cost of any single item can still be measured in single digits. For a cheap Robson Street date, take your partner to Starbucks and then bring your java along for an extended browse.
1092 Robson St., 688-0609

Mayfair News

Everything from Harper's to Home Builder to Scientific American in Italian, to the latest edition of the French magazine Photo, the one that always seems to feature a naked woman on the cover. Also newspapers from across North America and around the world.
1535 W. Broadway, 738-8951

McNews

Near the Seabus print outlet offers serious business-oriented publications for the busy commuter.
1460 Lonsdale Ave., North Vancouver

A SLANTED POINT OF VIEW

Tired of perusing the *Province* for your daily dose of culture? Vancouver is also home to *Rice Paper*, a culture and art magazine about the Asian-Canadian experience. Started by the Asian Canadian Writer's Workshop six years ago, the magazine showcases Asian-Canadian writers and provides a forum for cultural and artistic dialogue. Oh, and for those who are now hopping up and down about the "Slanted point of view" headline above – gotcha! That's *Rice Paper*'s subtitle.

WATER MUSIC

On the air since July of '98, radio station CJKW has the most intriguing format of any radio station anywhere: all whale, all the time. The station's on-air sounds stem from a completely anaerobic source – a microphone, placed underwater in the northern Vancouver Island whale refuge of Robson Bight, where pods of orcas frequently pass the time rubbing their tummies on the rocky beach. When things get dull, the station does sometimes substitute recorded whales sounds, many from the Vancouver Aquarium's extensive collection of orca whale recordings. Intriguing as it all is, CJKW's broadcast audience is limited. It can only be heard within a 10-kilometre radius of Robson Bight, or else via the live feed at the Aquarium. And for those who wondered, the KW in the call sign stands for Killer Whale.

Cheap Seats

These days, the real trick to getting full-value from a $10 movie ticket is to head to one of the numerous megaplexes in the city. Once you're in the door, no one so much as looks at your ticket ever again. Pick the right plex and you can wander from flick to flick, killing the better part of day and bringing the cost per movie down to a more than reasonable $2.00. What follows is a list of options for mega-viewing.

Fifth Avenue Cinemas

2110 Burrard St., 734-7469

Granville Cineplex Odeon Cinemas

855 Granville St., 684-4000

Silver City Coquitlam

170 Schoolhouse Rd., Coquitlam, 523-2911

Silver City Guildford

15051 101 Ave., Surrey, 531-1716

Silver City Metropolis

4700 Kingsway St., 435-7474

Silver City Riverport

Corner of No. 6 Rd. and Steveston Hwy., Richmond, 277-5993

Station Square Cineplex Cinemas

6200 McKay St., Burnaby, 435-3575

Tinseltown Cinemas

3rd Floor, 88 W. Pender St., 806-0799

Magpie Magazine Gallery

Photo: Robert Ballantyne

Eastside location adds a slightly funky, leftish intellectual tone to one of the city's premier mag shops. Narrow aisles, but worth the effort.

1319 Commercial Dr., 253-6666

The Newsroom

Kerrisdale location makes for a large gardening section, along with wide variety of other titles. *2256 W. 41st Ave., 263-0588*

Look Ma, I'm a Star

Photo: Blaine Kyllo

Fame is fleeting, 'tis said, which is why it's such a good thing that some enlightened soul at City Hall decided that the greats of the B.C. entertainment world would be forever memorialized with their own star on Vancouver's own Walk of Fame. Located on the pavement of the 800-block of Granville, the walk has stars – round little plaques, actually – for such noted greats as Calvin Winter, Holly Maxwell, and Drew Burns (George's nephew?). True, folks we actually know are also there, including Bryan Adams, Sarah McLachlan, and eternal impresario Hugh Pickett. And because showbiz snobbery applies just as much to pavement stars as the real thing, the Orpheum Theatre has an exclusive walk for six 'round back, just outside its stage door on Seymour. Who're the lucky immortalized? Bob Hope, Victor Borge, Reveen, Nana Mouskouri, Mitzi Gaynor, and most recently, Harry Belafonte. The secret is what those six did to get immortalized together.

The 1970s and '80s were memorable decades for Vancouver musicians making it big across Canada and elsewhere, spawning Top 40 hits that we either remember with fondness or disdain. You be the judge:

D O A

Photo: courtesy Sudden Death Records

Who cares if they could never sing: DOA are still the best riposte when anyone tries to tag Vancouver as the home of Bryan Adams. Founded in Vancouver in 1978 by singer guitarist Joey Shithead (aka Joe Keithley, photo left), DOA's ranting power chord tunes put disco in the grave for a good two decades, and inspired Michael Turner's book *Hard Core Logo*, which Bruce MacDonald turned into a movie, which in turn inspired the older but still hale Shithead to dust off his vocal chords and head back into the studio for another session of high-pitched screaming. The result, a CD entitled *Festival of Atheists*. In recent years, Shithead has gone on to form a label, Sudden Death Records and join an Internet radio station, MyCityRadio.com. His secret? Judging from the packing material that accompanied his photo, breakfast cereal Special K.

L o v e r b o y

Described in the book *Mondo Canuck* as a "hoser cockrock outfit," Loverboy's hits included "Everybody's Working for the Weekend" and "Turn Me Loose." And believe it or not, the band still tours, playing big venues like Breakers in Point Roberts.

T r o o p e r

This band from the late 1970s made it big in Canada but not south of the border. Hot songs included "The Boys in the Bright White Sports Car," "Raise a Little Hell," and "One for the Money, Two for The Show."

Photo: Victoria Renolds

Neko Case (photo above) Drummer and sometime singer for MAOW, went solo and managed to fuse punk, rockabilly, pop, and country into a new thing called "insurgent country." Is in reality an American citizen, despite having a degree from the Emily Carr Institute of Art and Design and working with local label Mint Records.
Best known album: *The Virginian*
Latest album: *Furnace Room Lullaby*

Bif Naked
Survived an indulgent early career in the land of hardcore punk, and has developed a reputation for intense rock and roll music with honest, personal lyrics. Now a proponent

of a "straight edge" lifestyle — no drinking, smoking, drugs, or red meat — that hasn't kept Naked from acquiring a dozen tattoos.
Best known album: *I Bificus*
Latest album: *I Bificus*

Veda Hille

Native Vancouverite is known as a pianist, but can also play the guitar. Has written music for dance, film, and solo recordings, including an album based on the life of Emily Carr, and a five-minute aria based on the calls of Canadian songbirds.
Best known album: *Path of a Body*
Latest album: *You Do Not Live in This World Alone*

Kinnie Starr

Resolutely independent, Starr was aggressively pursued by labels after they noticed her. She signed with Mercury Records, which was then absorbed by Island. But Starr and Island didn't see eye to eye, so Starr left, formed her own label, and forges on.
Best known album: *Tiny*
Latest album: *Tune Up*

Bryan's Songs

Photo: courtesy Bruce Allen Talent

Bryan Adams is known the world over. Love 'em or hate 'em, his Oscar-nominated movie ballads are common cultural currency from the basements of Surrey to the speed-crazed taxi-cabs of Istanbul. There are a few other things, however, about North Van's most famous native son that are perhaps less well-known. The "Summer of '69" – when Adams was 8 – may have been when he "bought his first real six-string," but it wasn't until the seventies that he made his first forays into recording. Not surprisingly, given the times, these now-impossible-to-locate bits of vinyl owe little to rock and an awful lot to disco. At the time the future superstar was also working as a dish duck at the Tomahawk Barbecue on the North Shore. His first serious recording gig came around 1977, when at age 16, he was asked to do vocals for Sweeney Todd on a recut version of "Roxy Roller." It wasn't until the early 1980s that his leather-clad rock persona solidified, but when it did it was something to see. Warming up for Vancouver glam band Loverboy, Adam's show-stopping stage effect – done during the tune "You Want It, You Got It" – consisted of a pair of roadies popping up from behind an amp stack with a white cotton sheet spray painted to read "Toyota." He still blew Loverboy off the stage, which is likely why they dumped him a few gigs in to the tour. Quite obviously, it didn't hurt his career in the slightest.

Priscilla, Queen of Pilates

One of the more unlikely residents of Terminal City is none-other than Terence Stamp, the drag queen star of *Priscilla, Queen of the Desert*. Stamp lives part time in Kitsilano, devoting his days not to haute couture and camisoles, but to the study of pilates, an kind of uber-athletic yoga. It does wonderful things for your figure, darling.

Secret Seating II

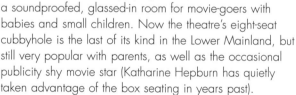

When the Ridge Theatre on Arbutus Street was built in 1950, "crying rooms" were commonplace, supplying a soundproofed, glassed-in room for movie-goers with babies and small children. Now the theatre's eight-seat cubbyhole is the last of its kind in the Lower Mainland, but still very popular with parents, as well as the occasional publicity shy movie star (Katharine Hepburn has quietly taken advantage of the box seating in years past).

Even more exclusive is the balcony for two at the Granville 7 Cinema. Enter Theatre 5 and just to your right is a closet-like entryway that leads to two – and only two – isolated, elevated seats – the world's most private balcony, perfect for whatever it may occur to you to do in those long minutes between onscreen explosions. Careful, though: unlike at the Ridge, this little cubbyhole is anything but soundproof.

Tools of the Trade

So you wanna be in showbiz? Here are some places where you can learn how.

Vancouver Film School

Its most famous alumnus is actually a drop-out, although he's listed as a graduate (Class 25, October 1992): Kevin Smith, director of the films *Clerks, Chasing Amy,* and *Dogma,* dropped out and used the money for his first feature.
420 Homer St., 685-5808

UBC Department of Film

Graduates include Mina Shum *(Double Happiness),* Kathy Garneau *(Tokyo Cowboy),* and Lynne Stopkewich *(Kissed). 822-6037*

Praxis Centre for Screenwriters

Run by Simon Fraser University, the Centre offers many free workshops and screenwriting seminars, as well as a huge library of film scripts.
300-12 Water St., 682-3100, www.praxisfilm.com

Dave Hardy Film School

Former head of instruction at the Vancouver Film School, Hardy left to set up his own shop because he felt the VFS was more interested in profit than pedagogy. His workshops now offer the best deal in town for learning the basics of filmmaking.
2652 W. 3rd Ave., 734-0508

Third Space Film Workshop

Offers the chance to make a five-minute film, and attend workshops from local luminari like Lynne Stopkewich.
411 W. Hastings St., 270-2536

Cineworks

Formed a score of years ago by a passel of SFU film school graduates, Cineworks is a non-profit film co-operative offering professional workshops, mentoring support, and low-cost rentals on equipment. Some of the toys available at the Howe Street office (next to Pacific Cinémathèque) include lights, cameras, studio action, digital editing suites, and more, all about half the going industry rate. Members pay an annual $100 fee and put in 10 volunteer hours. Films from Cineworks alumni have included Mina Shum's *Double Happiness* and *Drive She Said*, and Anne Wheeler's *Better than Chocolate*.
1131 Howe St., 685-3841

alternative cinema

Want to see a movie but not really interested in the latest Adam Sandler debacle? From retro to documentary to films in different tongues, there are a number of alternative venues:

The Blinding Light!!

The alternative alternative theatre, the Light!! is the Vancouver venue for all that is offbeat and experimental in film. Screenings to date have included new Vancouver shorts, experimental animation, found-in-the-back-room home movies, and industrial films from the 1950s and '60s (best title so far: *Myocardial Infarction: The Nurse's Role*). Is also the site of the Vancouver Underground Film Festival.
36 Powell St., 878-3366

Pacific Cinémathèque

Since 1972, Pacific Cinémathèque has featured alternative films from around the world, including quite a few from Hollywood. Screenings are organized into themes – i.e., Cuba, Film Noir, or the Hong Kong Action Flick: A Retrospective – so if you like one you can come back for more, and if not it's time to look elsewhere for a few weeks. Schedules are in available in cooler record and video stores and in many cafés around town.
1131 Howe St., 688-FILM

Raja Cinema

Deep in the heart of farthest Collingwood, next to Legion Branch 48 and kitty corner from Big O Tires, stands the Raja Cinema, a modest little single-screen movie house that nonetheless manages to bring in the best of the flicks from the world's movie-making capital, Bombay. For viewers unfamiliar with the Indian masala genre, expect a blend of raw violence and musical production numbers, a kind of *Die Hard* meets *The King and I*. And if Kingsway and Joyce is too far off the beaten tiger track, there's another Raja at 639 Commercial Drive (253-0402). Occasionally, movies at the Raja even feature English subtitles.
3215 Kingsway, 436-1545

Ridge Theatre

In 1999, devoted film-goers were disappointed to hear that Ray Mainland, owner of the Ridge, was going to sell his cinema to Leonard Shein's Alliance chain. After all, the Ridge was a mainstay when it came to rep cinema double-bills. But business had taken a turn for the worse, and Mainland was forced to lay off savvy programmer Jack Vermee, who had helped build The Ridge reputation. Vermee went back to the Van East, which is where he got his start in the first place.

Everything changed when Mainland was killed in a car accident, however. While Alliance tried to move in immediately, the will ended up in probate, and until it is executed, the Ridge is in limbo. Which is great for film fans, because until the legal stuff gets cleared up, the Ridge's long-time employees are running the show, even going so far as to hire Jack Vermee back as programmer.
3131 Arbutus St., 738-6311

Vancouver East Cinema

The Van East has been it all. Starting out as an art theatre, it was transformed into a Chinese-language cinema, and has now become a reperatory cinema again, showing independent features and art house fare. It's a reliable spot for the East Side crowd to get their Euro-flix fix.
2290 Commercial Dr., 251-1313

Video In Studios

This artist-run collective, over 25 years old, offers courses and workshops for video-makers. Producer's Nights, held on irregular Thursdays, is the time to schmooze with video types. For video viewers, Video In presents monthly screenings along with special events at regular intervals throughout the year. All screenings are in Video In's warehouse-like space on Main Street. For further information, look for their free guide, or check out the website at www.video-in.com.
1965 Main St., 872-8337

Photo: Blaine Kyllo

Video In

If you know what video is (hint: it has nothing to do with MTV), you can learn to make it at Video In. Part of a nationwide video collective, Video In offers training in video production, state-of-the-art computer editing, and cutting-edge equipment rental and editing facilities at the best rates in Vancouver. Membership is $75 per year, but this amount can then be applied towards equipment and editing suite rentals. And if you don't know video from a hologram, Video In also offers regular evening screenings of its members' endeavours.
1965 Main St., 872-8337

Women in Film

For women in the film industry, be it film, video, television or multimedia, the Women in Film Vancouver Society is a non-profit society that offers support, mentorship, training programs, and oportunities for advancement in the industry. Annual membership varies, depending on your experience level and degree of involvement. Though slightly pricey, the Women in Film production binder/book is the sought-after bible of the independent filmmaker. *1431 Howe St., 685-1152*

Youth in Film Project

Quentin Tarantino began his career in a video store. On the off chance that's not working for you there's always the Youth in Film Project, a Capilano College program geared for youth with an interest in the film industry. Particpants are introduced to the various jobs involved in making movies, including lighting design, set design, hair, make-up, and sound engineering. Should something capture your interest, they'll pair you up with a "mentor," a film industry professional who will take you to the set, point out the difference between a gaffer and a best boy, and give you some tips on how to get ahead in show biz. No spots for groupies, but they generally figure things out for themselves. *929-7981*

Big Screens

It seems fitting that in the country that invented massive floor-to-ceiling cinema, there should be not one but two IMAX-style theatres. Programming-wise, the CN Imax at Canada Place *(682-4629)* seems to favour large movies about big critters (elephants, whales), while the Alcan Omnimax at Science World *(443-7440)* tends towards large movies about wide open spaces (Antarctica, Everest). Both are great places to take kids.

Cheap Seats

Vancouver is blessed with a number of repertory screens, each with its own particular characteristics. The Denman Place Discount Cinema *(124-1030 Denman St., 683-2201)* in the heart of the West End goes for mainstream Hollywood at a cheap price. The Hollywood Theatre *(3123 W. Broadway, 738-3211)* in Kitsilano goes for mainstream double bills (and 2-for-1) with a theme (i.e., Tom Hanks night).

Erotic Cinema

They may not be your cup of tea, but isn't it nice to know the men with the raincoats have somewhere warm to go:
Fox Cinema: *2321 Main St., 874-3116*
Kitten Theatre: *1026 Granville St., 689-0786*
Venus Theatre: *720 Main St., 685-3344*

Life on the West Coast isn't all fleece and Gore-Tex. During those long and oh-so-slightly damp winter nights, Vancouverites drift indoors, taking up residence in drinking pubs and dancing clubs – places to watch and listen, places to play and participate in all ways intriguing, erotic, and sometimes downright dangerous. They're all in the pages that follow.

As is the secret of how good for you a martini can be.

Secret Nightclubs

There's a curious ritual enacted on Vancouver streets every weekend evening starting 'round 1 am. Well-dressed club-scene crawlers, having been unceremoniously evicted from the city's smallish stable of legitimate drinking holes, wander in ones and sixes down dark alleys, seemingly never to return. Is it a case for Mulder and Scully, a latter-day version of *Invasion of the Body Snatchers*? No, just a rational response to a terminal infestation of bureaucrats.

For some reason, the powers that be at city hall see drinking, clubbing, and carousing as a *bad thing*, and so limit such anti-social behaviour to a very few places, and dictate that it end shortly after midnight. Vancouverites, being as drunken and debauched as the next modern urbanite, have in response taken to disappearing after closing time to spots with light and noise and booze and flexible operating hours – everything a bar needs, in fact, except a liquor licence. For that reason, of course, they can be a tad tricky to find.

The most successful after-hours club has to be the one in a defunct café located just outside Gastown. Patrons pay a $20 cover to get in via an alley entrance, and are treated to two floors lights, DJs, overpriced drinks, and the late night company of the most beautiful of people. Those who mourn the Woom Shakti, an infamous unlicenced club, will be glad to hear that a new venture, 'tis said, will feature local and visiting musicians in the throes of improvization.

So how do you know where to go when the house lights come up in your regular bar? You could follow the other folks down the empty alleyway. Better yet, ask around at your favourite legit nightspot. Odds are – if you don't look like the fuzz – someone'll let you in on the secret.

Night of Dreams

Photo: Mandelbrot

Every last Saturday night in July, a phantasmagorical parade of lantern-bearing apparitions wends its way around the waters of Trout Lake in East Vancouver. It's the Illuminares Lantern Festival, in which participants wear masks, beat drums, juggle, spit fire, or simply walk and gawk. Illuminares is the handiwork of the Public Dreams Society, a non-profit group with a philosophical commitment to fostering the bonds of urban community. In the months leading up to the parade, the society holds craft workshops so that people can drop in and learn how to make a paper lantern or mask. Come the night of the festival, everyone gets a chance to show off their handiwork. Public Dreams also organizes the Parade of Lost Souls the last Saturday in October on Commercial Drive.

Photo: Blaine Kyllo

Naked, the new upstairs lounge at Ballantyne's Restaurant (432 Richards St., 609-2700), has what some would call a slightly suggestive name. Inside, the décor of low couches and long sheer drapes of fabric gives the room a sensuous *Arabian Nights* feel. For all that, however, on most nights the clientele remain fully clothed. True, at the book launch of *Exhibitions: Tales of Sex in the City* one local author extended the definition of low-cut to the point where it could just as easily have meant waist-high. And it's also rumoured that on other occasions Naked's tiny balcony has been put to the sort of use its couple-sized space would suggest. But on a night-to-night basis, the only real guarantee of seeing something nude is to go downstairs to Ballantyne's and have a peak beneath the bar. The pedestal upon which the long countertop sits, you'll discover, is made entirely of stylized female torsos, cavorting in a wide variety of positions. It's a shocker for some, though co-owner Salli Pateman says she's had no complaints so far. And should you happen to be one of those folks who like to lean back on the bar stool, the various lumps and knobs and other protuberances make wonderful places to put your feet.

Secret Talent

It's not always true that a bar with a house band is a place to avoid. Believe it or not, not all house bands suck. The Odds, for example, were the house band at The Roxy for years before making a name for themselves. The same can be said for Soulstream, the house band at Bar None. Specializing in '70s soul and funk, Soulstream, made up of some of the best studio musicians in Vancouver, has been playing the Yaletown bar on Monday and Tuesday nights for the past two years. If you want to impress a musician, take them to see a Soulstream set. You'll look like one who is in on the secret.

Secret "Scenes"

Planning an evening out but not sure what's going on where? Here's a guide to help you hook up with the crowd that's right for you:

BLUES
Fairview Pub
A Broadway institution, the Fairview is a mainstay of the Vancouver blues scene.
898 W. Broadway, 872-1262

The Yale
Oldest, grimiest, and most authentic of the city's blues yards, the Yale comes complete with a photo gallery of blues greats who have been there and sung that.
1300 Granville St., 681-YALE

LATIN
Latin Quarter
A tapas restaurant featuring live Latin bands.
1305 Commercial Dr., 251-1144

Mesa Luna
Complete with authentic gangster atmosphere. Cops arrive only about once a week.
1926 W. Broadway, 733-5862

DJ/TECHNO/HOUSE
7 Alexander Street

A small, intimate club dedicated to
the way of the DJ.
7 Alexander St., 899-1200

Chameleon Urban Lounge

Way down deep in the Hotel Georgia
is the city's funkiest dancing cavern.
801 W. Georgia St., 669-0806

Luv-A-Fair

Punk/industrial mainstay of the '80s,
still going strong.
1275 Seymour Ave., 685-3288

The Palladium

Formerly Graceland, nights dedicated
to house, industrial, and '80s retro.
1250 Richards St., 688-2648

Granville's New Beginning

Thanks to the post-World War I drive for temperance, it wasn't until 1925 that beer parlours became (once again) legal in B.C. Even then the levity was kept carefully controlled: drinkers had to remain seated at all times, and games and entertainment were not allowed. Critics of the Vancouver nightlife scene could argue that not much has changed since. But perhaps things are looking up. Signs of a new enlightenment can be seen in the opening of the **Lennox Pub** *(800 Granville St., 408-0881)*. Part of the Granville Street renewal, this new pub fills a big void in the neighbourhood; it's a comfortable spot without lineups, where you can have a drink without the bother of ordering food. The pub has a turn-of-the-century feel with lots of brass, wood panelling, and a long bar, while the beer list is extensive, containing such hard-to-find favourites as Belgian Kriek or Leffe. For non-beer drinkers, there's also a great selection of single malt scotches. The menu covers all the pub food basics to keep you nibbling while taking in the street scene at the corner of Granville and Robson. There's even a secret passageway: head up the risers towards the bathroom and just past the dartboards there's a steep narrow passageway on the right hand side. Climb up the pitch-dark stairway and you'll come to a landing with a two doors: one with a bright sliver of light coming out from underneath and a second, up another short flight of steps, completely, totally black. Read up on your Grimm's fairy tales before you make your decision whether to proceed.

Sugar Refined

Photo: Blaine Kyllo

What do Billy Idol, Marcia Brady, and the Chemical Brothers have in common? They've all paid a late-night visit to **The (Sugar Refinery)**, a cozy "photographic lounge" located in the seediest part of the downtown Granville Street strip. Manager Steven Horwood occupied the second-floor hangout spot in 1995 when he ran out of at-home space for his assembly sculpture. Realizing he would need creative sources of revenue to pay the rent, Horwood threw down some couches and began running his studio as an after-hours club. Its back-alley entrance quickly became a destination for ravers, artists, and hip restaurant workers, who appreciated the loft-party atmosphere and flexible closing time. The club gradually went legit, expanding its food counter into a licensed dining room and opening a streetfront doorway. "It just sort of evolved," Horwood explains. The same can be said of the nightly live entertainment, which now ranges from old-school jazz to poetry slams to doses of electronica. One thing that's hardly changed at all: those accommodating hours. The (Sugar Refinery) is still open until 3 or 4 am, depending on the season. *1115 Granville St., 683-2004*

The Real Enchilada

With all the talk of a Salsa revival, it's fitting to point out the most authentic Latino hot spot in the city may well be the **Pachanga Club** *(315 E. Broadway, 230-3321)*. True, it's not trendy. It's not even very pretty. But six nights a week they have the true down south sound, from hip hop Latino to Mexican Night to Reggae en Español. Dance lessons, as you might have expected, are definitely not included, but if you step next door into **Club Paradise** on Wife and Girlfriend night, you can "let her strut her stuff on stage." Even better is Friday's Cat Fight Night, in real hot oil. Ah, Latin culture.

Plaza Club

Movie theatre turned nightclub; 275-seater featuring Latin, house, and funk.

881 Granville St., 646-0064

Photo: Blaine Kyllo

Purple Onion

Bicameral nitespot in Gastown features fun and funky house band in one room and a dance floor and DJ in the other. Crowd is mid-20s to early 30s.

15 Water St., 602-9442

Sonar

Loud, heavy, and full of beat, this is one of the venues that host DJs from around the world.

66 Water St., 683-6695

Wett Bar

Willow-thin girls seemingly still in high school and spleen-shattering bass volumes. A quirky combination, but apparently successful.

1320 Richards St., 662-7707

FUNK
Backstage Lounge, Arts Club

1585 Johnston St., Granville Island, 687-1354

Bar None

1222 Hamilton St., 689-7000

Brickyard

Gastown club featurning bands
Wednesdays through Saturdays.
315 Carrall St., 685-3978

Columbia Hotel

303 Columbia St., 683-3757

Commodore Ballroom
(photo below)

Newly refurbished with oh-so-springy
dancefloor, the Commodore's still the
best mid-sized venue in town.
868 Granville St., 739-4550

Photo: courtesy House of Blues

Picadilly Pub

The place to get in touch with the up-
and-coming live local indie scene.
620 W. Pender St., 682-3221

Railway Club

Watering hole for the media crowd
occasionally plays host to a big-name
band for an impromptu concert.
579 Dunsmuir St., 681-1625

bingo mania

Photo: courtesy Planet Bingo

Ever wonder why Vancouver's streets are so deserted after dark? It's not the rain, it's the cards. Everyone's inside playing bingo. For those few who haven't yet clued in, here's a few spots where you can spend an evening bingoing.

Burnaby Bingo Country

302-7155 Kingsway St., Burnaby, 523-1221
Nightly jackpot: up to $7,500

Langley Bingo Palace

19664 64th Ave., Langley, 533-4224
Nightly jackpot: up to $10,000

Newton Square Bingo Country

7093 King George Hwy., 590-3230
Nightly jackpot: up to $7,500

Planet Bingo

2655 Main St., 879-8930
Nightly jackpot: $20,000

Royal City Bingo

555 6th St., New Westminster, 522-7355
Nightly jackpot: up to $7,500

St. Helen's Bingo

1739 Venables St. (at Astorino's), 255-4078
Nightly jackpot: up to $7,500

Richmond, Round the Clock

Where do you find a lady of the evening if it's only two in the afternoon? Well, you could drive to the downtown eastside, but that's just a bit too far for some, and a lot too grotty for many. For a better answer, look to Richmond. Smack in the centre of Vancouver's favourite bedroom communiy, the residential zone around Buswell Street and Cooney Road has over the past few years begun to distinguished itself as the region's leading centre for Asian-oriented brothels. The location – just off No. 3 Road and a hop and a jump from the Richmond Public Market – is conveniently close to both Vancouver International Airport and the Yaohan and Aberdeen Centre malls, making it an easy stopover spot for shoppers and highflyers alike. Cost of a visit – morning, afternoon or evening – hovers around $160, a bargain in comparison to the cost of an escort from the Yellow Pages. Perhaps the only drawback to the system is the party-pooping habits of the Richmond vice squad. Last February when they dropped in unannounced at 6611 Cooney Road, Richmond RCMP interrupted two clients and five women. Refunds, apparently, were not provided.

Hong Kong Headliners

Quick, name a famous Vancouver pop star. Bryan Adams? Sarah McLachlan? Too small. How about Nicolas Tse? Now there's a star. In the first week of its release, Tse's debut album sold a staggering 70,000 copies. Of course, he's playing to an audience of over a billion – in China. Vancouver is now one of the hottest recruiting grounds for the burgeoning Canto-pop scene. Other Vancouverites making it back east (or out west, depending on your viewpoint) include Sonja Kwok, Alex To, Vivien Cheung, and Sally Yeh. Though based in Hong Kong, the appeal of such stars extends to all of mainland China. Who knows – that could be Hong Kong's Madonna in front of you in the grocery store lineup.

Starfish Room
Venue for live local and international acts, as well as DJs.
1055 Homer St., 682-4171

Studebakers
Where old bands go for life-support. If they're two decades out of date and desperate (think Loverboy), odds are you'll find them at Studes.
6200 Kingsway, 434-3100

JAZZ
Capones
Yaletown restaurant and live jazz bar.
1141 Hamilton St., 684-7900

Hot Jazz Club
2120 Main St., 873-4141

Jazz Cellar
3611 W. Broadway, 738-1959

Rossini's
This restaurant-jazz venue has two locations.
Kitsilano, 1525 Yew St., 737-8080;
Gastown, 162 Water St., 408-1300

sing for your supper

Looking for a casual atmosphere where you can chat, drink, and chow down on good old pub grub? Try these neighbourhood pubs:

Avanti's Neighbourhood Pub
Commercial Drive's favourite pub, tucked behind a mini-mall.
1601 Commercial Dr., 254-5466

Bimini's Tap House
A Kitsilano joint, the couch seating by the fireplace is where to be. Also has a cold beer and wine store.
2010 W. 4th Ave., 732-9232

Darby D. Dawes Pub
2001 MacDonald St., 731-0617

Delaney's Pub
170-5665 Kingsway, Burnaby, 433-8942

Dover Arms
Amidst the West End's coffee bars and health food take-out joints, a breath of fresh air: beer, TV, and a hint of merry old E.
961 Denman St., 683-1929

**Elephant Walk
Neighbourhood Pub**
1445 E. 41st Ave., 324-1400

Given Vancouver's large population of Japanese students, karaoke has always enjoyed a big following here. In addition to these establishments, a number of Japanese (and Chinese) restaurants crank up the karaoke machine towards evening's end. So get with it. Swig back that last drink and sing "Proud Mary" like there's no tomorrow:

Big Boss Karaoke Pub
715 E. Hastings St., 215-8368

Club Paradise Karaoke
315 E. Broadway, 876-6386

Daddy Cool's Entertainment
2022 Paulus Cres., Burnaby, 420-1627

Good Luck Cabaret
147 E. Pender St., 605-8727

Melodyshake Karaoke Restaurant
1150-4380 No. 3 Rd., Richmond, 273-0688

Mike Family Karaoke
210-6200 McKay St., Burnaby, 431-9833

Or, perhaps you're not quite ready for the karaoke spotlight. In that case, you can rent private rooms at these Karaoke Box Clubs:

Crystal Karaoke Box

130-8400 Alexandra Rd., Richmond, 821-0660

Doremi Karaoke Box

125-8171 Ackroyd Rd., Richmond, 273-0005

Laser Star

1243 W. Broadway, 733-3383

Music Play Karaoke Box

4361 Kingsway St., Burnaby, 430-5484

Robson Karaoke Box

2nd Floor, 1238 Robson St., 688-0611

comedy tonight

Need to exercise your diaphragm? You'll get a great work out at these comedy clubs:

Gastown Comedy Store

19 Water St., 682-1727

Lafflines Comedy Club

26 4th St., New Westminster, 525-2262

Yuk Yuk's

750 Pacific Blvd., 687-LAFF

Fox & Firkin

With at least 18 beers on tap, many of them imports, the Fox is a restaurant, but feels like a pub. And there's a great back room for private gatherings.
1762 Davie St., 605-1112

Fireside Pub

421 E. Columbia St., New Westminster, 521-1144

Irish Heather

In the hear of Gastown's Gaoler's Mews, the Heather is true-blue Irish authentic. The best Guiness and Kilkenny in town.
217 Carrall St., 688-9779

Jeremiah's Neighbourhood Pub

Named for the man who chopped down the trees where West Point Grey now stands.
3681 W.4th Ave., 734-1205

The Jolly Taxpayer

Business crowd during the week, and sports teams out for good cheer after the game.
828 W. Hastings St., 681-3550

The King's Head

Pleasant neighbourhood pub where both indoor smoking and the music of James Taylor live on. Those who like both are in heaven. For the rest, it's nothing but fire and pain.
1618 Yew St., 733-3933

Lamplighter's

Pool tables, dart boards, and TVs. Beer. And a clientele unlike any other.
210 Abbot St., 681-6666

Lennox Pub

A bar. On Granville Street. Where you can order a beer. And no food. Without feeling guilty. Is Vancouver finally growing up?
800 Granville St., 408-0881

Morrisey Irish Bar

This friendly Irish pub is located at the south edge of the downtown Granville strip. Go for the pint and to hear great Brit pop from the past: The Smiths, U2, The Cure, and so on.
1227 Granville St., 682-0909

Pig & Whistle

An old Gastown mainstay.
15 W. Cordova St., 682-9386

Rose & Thorne Pub

Affectionately known as the RAT, this was a friendly, relaxed, down-home kind of pub. And at the end of September 2000, their 25-year lease came to an end. Rumour has it the institution may simply move to a new location.
755 Richards St., 683-2921

country livin'

Just because Vancouver is located 2,500 miles from Nashville doesn't mean the city can't line-dance with the best of 'em:

Boone County Country Cabaret

801 Brunette St., Coquitlam, 525-3144

Gabby's Country Cabaret

20297 Fraser Hwy., 533-3111

Pancho & Lefty's

10768 King George Hwy., 583-3536

the student crowd

Excessive drinking, constant posing, and intermittent puking — you're only 19 once, so why not enjoy it? Here's where to seek out others in search of higher learning:

The Blarney Stone

Irish themed frat boy bar with nasty bouncers. Prices are high, beer is watered, but ID is rarely if ever requested.
216 Carrall St., 525-3144

The Cambie

Downtown eastside prices with out the full-on grunge of a Hastings Street tavern, plus enough remaining rubbies to add a tad of authenticity. A favourite for those with lots owing on their student loan. *300 Cambie St., 684-6466*

Fred's Tavern

Taught, tanned, young, and beautiful, plus a cover charge and contrived line-up. What more could you ask for? *1006 Granville St., 605-4350*

Highland Pub

Simon Fraser University Campus, 219-3492

Kits Pub

A neighbourhood pub atmosphere for people from all over the Lower Mainland. *1424 W. Broadway, 736-5811*

Luv-A-Fair

Good for those nights when you're into the industrial thing. *1275 Seymour Ave., 685-3288*

Pit Pub

The on-campus place to imbibe. *6138 Student Union Blvd., UBC, 822-6511*

Photo: Mandelbrot

The Roxy

Still a favourite meet market, the Roxy has, over the years, become an institution. *932 Granville St., 331-7999*

Side Door Cabaret

For the more upscale crowd. *2291 W. Broadway, 733-2821*

Stone Temple Cabaret

Kits High heads downtown. Girls dance in circles while white boys in tevas swig from the bottle and do their best to get down. *1082 Granville St., 488-1333*

Wild Coyote

1312 S.W. Marine Dr., 264-7625

You're here, you're queer, but where to go? Vancouver's gay and lesbian clubs, of course.

Charlie's Bar & Grill
Dykes only Saturdays.
455 Abbot St., 685-7777

Chuck's Pub
Seediest gay bar in the city has a certain wistful charm to it. Sure, the décor and the patrons are all looking a little shop-worn, but it's comfortable and very friendly.
455 Abbot St., 685-7777

Denman Station
Head down the stairs and find a cozy, rec-room-like atmosphere.
860 Denman St., 669-3448

Doll & Penny's
The city's longest running drag show happens at this restaurant; the place to bring your visiting parents.
1167 Davie St., 685-3417

The Dufferin

They call it "sufferin at the Dufferin." Others look forward to the male strip shows which are called "Buff at the Duff." Further explanation is superfluous.
900 Seymour St., 683-4251

Photo: Blaine Kyllo

Fountainhead Pub

Those lamenting the city's less-than-plentiful gay club scene applauded the opening of this new pub in 2000. The outdoor patio is always full.
1025 Davie St., 687-2222

The Lava

Plays host to Electrolush Lounge, a wildly popular retro night every Thursday.
1176 Granville St., 605-1154

Photo: Blaine Kyllo

Though recently incorporated as yet another province in the entertainment empire of steak and workwear mogul Mark James, the Heritage House Hotel retains more than enough character to set it off from a run of the mill Kitsilano pub. It is, for example, the only heritage building in the city that concurrently plays host to three different gay (or gay-friendly) bars. Downstairs, the lesbian-leaning **Lotus Cabaret** has a big bar for drinking, small alcoves for sitting, an adequate sized dance floor, and an upbeat and friendly atmosphere. Formerly an exclusively lesbian bar, the crowd now is mixed; the club also plays host to a fetish night on the last Saturday of every month. The elegant **Charlie's Bar & Grill** on the main floor is rolling in space but just a tad hurtin' for customers. Best, most obscure, and also most endearing of the three is **Chuck's Pub**. More than slightly seedy (don't be surprised to get flamboyantly groped by at least one badly aging queen), Chuck's feels like a '50s-style tavern, with comfortable wicker chairs and the absolute cheapest draught in town. It's also home on Friday evenings to Funny Girl Night, an amateur drag queen revue. None of the acts has even a smidgen of talent, but patrons and performers all seem to know each other, and when the lip-sync comes on, everyone sings along. *455 Abbott St., 685-7777*

A Nobel Prize is surely the ultimate accolade, the sign that in your chosen field there is no one smarter or more accomplished. So how do you win one? You could labour away at the lab bench for years, advancing the scope of human knowledge and making deductions so difficult they've eluded all the best minds in the world. Or you could drink at **Delilah's** *(1789 Comox St., 687-3424)*. That's what UBC scientist Michael Smith did. Smith (who sadly passed away in October 2000), had so indulged in the West End restaurant's famous cocktails that when the Nobel committee rang from Stockholm at 4 am Vancouver time to let him know he was the winner of the 1993 prize for chemistry, Smith snoozed blissfully through the call. He heard about his win on the radio, much, much later on in the morning.

Photo: Blaine Kyllo

Our lawyer cautions us to add that not all patrons of Delilah's will win the Nobel. And Smith himself believed that Delilah's was not entirely responsible for his success. "I also sleep naked and wear Birkenstocks to work," he said. "That may have had something to do with it."

The Lotus

Gay-friendly. Whatever their persuasion, patrons will find a pleasant little dance floor and lots of comfy alcoves.
455 Abbot St., 685-7777

Numbers

1042 Davie St., 685-4077

Odyssey

The city's top gay dance club.
1251 Howe St., 689-5256

Royal Hotel

1025 Granville St., 685-5335

Sublime

(photo below)
After-hours dance club.
816 Granville St., 874-1969

Photo: Blaine Kyllo

The Whistler
Watering Hole

Black's Pub
Mountain Square, Westbrook,
Mountain Square, 604/932-6945

Cinnamon Bear Lounge
Delta Whistler, Delta Whistler Resort,
604/932-1982

Crystal Lounge
4154 Village Green, 604/938-1081

Dubh Linn Gate
Pan Pacific Lodge, 604/905-4047

Hoz's Pub
2129 Lake Placid Rd.,
604/932-5940

Mallard Bar
Chateau Whistler Resort,
604/938-8000

The secret to getting down in Whistler is to realize that though a hundred different nationalities may stroll the streets by day, come nightfall the only thing that matters is age. Hidden beneath the Pharmasave at the entrance to the Main Village, **Tommy Africa's** (604/932-6090) caters exclusively to the 18 to 22-year-old crowd: infinite volumes of beat, absolutely zero light. Person-to-person interaction is entirely mediated by pheromones. Occupying a cavernous space beneath the Amsterdam Café in the Village Square, **Maxx Fish** (604/932-1904) reels in a similar demographic. Far more fun than actually dancing is to stand outside and watch as teens in mini-skirts and halter-tops scamper up eager as chipmunks, only to get told to wait in line. First they pout, then they smoke, trying to maintain a semblance of cool as they hop from one stilletoed foot to another. Finally, the warming smoke gone and the goosebumps on shoulders and thighs swollen to resemble blueberries, they look around wildly for shelter, the ugly truth dawning in their eyes: Whistler isn't California after all.

Even in their desperation, only a few will head to **Garfinkel's** (604/932-2323), at the entrance to Village North, where the cut-off age can reach as high as 26 – even 29, if you count the occasional aging liftie trying to stretch out the charming wastrel routine for yet another year. **Buffalo Bills** (604/932-6613), across from the Whistler Gondola, and the **Savage Beagle** (604/938-3337) in the Village, cater to the 30-something crowd. Bills is bigger, with a pool table and video ski machine, smallish dance floor, and music straight from the 1980s. For the ultimate Whistler experience, however, head to the **Boot Pub** (604/932-3338), on Nancy Green Drive, just off Highway 99. The Boot advertises itself as Whistler's living room, and more than delivers on the promise: throngs of grubby Aussie lifties – most of whom seem to know each other – cram the room, bouncing to the beat while spilling pitchers of draught over the floor and their mostly unwashed clothes.

Secret Booze Can

On a hot summer night, getting a drink in any of the jock-packed pubs near Kits Beach can be more strenuous than a night of digs and spikes on the volleyball court. Fortunately, for those in the know, there's an alternative just down the street at 1407 Laburnum, where the Canadian Legion operates its Billy Bishop branch. True, in days of yore you had to have served your country to drink at this spot, but the Legion is eager enough for customers now that fraternal memberships can be had by nearly anyone with a taste for a quiet pint by the beach, and a reasonable taste for Morris-dancing and old World War II dancehall tunes.

blast from the past

Photo: Blaine Kyllo

Despite everyone's beliefs to the contrary, the retro lounge scene is still here — at least for now. Have a martini and chill out waiting for the end:

Babalu
654 Nelson St., 605-4343

Bistro Lounge
Barclay Hotel, 1348 Robson St., 688-8850

Georgia Street Bar & Grill
801 W. Georgia St., 602-0994

Waldorf Grove Pub
1489 E. Hastings St., 253-7141

Meet Markets

Searching for that special someone who drinks, dances, and returns your flirtations? Slip into your best I'm-available wear and try your luck at any one of these places:

Au Bar
The city's latest hotspot: bulging beefcake boys and doe-like ladies in ultrashort skirts. Either this place is a sophisticated piece of performance art, or the ultimate '80s pick-up palace. You decide.
674 Seymour St., 648-2227

Bar None
A bit of dash-and-fancy for the yuppie Yaletown set.
1222 Hamilton St., 689-7000

Big Bam Boo
1236 W. Broadway, 733-2220

Gotham
Stockbroker heaven at this très-expensive steakhouse. Flash the Platinum Visa at the bar for best results.
615 Seymour St., 605-8282

Richard's on Richards

Still going strong; survived its polyester suit reputation from the '80s.

1036 Richards St., 687-6794

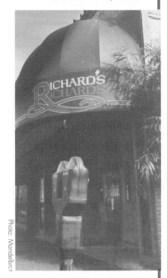

Photo: Mandelkrei

The Roxy

932 Granville St., 684-7699

Shark Club

180 W. Georgia St., 687-4275

Urban Well

Young-skewing clientele looking for same.

1516 Yew St., 737-7770;
888 Nelson St., 638-6070

Voda

Chic watering hole where those who want to be seen go.

Westin Grand Hotel, 783 Homer St.,
684-3003

Yaletown Brewing Co.

The restaurant's pub is the best place to find a hot techno-geek.

1111 Mainland St., 681-2739

sports bars

Sports bars are a rather odd phenomenon: crowds, mostly male, drinking beer and watching sports on TV. All that's missing is the La-Z-Boy rocker and a vat of nachos (oh, wait, it's there too):

Boomers Sports Grill

10388 Nordel Crt., 930-8727

Cinnamon Bear Lounge

Delta Whistler Resort, 4050 Whistler Way,
604/932-1982

Mahoney's Sports Grill

222-1025 Robson St., 662-3672

Malone's

400-525 Seymour St., 681-1591
608 W. Pender St., 684-9977
2202 Cornwall St., 737-7777
2300 Rocket Way, 464-5551

Photo: Blaine Kyllo

Shark Club

80 W. Georgia St., 687-4275
20169-88th Ave., Langley, 513-8600

late night nibbles

It's two in the morning, the bars have closed their doors, and you realize you haven't eaten since that breakfast burrito. No wonder the world is spinning. What to do?

Benny's Bagels

2505 W. Broadway, 731-9730
Open 24 hours

Buffalo Bill's

4122 Village Green, Whistler, 604/932-6613
Monday till Saturday till 2 am
Sundays till 1 am

DV8 Lounge

515 Davie St., 682-4388
Friday and Saturday till 4 am
Sunday to Thursday till 3 am

Gigi's

189 W. Broadway, 873-2696
Monday to Saturday till 3:30 am
Sunday till 2:30 am

Hamburger Mary's

1202 Davie St., 687-1293
Friday and Saturday till 4 am
Sunday to Thursday till 3 am

Martini's

151 W. Broadway, 873-0021
Friday and Saturday till 3 am
Sunday to Thursday till 2 am

Naam

2724 W. 4th Ave., 738-7151
Open 24 hours

Something's Brewing

Vancouver's got its fair share of great local breweries, but there are also a number of brew pubs and restaurants that offer their own concoctions brewed on the premises. Here are some of them:

The Creek Brewery and Restaurant
1253 Johnston St.,
Granville Island, 685-7070
Specialty: Helluva Hefewiezen

Howe Sound Inn and Brewing Company
Squamish Town Centre,
1-800-919-ALES
Specialty: Nut Brown Ale

Sailor Hägar's Brew Pub
221 W. 1st St., North Vancouver,
984-7669
Specialty: Narwhal Pale Ale,
Hägar's Belgian Wit Ale

Nelson Cafe

655 Nelson St., 633-2666
Sunday to Wednesday till midnight
Thursday to Saturday till 3 am

Steamworks
Brewing Company
375 Water St., 689-2739
Specialty: Cole Porter,
Lions Gate Lager

Yaletown Brewing Company
1111 Mainland St., 681-2739
Specialty: seasonal brews

And for those constantly in search of the finest of local brews, the Royal Canadian Malted Patrol is an organization dedicated to continued vigilance in this pursuit. Investigations are ongoing, and normally held weekly. For Information, contact recruiting officer Duncan Ainsley at 734-1072.

Steeps Grill

Roundhouse Lodge on Whistler, 604/905-2379
Monday to Saturday till 2:30 am
Sunday till 2:00 am

The Vineyard

2296 W. 4th Ave., 733-2420
Open 24 hours

Wong Kee

105 E. Broadway, 873-1711
All week till 3 am

Wonton Noodles

1991 E. Hastings St., 253-8418
All week till 5:30 am
4008 Cambie St., 877-1253
Friday and Saturday till 5:30 am
Sunday to Thursday till 3 am

You'd have thought a city so young would have had little chance of getting up to much in the way of mischief. But though laid-back in other endeavours, in the low-down world of depravity, vice, and corruption this sweet young city has shown a truly inspired zeal. On a number of occasions Vancouver has reached depths of such astounding baseness that the entire straight-laced world has tuned in to be shocked, appalled, and irresistibly intrigued. Celebrity strip bars, leather-clad lesbians, bank-robbing cops, corrupt politicians, and hastily covered-up murders. It's all here. Though the streets of Vancouver are often awash with rain, those gutters are never entirely clean.

Aliens in
Our Midst

Area 51 may be home of the little green men on *The X-Files*, but out in the real world, the favourite stomping ground of UFOs is right here in British Columbia. According to statistics carefully compiled over an 11-year period by the University of Manitoba's Chris Rutkowski, the west coast accounts for almost half of Canada's UFO sightings. One of the aliens favourite spots is the North Shore mountains, particularly the area just behind Grouse. In the summer of 2000, a group of four hikers out partying at a cabin on Mount Fromme found themselves surrounded by bizarre flashing lights, while incredibly deep-pitched vibrations made the entire forest thrum. The four high-tailed it back to town, escaping the near-inevitable abduction. Others aren't so lucky. For years, the folks at UFO*BC have, through their hotline (878-6511), collected vivid reports of sightings, crash retrievals, and abductions, many of which are now posted on their website: www.ufobc.org. Among the most recent cases is a Vancouver apartment dweller who awoke to find two naked lizard creatures, eight feet tall, standing over her bed examining her. The alien pair were evidently conducting some sort of test, telepathically inducing pleasant thoughts of romance, then gauging her reaction as they inserted grisly *denouéments*. The woman escaped only after mentally cloaking herself in a field of white light. For those interested in something a little more concrete, UFO*BC also does a brisk trade in stick pins and bumper stickers. Really.

Raging Bully

Photo: Blaine Kyllo

Though the food is certainly top drawer, Section (3) Restaurant *(1039 Mainland, 684-2777)* is likely better known for its name. Or its old name. Once upon a time it was known as DeNiro's, a tribute to owner Salli Pateman's fondness for actor Robert DeNiro. Indeed, Pateman was such a fan that once she had DeNiro's up and running, she a sent a gushing note to the actor, explaining the concept, telling him how much she admired his brilliant performances in everything from *Serpico to Dog Day Afternoon*, and inviting him for a free meal any time he came to town. What she got back was not the usual Mr. DeNiro-thanks-you-and-here's-a-stock-shot-for-your-trouble. Instead, Pateman got a letter from Mr. DeNiro's attorneys threatening legal action if she did not immediately cease and desist with her restaurant moniker. To this day, DeNiro's response mystifies Pateman. True, he has his own restaurant in New York, but it's not like he's planning a west coast expansion. And as she's since learned, there are several other as-yet-unharassed DeNiros in places such as San Francisco and London. But rather than get in a legal pissing match with a celebrity she once admired, Pateman chose to switch. Her eatery's now named after the legal code under which DeNiro threatened to sue.

The Spirit Moved Me

Located on Oak Street's church row, the reserved and respectable Kabalarian Philosophy headquarters looks like any other religious building. Members of the order believe in positive thinking, numerology, and the ability of disembodied minds of dead people to take control of the living. That last part explains the group sex. Lawsuits filed against the Kabalarian Society allege that before his death in 1964, Kabalarian founder Alfred J. Parker regularly involved underage female members of the order in ritualistic group sex. After Parker passed on to the other side, Ivon Shearing took up the leader's staff,

Just passing through

A few of the great names of the past who have made pitstops in Vancouver:

Photo: Vancouver Public Library

Jack Benny
Storming the vaudeville circuit in 1922 with buddy Zeppo Marx, Benny swung by Strathcona's Ferrera Court apartment building to visit one of Marx's friends. There he met a local rabbi's daughter, Sadie Marx, soon to be renamed Mary Livingstone, but later to be known as Mrs. Jack Benny or just "Oh Mary." The romance didn't exactly bloom right away, however. At the time she was only 12.

Babe Ruth
Babe Ruth stopped by on November 29, 1926 as part of his $100,000 tour of the vaudeville circuit to pose

with the mayor and police chief. The next year the Sultan of Swat would hit 60 home runs.

Sir Arthur Conan Doyle

The creator of Sherlock Holmes had already come and gone from Vancouver (where he had lectured on his pet subject, spiritualism) when the *Komagatu Maru* sailed into Vancouver filled with would-be Sikh immigrants on May 23 1914, but he was still in the country. Reading newspaper accounts of the boat's arrival, and later forced departure, Doyle cleverly deduced the Moriarty-like force responsible: "The whole incident seemed to me to be so grotesque — for why should sun-loving Hindoos force themselves upon Canada — that I was convinced some larger purpose lay behind it. That purpose was, as we can now see, to promote discord among the races under the British flag. There can be no doubt that it was German money that chartered that ship."

Sultan of Brunei

His Highness, Paduka Seri Baginda Sultan Haji Hassanal Bolkiah Muizzaddin Wadaulah, showed up in 1995, looking to pick up a waterfront *pied-à-terre* in West Van. Local opposition to his wild parties and helicopter pad scared the poor sultan away.

but it seems that spirit was still out there. Some three decades later in 1997, Shearing in turn was convicted of 12 counts of sexual abuse involving seven different women. Two of the women later filed lawsuits, which may be why — for the moment anyway — the Kabalarians are keeping their heads down.

Scandal, Anyone?

In February 1996, on the eve of Glen Clark's accession as Premier, BC Liberal house leader Gary Farrell-Collins called a press conference to unveil what a major financial scandal. BC Hydro chairman John Laxton was secretly offering shares in a lucrative Hydro subsidiary to members of the NDP.

The media response was instant and overwhelming. The *Vancouver Sun* ran seven full stories plus a lead editorial, all screaming with word "scandal." On the op-ed page, the editorial writers completely wigged out. "Hydro officials abused their positions to provide cushy deals for relatives and friends of the NDP," read the headline. "What these men did may have been legal, but it was totally immoral," read the editorial.

Damaging stuff. There was only one problem. None of it was true. There was no secret share offering. There was no cushy insider deal. Over 90 percent of the investors weren't members of the NDP.

As it turned out, the Liberal party knew at the time its allegations were nonsense. As it turned out, so did the newspaper. But an election was close, and the hated NDP looked set to make a comeback. A scandal was needed, facts be damned.

It took more than four years, one inquiry, one criminal investigation, and the judgment of a Supreme Court justice to establish what the true insiders had known all along: the so-called Hydrogate scandal was no scandal at all. In the meantime, BC Hydro president John Sheehan had been fired, the Hydro subsidiary had been sold off at a loss, and Hydro chair John Laxton was first fired and then publicly vilified as the kind of Howe Street sharpie more regularly seen swimming through the lower reaches of the VSE.

Laxton, who, thanks to his role as a crusading lawyer, had to that point enjoyed a kind of honeymoon with the press, should have known something was up when he rented out his waterfront house as a film set for a Leslie Nielsen comedy. The name of the film? *Wrongly Accused.*

Coup D'etat

Photo: Wayne Leidenfrost/The Province

On the night of March 2, 1999, BCTV reporter John Daly staked out Premier Glen Clark's eastside house, apparently on a "hunch" that police might show up. Lo and behold, sometime after supper a crew from the RCMP commercial crime unit arrived to execute a search warrant. TV viewers were treated to dramatic footage of the Premier and his wife pacing through the kitchen while the Mounties rifled through his upstairs rooms looking according to their warrant for evidence of a tie-in between Clark and a construction contractor and would-be charity casino operator named Dimitrios Pilarinos.

The timing of the raid was curious. Pilarinos' casino application had been definitively turned down several weeks earlier. The raid, what's more, turned up seemingly very little: plans for a deck Pilarinos had built on the back of Clark's house; bills for the work for close to $13,000; checks showing Clark had paid in full. Hardly the stuff of Watergate, but then the substance hardly mattered. The optics produced by Daly's TV footage were political damnation. Within weeks BC Premier Glen Clark had resigned.

Clark's passing went by-and-large unmourned; with a personality set permanently on "abrade," he was a difficult leader to love. Still, it's curious that Daly happened to be there, camera crew in tow, at just precisely that time. Or maybe not so curious.

A key figure in the RCMP investigation was Staff Sergeant Peter Montague, former media relations officer for the RCMP who once remarked, in reference to the

Emperor Haile Selassie

Haile Selassie, Emperor of Ethiopia and living Jah to millions of Rastafarians worldwide, arrived in Vancouver together with his pet chihuahua Lulu in 1967. He was on his way to visit Expo '67 in Montreal. During his brief stopover in town, he was entertained by Vancouver Mayor Tom "Terrific" Campbell, a man who a few months later would try to have all of Vancouver's hippies rounded up and placed in detention in a single central location — with gassing presumably to follow. Selassie would have approved of this, of course, for 'tis a little-known fact that the Lion of Judah hated his dreadlocked followers with an abiding passion. Selassie was deposed in a coup in 1973. Campbell himself only lasted until 1972.

Amelia Earhart

The American aviatrix was here on the lecture circuit in February 1933. Like another Vancouver visitor, Elvis, her later disappearance and presumed death was to prove no match for the resurrecting power of the tabloid press.

Elvis Presley

The Pelvis set a record for shortest-ever appearance right here in Vancouver, disappearing just five songs and 15 minutes into his September 3, 1957 Empire Stadium gig. Fans complained that $2 admission was a scam. And you thought the Oasis concert was a ripoff.

mounties' actions during the Gustafson Lake standoff, that "smear campaigns are our specialty." Daly has said he considers Montague a close friend. Daly has also said that no one in the police department told him about the impending raid. Of course, that doesn't rule out the possibility that the RCMP slipped the information to someone else, who then passed it on to Daly.

Leo Knight is well connected to both the media and the police. An ex-cop, he now writes a law and order column for the *North Shore News*. Knight knows both Daly and Montague. And curiously enough, he too was on hand the night of the raid, skulking behind some trees while the Mounties raided Clark. Knight even admits to chatting with Daly. And judging by his columns, he has a serious beef with the NDP.

Knight's not the only one in this affair with a known political leaning, of course. In advance of the 1997 provincial election, "smear-campaign" Montague was asked to run for Gordon Campbell's Liberal party. For a time he seriously considered it. That doesn't mean his investigation was biased, of course. Indeed, when questioned on this point Montague's superior stated that the mere appearance of political motivation was not enough to take him off the investigation.

Twenty-two months after the raid, prosecutors finally unveiled the results of their investigation, jointly charging Clark and Pilarinos with fraud and breach of trust. At a press conference that day, Clark commented that given the time and effort the RCMP had spent on the case, prosecutors were almost obligated to lay charges. Sometime in 2001 a B.C. Supreme Court judge will get to decide whether the construction of a deck for which Clark paid the going rate induced the Premier to look favourably on Pilarinos' casino application which the government turned down.

By the time a verdict is reached, the NDP's mandate will have expired and Gordon Campbell's Liberal Party will almost certainly have taken power. Citizens of B.C. will then be able to feel proud and secure in the stable workings of the democratic process. At least until the police discover another politician they don't like.

Among the most famous visitors to Expo '86 were the still-happily-married (on the outside, anyway) Prince Charles and Princess Diana. Among the most obscure was a sweet young 17-year-old from Prince George by the name of Kathryn Gannon, here with the rest of her dance troupe to entertain the visiting royalty. But then little Kathryn didn't really make her splash until the age of 22, when she took off her clothes on stage for the first time. By age 26, she was performing the horizontal mambo on video screens everywhere under her porn star name of Marylin Star. It was the glamour of being a full-time professional shag-monkey that got Gannon into the swankiest New York parties, at one of which she met James McDermott, CEO of a major Wall Street investment bank. McDermott and Gannon were soon a couple. Indeed, so devoted was the Wall Street tycoon to the young starlet that, according to the U.S. Securities Exchange Commission, he soon provided her with insider trading information, allowing her to net $129,000 in illegal profits. The SEC was not amused. McDermott was tossed from his $6 million a year CEO job. Gannon fled to Vancouver, into the arms of, in fact, another big-shot financier. Michael Gilley is perhaps best known as the former CFO of Cam-Net Communications, a telephone services reseller that went south taking some $100 million of investors money along with it. Gilley, however, came out fine. Certainly well off enough to cover the cost of legal expenses for a special someone.

Gannon became Mrs. Gilley on Valentine's Day, 2000. Just over two months later, Gannon was arrested by the RCMP after an extradition request came in from the U.S. She would have spent time in jail, but her new hubby coughed up the 50 large for the bail, and if the couple's marriage hadn't broken up less than a year later, would likely have helped her with her legal fees as the extradition hearing moves forward.

Instead, Gilley's money will be paying for his defence. He was charged with assaulting Gannon in September 2000, after taking her wedding ring in what police called "a wrestling match," and pushing her out of the house. Good love, it seems, is hard to find.

Muhammad Ali

The Greatest fought a heavyweight match against not-so-great George Chuvalo (who?) at the Pacific Coliseum in 1972.

Photo: Ralph Bauer/Vancouver Sun

Liberace

The famed master of flamboyance stopped by — glittering grand piano in tow — for a one-night appearance on the Vancouver stage way back in 1956. And his comment upon seeing our city for the first time? "I wish my brother George was here."

Photo: Vancouver Public Library

Count Basie

All those hep cats jiving to the (mostly taped) sounds of swing will be happy to know that Vancouver has a long history as a Swing City. Just look at how many of the greats stopped in to play. Benny Goodman was here many times, including appearances in 1960 and 1979. Louis Armstrong appeared in 1964, Duke Ellington a few years before that. And, arguably the greatest of them all, Count Basie and his whole huge orchestra appeared in Vancouver way back in 1951.

Clark Gable

Not yet the man who frankly didn't give a damn, Clark Gable swung through town in the early '30s and managed to spend several hours wandering round the site of what would one day be Langara College. At the time, of course, it was the Shaughnessy Golf Club.

Bing Crosby

In town for yet another walk round the golf links, crooner and comedian Bing Crosby managed to make it on the road to deepest, darkest Killarney in time for the opening of the Killarney Community Centre. In gratitude, the denizens of this most distant of Vancouver neighbourhoods rewarded Bing with a room named in his honour.

The Vancouver Syndrome

Maybe it's something in the water. Maybe it's because all the male Vancouverites are out climbing trees and crunching rocks. Whatever the reason, Vancouver is the only place in the known world where getting accused of murder is the best place to meet a babe. Born and bred Vancouverite Kathy Macdonald got her first look at her current beau, bank robber and autobody man Shannon Murrin, while sitting in the jury box pondering whether he was guilty of killing an eight-year-old Kelowna girl. North Vancouverite Gillian Guess (above) hopped into the sack with gang leader and accused killer Peter Gill while serving as a juror at his murder trial. She had a feeling he was innocent. Macdonald, too, would eventually conclude that Murrin was not guilty.

True, there were subtle differences between the two. Guess started sleeping with Gill while she sat in judgment at his trial. Macdonald's relationship with Murrin began only after he'd been tried and found not guilty. Guess ran around bragging of her accomplishment, almost daring the police to do something. Macdonald was cautiously circumspect. Guess loved to kiss and tell. (Recounting her first sexual encounter with Gill, Guess she said, "I've had inoculations that lasted longer.") On the topic of her sex life, Macdonald has stayed mum. A last little difference: Guess was charged and convicted of obstruction of justice, and sentenced to 18 months in jail, while Macdonald, together with Murrin, is writing a book about police abuse of power and their life together since the trial.

Still, the cases are similar enough to have the B.C. judiciary worried. On the first day of a recent murder trial, B.C. Supreme Court Justice Wally Oppal turned a stern eye to the members of the jury — male and female — and warned them that, "You cannot develop any kind of social relationship with any of the accused." In issuing the warning, Oppal said, he wanted to avoid any further repetition of what he called "The Vancouver Problem."

ghostly appearances

Even though Vancouver is a relatively young city, it's had its fair share of spooky sightings. Here are a few, the first two culled from Robert Belyk's book *Ghosts of British Columbia*:

The Haunted Walkway

In the summer of 1985, the owner of a Coquitlam apartment complex was feeling very pleased with himself. The load of granite slabs for the building's new walkway had come at a very reasonable price. It wasn't until tenant Lucille Schneider turned one over that residents found out why: the flagstones were actually tombstones, picked up cheap when the nearby Woodlands school for the mentally disabled turned its small cemetery into a park.

And it was then that the hauntings began: TV sets would change channels while no one was in the room, appliances would turn on by themselves, footsteps would be heard padding through empty rooms.

For the children living in the building, the tombstones held an eerie fascination. Lifting up the slabs to read the names of deceased children became a kind of game. After that, tenants began seeing the faces of children at their windows, and waking in the middle of the night to find their beds shaking violently of their own accord. For one family, it was the last straw. They moved out, and other families threatened to follow. The owner gave in, and had the grave markers picked up and carted away. To where, he didn't say.

Phantom of the Nursing Home

More than a few pained souls passed their final moments gazing out from the verandah of the Arts and Crafts mansion that housed the Oakhurst Nursing Home, so it was perhaps only fitting that a few of those dearly departed would opt to hang around for a while at the abandoned building at Oak Street and 58th Avenue. In January 1995, one of those spirits made its presence known to the crew of the film *One Foot in Heaven*, who had set up to do a week-long shoot in the mansion.

On his overnight shift, assistant location manager and

A MONSTER MADE IN VANCOUVER

Pratt is hardly a name made for glory. Think of the connotations: "pratfall," meaning humiliating failure, or "prat," meaning a foolish person, or a set of buttocks. Thus it was that when 22-year-old Bill Pratt laboured in Vancouver, first as a longshoreman, then as a stagehand at the old Orpheum Theatre, and finally as a carpenter on the site of the PNE, he was not what one would call gloriously successful. It was likely to escape the curse of being a Pratt that Bill himself changed his name when he set out for Hollywood to seek fame and fortune. His new name: Boris Karloff.

GASSY JACK'S LOST WAGES

Given the hue-and-cry over Swiss banks hiding away the assets of those they knew were unlikely to return, it's worth taking a look at the actions of our own provincial treasury.

When Jack Deighton, Vancouver's founding father, died in his bed in 1875, the disposition of his hotel and other properties left a substantial legacy of $5,878. A $1,600 lawsuit with his ne'er-do-well brother Tom, plus $4,278 in lawyers' fees, ate up all but $304; however, even that was a tidy sum for the time. Alas, Jack's son died only a year after his father, and his wife Madelaine — a Native Indian from somewhere up the Fraser Valley — left to be with her own people. The money was never claimed. At a conservative interest rate of five percent, Jack's legacy now amounts to some $123,000. Where, we wonder, is the Committee for Oversight of the Rightful Restitution of the Unfortunate Pioneer's Treasure?

night watchman Jordan Winter reported that on several occasions he heard a muffled cry emanate from inside the building, like the sound of a sick child, or perhaps one being strangled. Once, Winter even saw a ghastly face appear in the window over the verandah, but when he went inside to investigate, he found nothing. Makeup artist Elissa Frittaion heard the same strangled cry in broad daylight coming from a spot outside the mansion in the vicinity of a gnarled old chestnut tree. When she looked there was nothing, but that wasn't the end of her spiritual experiences.

Trying to pass the long hours of idleness that are a part of any film shoot, Frittaion wandered one bright sunny afternoon into the octagon-shaped verandah on the first floor. Right away she felt uneasy – unwelcome somehow – and quickly turned around. It was then that she felt "a strange pressure, like a wave of water," pressing on her back and upper legs, forcing her out of the room. Unnerved, she sought out the company of fellow crew-member Mariah Krawley, and together the two came back to investigate. This time both women were forced out of the room by the same irresistible pressure. Someone or something clearly did not want them there. Frittaion took the hint, and never set foot on the haunted verandah again.

What, one wonders, will that unfriendly entity do when, as planned, the half-timbered old mansion is renovated, subdivided, and incorporated into a new condo development? If the ghost is a true Vancouverite, odds are it will lobby for a development freeze, bringing a whole new meaning to the acronym Nimby: "*Necromancer* in my backyard."

A Ghost Named Charlie

Quite a few folks in Vancouver are aware that the Vancouver Art Gallery has a ghost. Quite a few more have been told the story of the *Komagata Maru*. Very few have ever put the two tales together.

The ship *Komagata Maru* arrived in Vancouver harbour on May 23, 1914, filled with 376 would-be Punjabi immigrants, most of them Sikhs. It had been chartered by a group of local Sikh activists to circumvent a Canadian order-in-council requiring immigrants from India to arrive directly from the sub-continent. Despite complying with the regulation, the immigrants were not allowed to land, and the ship was forced to leave port two months later.

In the aftermath of the affair, local authorities set about trying to infiltrate the local Sikh community to find out who chartered the ship. Inspector William Charles Hopkins was sent undercover to try and recruit informers. Not surprisingly, local Sikhs soon discovered the identity of one of his agents. On September 5, 1914, as informer Bela Singh entered the large Sikh temple at West 2nd and Burrard, one man took a shot at him, and another tried to slash him with a ceremonial sword. Both missed. Bela Singh pulled out two pistols of his own and let off 10 rounds, killing two of his attackers and injuring two more.

Put on trial for murder that October, Bela Singh was counting on the testimony of his controller, Inspector Hopkins, to clear him. When Hopkins showed up at the courthouse, however, a local Sikh named Mewa Singh pulled a gun and shot him three times through the heart. Hopkins died. Bela Singh was acquitted; Mewa Singh was convicted of murder and hanged. Denied the opportunity to testify, or just annoyed by the outcome of the affair, Hopkins' ghost has haunted the courthouse — now the Vancouver Art Gallery — ever since. Gallery workers have even grown rather fond of the spirit, giving him the nickname "Charlie."

Ghost on Deadman

Untold generations of Native Indians and more than a few of Vancouver's early smallpox victims found their final resting place on the aptly named Deadman's Island. Have a few of these souls hung around long enough to see the island transformed into a naval installation? According to rumours on the base, a weird spectral glow sometimes appears in the trees on the island. The apparition slowly coalesces into the form of a despondent seaman, said to have hanged himself from one of the branches. When equipment disappears from the base, this unhappy spectre is usually held to blame.

THE COLD SQUAD

Got a stiff on your hands? Don't call the Cold Squad. Not unless you've had it hanging about the house for a very long time. Operating out of a little office in the sprawling depths of Surrey, the 20-man Cold Squad unit — a joint project of Vancouver police and the RCMP — investigates homicides that have remained on the books for years or even decades.

The Squad's proudest moment to date was cracking the case of murdered Squamish teenager Judy Howey, who in 1964 was found buried underneath a tree in a wooded patch where the Sea to Sky Highway now runs. Squamish RCMP had their suspicions, but for 35 years lacked the evidence to make an arrest. Within a few short months of reopening the case, the Cold Squad had set up an undercover sting operation and cadged a confession from a now-46-year-old landscaper. In the fall of 2000, a Squamish jury found him guilty.

SCENE OF THE CRIME

In *Burnt Bones*, the psycho thriller by Vancouver writer Michael Slade, a Vancouver police inspector named Kim Rossmo employs a homemade geographic profiling program that pinpoints the areas frequented by likely murder suspects, and winds up saving the day. *Burnt Bones* is fiction. Indeed, Michael Slade himself is fiction, the *nom de plume* of no less than three Vancouver writers. But Detective Inspector Kim Rossmo is real.

The first working cop in Canada to earn a Ph.D. in criminology, Rossmo's research in the geographic profiling of serial criminals led to the development of an ingenious program called *Geographic Profiling Software*. The program uses a computer

Canadians aren't supposed to do bad things. We're quiet. Polite. Fond of peace, order, and good government. Strange, then, that in the heart of ordered conformity that was Vancouver in the early '60s, three cops – duly sworn representatives of the forces of Peace and Order – should take to robbing banks. On the other hand, they were very good at it. On their first ever bank job, on Christmas Eve, 1962, Vancouver police constables Leonard Hogue, David Harrison, and Joe Percival hit the Bank of Commerce on Kingsway in Burnaby and came away with $106,000 (equivalent to about $600,000 today). Quite a score. Far better than their initial forays into crime.

The trio's first cash job came at a Dairy Queen, where they discovered that the DQ made a habit of storing the evening's cash receipts in the freezer. For a time, nary a Dairy Queen freezer was safe. Hogue, however, wasn't happy being just an ice cream bandit. He'd gotten into crime for the cash; he had six kids plus a wife to house and clothe. And thus they moved on to banks, with stunning success, at least at first.

Next time out at a Simpsons-Sears hold-up, a beyond-the-line-of-duty credit manager gave Hogue a shove, knocking a Loomis bag with $88,000 out of his hands. And on January 16, 1965, they hit the Bank of Nova Scotia in Dunbar, but ran out in a panic with only $13,000 when the getaway driver sounded the horn too early.

It's a wonder that they continued. Hogue, in particular, had what he wanted. Early in 1963 he'd traded in his two-bedroom shack for a sizable split-level rancher at 1796 Harbour Drive in Coquitlam. After the initial big bank job, Percival quit the force and went into real estate, the better to launder his takings. Harrison also left the VPD, moving to Nelson and joining the force there. But for all three, it was no longer just about money, but about the thrill.

For their last big caper, they planned a daylight robbery of the CPR yards on West Pender, where a shipment of disused bills lay waiting for eventual destruction at the mint. Disguised as a CPR policeman, a mail carrier, and a train engineer, the three made their way into the rail yards and in five minutes made away with nearly $1.2 million. Alas, there was one problem. For security reasons, someone had taken the precaution of mutilating the bills by drilling them with half-inch holes. It appeared the money was worthless. Hogue urged his partners to destroy the incriminating evidence. Instead, Percival came up with a way to doctor the money, cutting patches from some bills and taping them on to others. The results looked good, and soon all three began passing the doctored bills.

Eventually, a bartender in Edmonton got suspicious of the guy who kept paying for his drinks in 20s, and Percival was caught. Hogue immediately fell under suspicion. Instead of going into work, he went to borrow a .357 gun from a friend of his, a CPR cop who – police believe – had tipped off the three about the cash shipment in the first place. Hogue rented a car, a big station wagon. And then he disappeared. Three days later, when he still hadn't shown up for work, two VPD cops show up at Hogue's Harbour Drive door.

They found his wife dead, executed with a single bullet through the head. All six kids had been similarly killed. And at the end of the hall in the master bedroom, they found Constable Hogue, a bullet through his left temple, a .357 handgun on the floor by his left hand.

Murder-suicide, the coroner's jury ruled. A distraught Hogue had killed his wife and kids, then turned the gun on himself. At the time, the theory was accepted. Police were trying to track down Joe Percival, who had posted bail and then vanished. They were also running an undercover operation aimed at bringing David Harrison to justice. Both would eventually do time in B.C. jails.

But though there was no further investigation, a few folks noticed some anomalies with the murder-suicide scenario. For one thing, there were no fingerprints on the gun or on the many shells that lay scattered around the house. Nor was there any blood on the gun, or on Hogue's hands, as might be expected when a large-calibre gun is used to kill seven people at close range. Strangest of all, Hogue was right-handed. The man who killed his wife and children was a leftie.

mapping technique that specifies crime sites and then uses criminal psychology theory to predict the likely homes or workplaces of serial rapists, murderers, and arsonist suspects. Now used by Scotland Yard and the FBI, among others, the program has proven highly effective in narrowing down to a small area, often as small as a square kilometre, within which police can start investigating more closely by using such techniques as DNA testing and door-to-door investigation. Rossmo's "profiles" have been instrumental in solving or shedding light on such high-profile cases as the "tag-team rapist" in Surrey, the Clifford Olsen child murders, the Paul Bernardo/Karla Homolka murders, and the St. Louis "Southside Rapist" case.

About the only thing Rossmo's program isn't good for is mapping out a career. After receiving his Ph.D., Rossmo was offered a number of high-paying jobs with national police forces, among them the RCMP and FBI. He opted to stay in Vancouver, however, after then-chief Bruce Chambers promised him a bright future and bumped him from street cop to Detective Inspector. As Chambers discovered, however, change is worse than homicide to the average VPD cop; Chambers fell victim to a revolt from the rank and file. New up-from-the-ranks chief Terry Blythe has told Rossmo to put away the laptop and get back to walking a beat. After all, whoever heard of a cop who knew how to use a computer?

It's tough being Vancouver's top cop. Current chief Terry Blythe got the job over the figuratively dead body of predecessor Bruce Chambers, ousted by a revolt of rank-and-file cops upset with his community policing plans and his "too soft" attitude towards the drug scene on the downtown east side. Chambers thought more money should be made available for treatment centres. It seems that nothing ever changes in Vancouver.

In December of 1916, then-Chief Malcolm MacLennan wrote a report to the City Police Commission proposing that rather than arresting drug addicts, "some asylum should be provided for them … where they could be held until they had recovered from their desire for drugs." Three months later, in answering a call about gunfire at a house at 522 East Georgia Street, MacLennan was shot dead … by a drug addict.

Police Chief Walter Mulligan had his own ways of digging up extra cash, as recounted in the book *Top Cop on the Take*. Appointed in 1947 to stamp out corruption in Vancouver, Mulligan set about – rather like the bent cop in the movie *L.A. Confidential* – shutting down about half of the pimps and bookmakers in town and ensuring that the other half channeled some of their profits into his pockets. It went on for nearly a decade, turning police headquarters on Main Street into the centre of criminal activity in Vancouver.

Several times the *Province* came across evidence of corruption, but always backed away from publishing. Finally in 1955, an upstart rag called *Flash* published a major exposé alleging that Chief Mulligan was on the take. Reading the papers' charges in the Main Street police station, Mulligan's chief henchman, Detective Sergeant Len Cuthbert, pulled out his .38 service revolver and put a bullet through his own chest. Miraculously, he lived.

After the province launched a probe into Mulligan's activities, another senior cop, Superintendent Harry Whelen, put a bullet through his own chest. He died. In the end, the commission would find extensive evidence of police corruption. Before any charges could be laid, however, Mulligan fled south to California. The exercise was not a total loss, however. Covering it made the career of a young newspaperman turned radio reporter by the name of Jack Webster, later to become one of Vancouver's legendary journalists.

That's one small step for man. At a recent summer show in Milan, 23 year-old boy-model and Vancouver native Robert Perovich astounded the fashion world by picking up a whopping US$25,000 for shaking his booty on the catwalk. While such fees are standard for female members of the modelling tribe, poor and picked-upon male models can normally be had for US$1,500 or less. It's unjust and unfair, of course, for developing the attributes of a successful model – a breastless, hipless figure, Auschwitz profile, and glassy-eyed heroin stare – is just as challenging for men as it is for women. But such are the dictates of commerce. In this case, the long-overdue blow for equality was the result not of government fiat, nor even divine intervention – Perovich, a born-again Christian, prays daily for his agent – but a bidding war between Italian fashion houses Gucci and Dolce & Gabbana. Though they have yet to comment publicly, the Canadian Human Rights Tribunal is said to have watched the case with favour.

NUDE SWIMMING

For those in the throes of the wintertime blues, toss off your malaise, your chemise, and your undershorts, and join in the nude swim at Lord Byng Pool (222-6090). Sponsored by the ardent nudists of the Wreck Beach Preservation Society, the Saturday night nude swim takes place the third Saturday of every month throughout the winter. To preserve the naturist nature of the evening, optional clothing is not an option. An eastside group, Naked Iconoclasts Fighting the Yoke (NIFTY) runs a similar evening at at the Templeton Park School (718-6252).

Photo: Blaine Kyllo

Now a trendy upscale restaurant, the Bidwell Street building that houses Balthazar spent much of its life servicing more basic needs. Though built in 1918 as a luxury Spanish villa, the residence quickly fell on hard times as the local elite fled the West End for the newly opened enclave of Shaughnessy. By the early 1930s, the villa was home to Marcel's Beauty Salon, a spa operation run by "Madame Maxine," a French chemist who offered her customers therapeutic baths of mare's milk and goat's blood. Within a few years, Madame Maxine had found something more lucrative than blood baths, going whole hog into the service industry by transforming the former villa into a brothel. For a time business boomed, particularly with the influx of service men during the war years. After a spate of late 1940s vice-squad raids, the building re-opened as a "grand pension," a fancy-sounding front for the main business which remained prostitution. By the 1970s, however, public tastes had changed and the villa's owners decided to offer up a different kind of dish, renovating and transforming the old Spanish bordello into a series of fine dining restaurants, the latest of which – Balthazar – opened in 1999. The cocktail lounge, located roughly where the brothel used to operate, is called, appropriately enough, the Bordello Room.

ORDERING IN

There's more to Whistler than mountains and scenery. The Lovenest *(102 - 4338 Main St., 604/932-6906, www.lovenest.ca)* will deliver "romantic accessories" direct to your hotel room. What comes next is up to you.

dress for duress

Tired of the same old same old? Can't find a date who will do what you tell her? Looking for a spot to show off your new leather teddy? Maybe you're a candidate for **Muffs & Cuffs**, the women's only leather and bondage night, held four times a year in a secret dungeon. More information can be obtained by calling Womyn's Ware on Commercial Drive (254-2543).

For those who prefer their company mixed, or are cursed by a lack of female chromosomes, there's still opportunity in this city to try out that new leather head gag, flog someone, or simply be flogged. On the last Saturday of every month the **Body Perve Social Club** meets downstairs at the Lotus Cabaret at 455 Abbott Street. The evening is open to those of all persuasions: male, female, fetishists, bondage queens, masochists, sado-masochists, and those with just an unnaturally heightened appreciation for all-leather fashions. Participants must be suitably attired. Outfits range from full-length rubber catsuits to skimpy thongs to cheerleader outfits, and fabrics include everything from leopard skin to shiny PVC to chain mail. The crowd tends to be a more-or-less equal mix of hard-core fetish and fashion fetish enthusiasts, with a large gay-bi contingent (688-4947; www.bodyperve.com).

Photo: Blaine Kyllo

One place to find your attire is **Mor Rubber** (1263 Homer St., 683-AMOR), where you can get stock latex wears and, even better, custom made apparel.

Those without suitable bondage apparel have three options: they can wear a full tuxedo (also a fetish for some), they can doff their clothes (all of them) at the door, or they can check out **Mack's Leathers** at 1043 Granville Street (685-7777), where a simple whip or gag'll cost you less than $50, while a full set of crotchless leather pants and matching jacket

Sin City

Somewhere deep in the American psyche there is a persistent notion of Vancouver as Sin City. Partially it's a still-reverberating echo from the 1940s and '50s when gambling dens and gin joints ruled the city, and cops did what you paid them for. In the '60s, ours was one of the first towns to go with go-go girls. And in the new millennium, we're still one of the few towns in North America where the peelers still take it all off. So maybe the Americans have it right after all....

Photo: Mandelbrot

No. 5 Orange

The city's premier peeler parlour. Local residents used to set their watches by the nightly chants of "Shower! Shower!" emanating from the No. 5, as the clientele egged the girls on for the finale. And what a clientele: the guest list at the No. 5 over the years reads like a who's-who of visiting celebrities: Sylvester Stallone, Bill Murray, John Candy, Ted Danson, Judd Nelson; rock groups Aerosmith, Mötley Crüe, AC/DC; athletes Charles Barkley, Dennis Rodman, Wayne Gretzky (does Janet know?). Dancers of note include

infamous Italian MP (and former wife of art star Jeff Koons) Ilona Staller (a.k.a. Ciccolina), Kimberly Conrad (later to be Hugh Hefner's wife), and the future rock star Courtney Love.
205 Main St., 687-3483

OTHER PEELER BARS OF NOTE:

Cecil Hotel
1336 Granville St., 683-8505

Casey's Pub
3484 Kingsway (Metrotown area)

Club Paradise
315 E. Broadway, 876-6383

Cobalt Hotel
917 Main St., 685-2825

Drake Hotel
Show Lounge.
606 Powell St., 254-2826

Fraser Arms Hotel
1450 SW Marine Dr., 261-2499

Marble Arch Hotel
518 Richards St., 688-2724

Penthouse Cabaret
1019 Seymour St., 683-2111

can run you all the way up to $1,500. Spreader bars and hand cuffs not included.

And should you decide that having bought the whip, you'd like to bite the bit (or whatever), here's a few other pain-and-party sessions happening around town.

Club Inferno

This full-equipped BDSM and fetish facility provides ample opportunity for those into a no-alcohol-but-lots-of-flogging kind of fun. If you're not whip-equipped, don't despair – there are always instruments of torture on hand. www.angelfire.com/bc2clubinferno; clubinferno@hotmail.com

Studio Q

Similar to other dungeons, but Studio Q is for the queerly kinked only, so no cross-gender lusting. Parties are private and by invitation only. *408-0118*; www.diversitymag.com/studioq/; studioq@diversitymag.com

Vancouver and Fraser Valley (Pansexual) Munches

What could be better than kink in the Valley? It sure beats cruising King George Hwy. Note to the uninitiated: munching is not something done at McDonald's (usually). www.renaissoft.com/fd/munch; dee@renaissoft.com

Virago Projects

Organizes Dark Circus play parties and other BDSM events in Vancouver. *735-9921*; viragoprojects@excite.com

By Invitation Only

Reive and Naughtya host pansexual BDSM play parties dedicated to the kink in all of us. VancouverDungeon@hotmail.com

Mistress Madelaine

While it's true that bondage and domination require an active imagination, after a while even the most fervid fantasizer can get tired of pretending the living room is really a dungeon. So why not visit the real-life party dungeon of the lovely Mistress M. in East Vancouver, where you'll learn the finer points of domination in a sound-proofed space full of interesting equipment. *434-1881*

Vancouver Activists in SM

A non-profit society for gay and bisexual men into sado-masochism. Offers monthly workshops and demonstrations as well as regular play parties. *876-1914*

Leather and Levi's Nights

The name pretty much says it all. Call 685-7777 for more graphic information or check the bulletin board at Mack's Leathers (1043 Granville St.).

A Fantasy Nightmare

Photo: Vancouver Province

On the night of August 3, 1990, William Vander Zalm, premier of the province of British Columbia, met Taiwanese land developer Tan Yu at a bar in the Westin Bayshore Hotel, ostensibly to discuss a deal they had in the works for a piece of land adjacent to Vander Zalm's Fantasy Gardens estate in Richmond. At some point Tan Yu gave the premier $20,000 in cash, in unmarked $100 bills. Vander Zalm later refused to say what it was for. Yu didn't ask for a receipt.

Four months later on December 4, Vander Zalm got a telephone call from real estate agent and extravagant hat connoisseur Faye Leung. She was furious that Vander Zalm's dealings with Yu had cut her out of a $1 million

POLITICS IN THE PARK

Think Prime Minister Chretien's unleashing the RCMP on APEC protesters in 1997 was excessive? It wasn't the first time political protest in this town has been unconstitutionally circumscribed. In 1936, alarmed by the growing legion of radical unemployed making their home in the city, the Parks Board declared that Oppenheimer Park on the east side was the only place in the city where political gatherings, or even the public expression of political views, would be tolerated. The policy backfired just two years later in 1938, when a mass of angry unemployed occupied the city's main post office, leading directly to a full-scale riot.

PRIME MINISTERIAL MATERIAL

Kim is cuddlier. That was the slogan ex-prime minister Kim Campbell used at UBC to get herself elected Alma Mater Society frosh president in 1964. It's something she wishes people would forget. "That was just a whimsical spur of the moment thing that we wrote on construction boarding," says Campbell. By 1967, the Port Alberni native had moved on to bigger things. She was 20, AMS vice-president, and no longer living in her parents' house in Kerrisdale.

Now Consul-General in Los Angeles, it seems Kim's still fairly cuddly. While her term as Canada's representative expires soon, Campbell has announced she'll be staying on in Tinsel Town. The love of her life, actor Hershey Felder — who would still have been in diapers for three or four years after Campbell's cuddly electoral career began — is working on a career as a playwright and entertainer. Campbell plans to stay and help nurture him along.

real estate commission. She wanted the premier to come to a rendezvous later that night in the Fantasy Gardens parking lot to discuss the matter without any lawyers present. Unbeknownst to the Zalmster, she was also taping the conversation, and later turned the tapes over to the media. Here is a partial transcript of the conversation:

Leung: "Why should I be responsible? I feel like telling the newspaper: 'Okay, you want the true story? Look at this paper.' Look at what I've done, and what have I got paid? Not one little cent. Fantasy Gardens got paid."

Vander Zalm: "Oh yeah?"

Leung: "Do you think I've got any gas money? Do you think I got anything out of it? And I was supposed to get 10 percent that IAA was assigned over when Taiwan, when Tan Yu pay you that 10 percent for the Petro land and all those other lands. Well, I have not got a penny."

Vander Zalm: "I didn't get anything, either."

Leung: "The 20,000 cash, I even turn it over to you that night. I was supposed to hold it in trust. But I turned it over to you...."

Later, after trying to work out an arrangement with Vander Zalm, Leung gives up. "I have nothing to hide," she says. "Why don't I put it out to the press; what am I keeping it myself for? Why don't I just let them know?"

And with that she hung up. And then she followed her own advice. The truth never really came out about the Fantasy Garden deal and the $20,000, but Vander Zalm was ultimately driven from office.

A Bridge Too ... Slippery?

One of the strangest unsolved mysteries occurred on one of the city's oldest tourist attractions – the Capilano Suspension Bridge – early in July 1999. Nadia Hama, thrice-divorced mother of three, took her kids for a day out at the bridge which crosses the 100-metre-deep canyon. She walked out on the narrow, bouncing decking carrying her youngest – a baby with Down's syndrome – over her shoulder like, according to one witness, "a sack of potatoes." Seconds later, the child was spinning through the air on its way down into the chasm. Hama neither screamed nor called out, but instead whipped out her cell phone and called her estranged husband. "Your son's dropped off the bridge," she told him. Miraculously, the child lived. Tree branches softened his fall, and he landed, safe and sound, at the bottom of the canyon, just inches from the roaring Capilano River. Hama claimed her son slipped from her arms, but not many were convinced. The highly suspicious North Vancouver RCMP performed an investigation, but since nobody had actually witnessed the incident, their suspicions remained just that. Social Services, which had initially seized all of Hama's children, returned them to her care. And so far as anyone knows, there have been no further field trips to the bridge.

A Nearly Good Getaway

Photo: Mandelbrot

A burglar-proof vault, 2,000 safety deposit boxes chock full of cash and jewelry, and five desperate men armed with pickaxes and a torch: all the makings of the biggest bank heist ever. Late one Friday night back in January 1977, a van pulled up behind the nine-storey Vancouver Safety Vaults building at 402 West Pender. One man scurried up the fire escape and smashed in a second floor window. His four partners passed up picks, sledgehammers, mallets, chisels, and several steel acetylene tanks, which the five of them then carried down to the basement vault.

BABES IN THE WOODS

On the morning of January 14, 1953, Vancouver police uncovered two small bodies buried under a light covering of leaf mould and pine needles near the edge of Stanley Park. They had been there for a least six years. The city's forensic experts identified them as the decomposed corpses of an eight-year-old boy and a seven-year-old girl. Near them lay a women's brown leather shoe, and the notched head of a shingler's axe. Forensics also showed that the two children had died from skull fractures that fit the axehead exactly. Police theorized that the children had been killed by their mother, who had then panicked and run off, leaving both shoe and axe behind. Lacking any idea of what the children had looked like, however, the police were stymied in their efforts to find the killer.

It was then that Austrian physical anthropologist Erna von Engel-Baiersdorf was brought in. Her task was to craft plaster likenesses of the two children, working from the broken and decomposed skulls. An exact reconstruction was impossible, of course, but von Engel-Baiersdorf's Viennese instinct told her that the children had been of a Nordic race, possibly Swedish or Norwegian. Photos of the two plaster casts were shown far and wide, but alas, they engendered no solid leads.

Recently, the famous Cold Squad had another look at the evidence. Thanks to DNA testing, the Cold Squad now knows where both psychic and police went wrong. The babes were not brother and sister, but two little boys. The case remains unsolved, despite the story being broadcast on A&E's *Investigative Reports*.

There was no alarm system, no security guard. Why bother? The safe was impregnable. It took the gang all night to hack and burn their way through the six inches of armour plate and 2.5 feet of reinforced concrete. They left Sunday morning by the front door, carrying some $10 million stashed away in cardboard boxes. From there the crooks made a nearly perfect getaway, driving unnoticed to the airport and boarding a flight that would have taken them to parts unknown. Alas for them, a baggage handler found a too-heavy box of coins suspicious and called the police, who met them on the tarmac after a forced landing in Winnipeg. Today, the basement vault is still there, pretty much as the gang left it. Go down the stairs by the elevator. Look for the door by the Federal Express drop. If the superintendent is there, knock and ask if you can have one of the now-empty safety-deposit boxes as a keepsake. The thieves left quite a few of them scattered around on the ground.

The Errols of His Ways

Photo: Vancouver Public Library

By 1959, Errol Flynn was well past his acting prime. His days as Captain Blood and Robin Hood were long gone; his swash had noticeably buckled. But when he arrived in Vancouver for a short visit in October of 1959, it was still big news. It was even bigger news two days later, when Flynn dropped dead in a West End apartment in the company of his 17-year-old "personal assistant" (since you ask, a very comely female). His body was transported to the city morgue on East Cordova where a pathologist set about performing an autopsy. Wanting a souvenir, he cut off a piece of

Robin Hood's merry member and plopped it into a jar of formaldehyde. Aghast, Coroner Glen McDonald re-attached the missing piece with scotch tape, and shipped the body off to L.A. for burial.

But the story doesn't end there. Somewhere between the apartment and the morgue, the key to a safety deposit box that Flynn habitually wore around his neck disappeared. Three weeks later, Flynn's lawyers had the Swiss safety deposit box opened up, expecting to find a half million dollars in cash and various stock certificates.

It was empty.

Unhappy New Year

Photo: Vancouver Province

"Spend New Year's Eve with the Three Tenors!" Thus went the advertising slogan for the most disastrous concert ever to hit Vancouver – the Terminal City stop in the worldwide tour of opera greats Luciano Pavarotti, Placido Domingo, and Jose Carreras, scheduled for New Year's Eve 1996 at BC Place Stadium.

Tickets prices for the much-hyped event were astronomical, as high as $2,000 a seat. Initially, that is. As Vancouverites failed to respond, and it looked like the stadium might be half-empty, prices fell, and fell again (much to the annoyance of the folks who had shelled out top dollar). Vancouver promoter Tina Vanderheyden warned that the show would be cancelled if more tickets weren't sold. By the end, as one local columnist quipped, they were practically giving tickets away at 7-11 with every Big Gulp or Slurpee.

Even the gods seemed to frown on the event. The tenors arrived in town in the midst of the worst snowfall to hit the city in a generation, distinguishing themselves immediately by their arrogant fussiness. Pavarotti insisted on having all his own cooking pots in his suite at the Pan Pacific, and when a particular brand of white kidney bean that he needed for some concoction or other was not among the kitchen supplies, he sent a young hotel minion out into the snow-choked streets to find a can.

HOUDINI'S VANCOUVER ESCAPE

Though Harry Houdini was killed by a Canadian, it was not, thank goodness, a Vancouverite. (Instead, it was an overachiever from McGill who caught the famous escape artist with a surprise punch to the gut, causing a fatal rupture to his kidney.) Houdini did appear in Vancouver,

The concert itself was schmaltz, a mix of "Best Of" opera outtakes and modern pop ballads; Jose Carreras' tortured ESL version of "Moon River" provoked outright laughter. Worst of all, at a quarter of midnight, the tenors ended their concert with no encore to follow, leaving attendees to welcome the New Year without them. Disbelief was the only thing keeping outraged fans from charging the stage.

And the aftermath? The snow melted. Vanderheyden's promotion company went belly-up. The world tour promoter, Matthias Hoffmann, wound up in jail in Germany on fraud charges. And, going through Pavarotti's room after he had departed, cleaning staff at the Pan Pacific came across a large can of exclusive white kidney beans. Unopened.

though. In the 1920s, he was hung upside down in a straightjacket from the Sun Tower building on the edge of Vancouver's Victory Square. Thousands of bowler-hatted Vancouverites turned out to watch. The *Vancouver Sun* even managed to send a photographer. Of course, it did happen on their doorstep.

Arsenic and Old Signs

Though now shuffled up to the front of the lot and obscured by a paste-on Toys R Us banner, the BowMac sign on West Broadway was once a wonder to behold. Erected in 1959 on the site of the Bowell Maclean car lot, the red and blue sign stood 10 storeys tall, boasted 3,500 lamps, and used enough electricity to power a small town. On a clear night it was visible from ten miles away. It was the largest free-standing electrical sign on the world, and the only one ever to harbour a murderer.

Rene Castellani was a man of many talents. In June of 1965, as promotions manager for radio station CKNW, he sat atop the BowMac sign for a full week, vowing to remain up there selling cars live over the airwaves until every car on the lot was sold. That same summer, he was also slowly killing his wife.

Poisoning her, in fact, with arsenic, so slowly that no one – not the cops, not her family, not the strawberry blonde switchboard girl he planned to marry after his wife was safely out of the picture – would ever suspect a thing. The arsenic had been filtered out from a commercial poison, and mixed in small doses into vanilla milkshakes – his wife's favourite treat – so that she wouldn't notice the taste. As her health failed and she entered the hospital to be puzzled over by confused doctors, faithful hubby Rene kept on bringing in her daily dose of vanilla-covered arsenic. By July, she was dead, and Castellani was scott-free. Almost.

Unfortunately for him, a puzzled medical intern at the hospital had ordered some post-mortem tests on Castellani's wife. They came back positive for arsenic. A search of Castellini's home revealed the poison beneath the sink. It looked suspicious. The clincher came from a lab analysis of the dead woman's hair which showed a steady intake of arsenic, with the exception of a one-week period which coincided exactly with the time hubby Rene was atop the BowMac sign selling cars. Castellani was convicted and sentenced to death, later commuted to life in prison. Think about that next time you go out to Toys R Us to pick up a new Barbie.

Murder at the Penthouse

Photo: Joe Denniston/Vancouver Province

The Penthouse strip club, at 1019 Seymour Street, has been making news since its inception. Indeed, it was christened by a headline. Raided on opening night in 1947, owner Joe Philliponi decided to rename the establishment — then called the Eagle Time Athletic Club — after reading the next day's headline: "Police Raid Penthouse." It made for more news fodder for the next 28 years, as celebs like Gary Cooper and Frank Sinatra came to ogle, and the likes of Sammy Davis Jr. came to sing. In 1975, it attracted major headlines when police raided the place and charged virtually the entire Philliponi clan with living off the avails of the working

And the Winner Is ...

What's the most dangerous section of the city? That depends on the felony you're most afraid of. For crime reporting purposes, the City of Vancouver has been broken down into four separate police districts, which makes comparisons quick and easy. Those who are really keen to get a grip on crime can get a complete breakdown of all crimes committed within a five-block radius of their very own house, compiled by researchers at the VPD Information Section (665-3456). The fee is $35/hour, with a two-hour minimum — far less than the cost of a boosted stereo.

District 1
downtown and West End

District 2
north of Broadway, west of Main
including Gastown, Chinatown,
Strathcona, and East Side

District 3
south of Broadway, east of Main
including Mount Pleasant,
Renfrew, Killarney

District 4
west of Main
including Kitsilano,
Shaughnessy, Kerrisdale

girls who came to the club to pick up customers; after that, Vancouver prostitutes would ply their trade in the streets. But the biggest of all headlines about the Penthouse came not for something that happened at the club, but for something that happened next door, at 1033 Seymour, on the night of September 17, 1983: Penthouse patriarch Joe Philliponi was found dead on the carpet of the Penthouse office, a .22-calibre bullet hole through his temple, the door to the office safe wide open. Gambler and small-time hood Scott Forsyth was convicted of the killing. An acquaintance, Sid Morrisoe, got 25 years as an accomplice. And there it would have rested, had not Sid's daughter Tami set out to prove Dad was innocent.

Believing the real culprit was Joe Philliponi's younger brother Ross, she set out to ingratiate herself with the clan. She married a Philliponi relation, Sal Ciancio, and began wearing wires for the RCMP. The investigation went on for years, during which time, according to Tami, she gathered evidence of Ciancio's involvement in a half-dozen killings. RCMP finally pulled her out and put her in a witness protection program. Tami then went public. Her story was widely published, and she was interviewed in disguise for TV. She even had her own website, in which she claimed Ross had his brother killed and framed her daddy for the crime; Ross called her a nutbar. And when the RCMP finally laid charges against Tami's erstwhile husband, they were for minor weapons offenses, not murder. Even these were eventually dropped. Nothing else ever came of Tami's campaign.

AUTO THEFT

The winner is District 3 at 2,742 per year (approx. 7 per day). The runner-up is District 4 at 1,972 per year (approx. 5 per day).

ASSAULT

The winner is District 2 at 1,299 (approx. 4 per day). The runner-up is District 3 at 1,183 (approx. 3 per day).

SEXUAL ASSAULT

The winner is District 2 at 130 per year. The runner-up is District 3 at 120 per year.

B & E's

The winner is District 4 at 4,979 per year (approx. 14 per day). The runner-up is District 3 at 4,028 per year (approx. 11 per day).

ATTEMPTED AND ACTUAL HOMICIDE

The winner is District 2 at 26 per year. The runner-up is District 3 at 9 per year.

The Death of a Shaughnessy Maid

3543 West 25th. It's an address that should be engraved in the city's collective memory, for it was on this little lot near Dunbar Street that one of the most outrageous crimes in the history of Vancouver took place. It was a case of murder and cover-up that would make headlines all the way to London, threaten a government, and demonstrate the degree of corruption possible when those who make laws and those who make vast sums of money all swim together in the same small pool. Fittingly, the case began not in Point Grey, but in another, richer neighbourhood: Shaughnessy.

Just before noon on the 26th of July, 1924, houseboy Wong Foon Sing was peeling potatoes when he heard a sound like a car backfiring in the lane. Seeing no cars outside, Sing plopped the potatoes back in the bucket and went down into the basement to check on "Nursie," 22-year-old nursemaid Janet Smith. He found her lying on the floor, a .45-calibre service revolver by her hand, and a great gaping hole in the back of her head. She was very, very dead. Sing ran up the stairs to call his employer. And that was the last honest action by anyone associated with the case.

Sing's employer was a 38-year-old society type named Frederick Lefevre Baker. Though not especially wealthy in his own right, Baker had all the right connections. His older brother had married the daughter of General Alexander McRae, the lumber baron who built Hycroft. His own best friend was Jack Nichol, son of Walter C. Nichol, former publisher of the Province newspaper and then B.C. lieutenant-governor. Thus it was that when Baker called the police, a constable was sent out with dispatch.

Within minutes of examining the scene, the policeman had managed to smear any and all fingerprints that might have been on the weapon. More evidence was destroyed when Smith's body was sent not to the morgue to be autopsied — as was the procedure — but straight to the mortuary for embalming. By the time the coroner had retrieved the body, the evidence was hopelessly muddled. He did note the complete absence of any powder burns on her hands or face, which normally would have resulted from having fired such a weapon. Despite this, however, the verdict of the coroner's court was accidental death: lacking anything to do on a Saturday morning, Smith had gone into the attic, retrieved her employer's old service revolver, taken it down into the basement, and either from depression or stupidity, pointed it at her head and pulled the trigger.

And there the matter lay. Certainly the authorities weren't anxious to explore the murder. But in the close-knit world of Shaughnessy nursemaids, rumours began to circulate of a wild party at the house at 3851 Osler on the eve of Janet's death. Nichol was said to have been there. There was speculation that Smith had been raped and then killed. Nursemaids in the area pointed out that as a perpetually happy 22-year-old, engaged to be married to a logger up the coast, Smith was an unlikely candidate for suicide.

One of the nursemaids took her concerns to her

Secret Use for a StarTAC

The StarTAC 3000 has to be among the most popular model of cell phone. Small and light, with a neat flip-top speaker, it looks and feels as if you're yapping on Captain Kirk's communicator. Perhaps that's why so many have sold. Coming back from a big night at the Great Canadian Casino, a pair of Richmond men discovered a new use for the StarTAC. The pair had done well at the tables — a fact which had obviously registered with someone besides the unhappy cashier. At the corner of Bridgeport and No. 3 Roads, the two were ambushed by a gang with two cars and a number of automatic weapons. Bullets slammed into their SUV, passing through the front doors and into the interior. The man in the passenger seat felt something sink into his gut. The driver, unhurt, sped away and managed to lose the assailants. Fearing he was seriously wounded, the passenger looked down at his waist to where his StarTAC, still in its clip, had been neatly dented by a sizable lead slug. Without it, he'd very likely be dead.

BURIED TREASURE IN STANLEY PARK

In 1942, thieves robbed the Bank of Montreal at Prior and Main Streets, escaping with $56,500 in cash. Three years later, police were approached by a woman who said that at least half the money was buried at Brockton Point in Stanley Park. She said her boyfriend had taken her to the hiding place one rainy night; shortly afterwards he was shot to death by persons unknown. In her statement to police, the woman said that the money was "in a clearing in a clump of trees, bordering the cricket pitch at Lower Brockton Point." The police dug for days, but nothing was ever found. Today, the cricket pitch is still there, now mostly occupied by a loitering gang of adolescent geese. Just below the field stands a small clump of cedar trees with what could be a clearing inside. The minimum fine for digging on city property is $500.

minister who, being a Scot like the deceased, mobilized the Scottish lodges to agitate for an inquiry. When a second coroner's inquest was held in early September, the verdict came back murder. The only question was: by whom?

Baker was not thoroughly investigated, even though information from police in London – where Baker had lived for a few years after the Great War – suggested that he had been heavily involved in a drug ring that supplied cocaine and opium to an upper-class clientele. Instead, investigators concentrated on the houseboy. Sing was taken in repeatedly and questioned by police. Each time his story was the same.

Then on March 10, 1935, Sing vanished. Authorities said he had escaped justice by fleeing back to China. Local Chinese associations said he'd been kidnapped – and so it turned out. Seven weeks later on May 1, Sing was found wandering, bruised, and delirious on Southwest Marine Drive. He told a hair-raising story of having been held captive in a house and tortured repeatedly by a group of men who wanted him to confess his crime. Sing had refused.

Incredibly, B.C. Attorney-General Alex Mason then decided to put Sing on trial for Smith's death; not because he really believed Sing had done it, Manson explained to a newspaper reporter, but in the hope of "smoking out the real perpetrators." In a way, it worked. The murderer was not found, but during Sing's trial, evidence emerged that his kidnappers were none other than officers of the Point Grey police department (it was then a separate municipality), and there were strong suggestions they'd been acting on orders from the Attorney-General himself. Questions were raised in the legislature, and for a while it looked as if the government might fall.

As for Sing, he beat the trumped-up charges. So too did the Attorney-General, though only barely. Four Point Grey policemen, including the chief, were put on trial for Sing's abduction, but all escaped conviction. For safety's sake, Sing left the country for China in 1926.

Janet Smith's killers were never found. Indeed, after Sing's trial, there was a determined effort to put the entire affair in the past. Over in Dunbar, the house where Sing had been held was demolished. A new house was built, with an entirely new street number. Some years later, the city even changed the street name, from West 25th to King Edward Avenue. The address of 3543 West 25th was no more.

What is the secret to a healthy urban existence? Following your bliss? Creating community with the ones you love? Connecting on a karmic level with the busy human beings around you while never losing that underlying tie to the wholesome thrum of Mother Earth? Maybe. But for all that you need the self-help section. In *Secrets* "Living" we let you in on the truly important resources no modern urbanite can do without: the place to get your nose, knee, or neck pierced; the deli with the air-freighted French baguettes; the psychic who can psychoanalyze your sick pooch and feel his doggy pain; the people who, for a modest fee, will bring you spuds, bud, booze, and tobacco; and perhaps more critically, the people who, for a slightly less modest amount, will take your kids away and amuse them on a Saturday.

Sorry, No Hooters Here

Long-time residents of the Drive could be forgiven for wondering where they'd spent their lunch hours after the *Utne Reader* article came out lauding the Drive as the hippest street in Canada, famous for its many topless bars. What had Joe's Café been hiding all these years? Turns out the *Reader*, being too cheap to send out a correspondent, had instead called up a local writer of their acquaintance and asked him for his favourite neighbourhood. In relating why he so liked the drive, this local scribe alluded to the Drive's fabulous collection of *tapas* bars. Faster than you could whip off your halter top the Drive was famous. Oh well, it is a pretty cool spot, full of Italian coffee bars, offbeat retail stores, bargain produce markets, and nary a free-range hooter in sight.

Secret Thrill Ride II

The city's ultimate thrill, as everybody knows, is the PNE's decades-old, all-wooden roller coaster, which rattles and creaks and threatens to give way as you swoosh and clatter around the rickety track. For those with a somewhat better developed sense of mortality, there's a somewhat more sedate ride available absolutely free in a tiny urban park located opposite Canada Place at the foot of Hornby Street. Entitled Working Landscape, this thrill ride — or art installation; call it what you will — consists of three large, low wooden disks, each geared to move at a different, celestially determined speed. The six-metre platform rotates weekly; the five-metre platform once a day; and for real daredevils there's the tiny, whirlwind three-metre disk, which rotates once an hour. Should any of these prove too terrifying, there's also an emergency stop button.

Paying For Your Crime

Back in the old days it took some serious wrongdoing to get condemned to a little cell in either Burnaby's Oakalla Prison or the larger B.C. Penitentiary in New Westminster. Nowadays folks pay for the privilege. Not so long ago, both sites were sold off and redeveloped with condos. A bit of the old flavour remains, though: at the B.C. Pen, the warden's old administrative building has been transformed with shops and restaurants, among them the Pen Café and Bistro (101-319 Governor's Court, New Westminster). Feel free to drop in some day for tea and sympathy with the Man. He gets lonely now that the inmates are all gone.

Bump in the Road

Lorraine Irving of the B.C. Genealogical Society delights in taking folks 'round Mountain View Cemetery, showing off such notable graves as Joe Fortes or murdered housekeeper Janet Smith. But the one grave she's never been able to visit is that of the cemetery's first occupant, Simon Hirschberg. A man of large appetites and sizable girth, Hirschberg had the misfortune to kill himself during a spate of rainy weather, just as trees were being cleared off the cemetery grounds. His pallbearers lugged him up the hill, looked at the obstacle course of mud and logs ahead, and quite sensibly gave up, choosing instead to bury him where he then lay – underneath Fraser Street, near the corner of 33rd. Substantial road work has taken place in the years since, but no one's ever come across Hirschberg; neither is there evidence of his ever having been moved.

Microclimates

Don't like the weather? Move a few blocks. Thanks to the profound weather influence of mountains, rivers, and ocean, the Lower Mainland is blessed with no less than 12 distinct microclimates. On one February morning at 7 am, Environment Canada recorded sunshine in White Rock, hail in New Westminster, rain in North Vancouver, overcast skies in West Vancouver, and snow at both Simon Fraser University and UBC. A postal worker's dream, and a weatherman's nightmare, or vice versa. On the bright side, it does allow Vancouver to carry on with our ongoing weather conspiracy, whereby we send continuous reports of rain back to gullible easterners, thus discouraging them from moving here.

Video Rentals

Applause Video

On top of a wide offering of new and old releases, they have a large foreign video section.
2595 Commercial Dr., 874-3133.

Black Dog Video

Film buffs will find Vancouver's best selection of "B" films, like *The Creature from the Black Lagoon* and Blaxploitation flicks such as *Blackula*.
3451 Cambie St., 873-6958

Cinephile

Specializes in avant garde films from all over the world. Knowledgeable staff make finding the right movie a breeze.
4340 Main St., 876-3456

Photo: Robert Ballantyne

Celluloid Drugstore

Video shop runs exactly like a pharmacy, only the medicine prescribed is film. Just tell Simon, or one of the other highly qualified video pharmacists, what ails you and they'll prescribe just the thing to buck you up. Need a good cry? Simon suggests *Ponette*, a French drama about a young girl whose mother dies. Exhausted? Simon suggests *Miller's Crossing* — guranteed to hold your interest without further wearing you down. Feeling a millennial angst over the decline of American world dominance? Simon says watch the entire *Rambo* oeuvre, then practice Sly Stallone poses before a mirror. And if the pharmacy is out of the video drug you crave, they will try to track it down for you. *1470 Commercial Dr., 251-3305*

Limelight Video

A popular spot with the UBC film school crowd, this little strip mall shop carries a great selection of independent and foreign films. *4-3701 W. Broadway, 228-1478*

Videomatica

Vancouver's largest specialty video store. Carries a wide selection of mostly foreign and classic films. Reserve your flick on the web and get a dollar discount. *1855 W. 4th Ave., 734-0411, www.videomatica.bc.ca*

Photo: Blaine Kyllo

Wildlife in the City

The cycles of nature are a wonder to behold, even in the heart of a big city like Vancouver. Indeed, it's in a large urban metropolis where man has eliminated so much of the natural primary productivity in favour of streets and homes and shopping malls that Nature gets especially inventive. Witness the scene at Kitsilano Beach on a summer Saturday: tourist drops French fry, which gets picked up by seagull, which gets picked off by one of the bald eagles nesting in the little park at the foot of Macdonald Street. The eagles quite thoughtfully leave the remnants — wings, feathers, beak — on the grass, thus providing outside work for city employees.

Even more fascinating is the case of the wild coyotes. According to biologist Kristine Lampa of the Stanley Park Ecological Society, some 200 of these 25-pound canines now make their home in the city, with another 2,000 spread around the Lower Mainland. The ones in Vancouver make their homes mostly in Pacific Spirit Park, in the Fraser lands, and in larger city greeneries such as Queen Elizabeth Park. For the most part, they have no affect on the human city dwellers, but occasionally, when little Fluffy or FooFoo the house cat gets sick of its kibble and sets out to hunt for songbirds, the natural cycle kicks in again. Far from chowing down on Tweetie Bird, little Fluffy ends up as coyote chow, prompting outraged owners to write long and self-righteous letters to the editor, making the newspaper much fatter and therefore — once they reach the dumpster or landfill — far better habitat for the coyote's habitual prey of mice, shrews, voles, and rats.

Wise Talk

Remember those bulky scientific calculators with the red LED screens? An indispensable weapon in the arsenal of any late-'70s Grade 8 pupil, they were the creation of Cecil Green, a UBC grad and the man behind Texas Instruments. Some of the millions Green raked in from those chunky adding machines went to found Green College, an elegant, integrated, campus-like place amid UBC's otherwise un-campus-like sprawl. By charter an interdisciplinary kind of place, Green College requires all its resident scholars to give one lecture per term, open to other members of the college and to the public at large; these are given in the college's elegant coachhouse. *822-8660*

Now If Only They Had Dessert

Photo: Mandelbrot

The best free meal in the city is on offer every spring in Punjabi Market. And it just so happens to come with entertainment. The yearly Baisakhi (or Vaisakhi) parade marks the anniversary of the day in 1699 when Sikh guru Gobind Singh baptized five followers and asked them to wear the five token symbols of Sikhism. But though ostensibly a religious procession, Baisakhi is really much more of a party. There are flower-covered floats, dancers, drummers, and countless numbers of families and businesses handing out free samosas, fruit, and *chai* (hot spiced Indian tea). Thanks to ongoing religious differences within the Lower Mainland Sikh community, there are now two Baisakhi parades to choose from. The Vancouver parade centres on Punjabi Market, but begins and ends at the more moderate Ross Street Temple. The fundamentalist Sikh faction centres on the Surrey Temple. For extra fun, watch B.C. politicians such as Ujjal Dosanjh and Gordon Campbell make a speech in Vancouver, then scurry out to Surrey to give the exact same speech all over again.

Whose Saree Now?

The trick to shopping in Punjabi Market, centred around southern Main Street, is persistence. Goods on offer include everything from $5 bracelets and other baubles to embroidered silk saree fabrics selling for upwards of $299 per saree-length (six yards). But as nearly everything arrives in shipments from Asia, the best bargains come when you've timed your shopping to coincide with a big container. Among the shops to try are Bombay Bazaar (6636 Main St., 327-1261), Guru Bazaar (6529 Main St., 327-4422), Chiffons Boutique (6655 Main St., 323-2394), and Memsaab Design (6647 Main St., 322-0259). And if the sarees aren't to taste, at least the samosas are always in fashion.

Time Savers

Short on time? Here are a few places that will save you time by delivering products or services to your home:

Dairyland Home Service
Delivers milk, eggs, cheese, juice, and other staple items.
6800 Lougheed Hwy., Burnaby, 421-4663

Churchill's Fine Cigars
Will deliver premium hand-rolled cigars to your door.
1062 Mainland St., 66-CIGAR

Dial-A-Bottle
Open until 10:30 pm. *688-0348*

Fresh Egg Mart
Delivers eggs only.
269 E. Georgia St., 685-1925

**Small Potatoes
Urban Delivery**
Delivers all-natural and organic goods, including groceries, produce, pet foods, and toiletries.
569 Powell St., 728-7783

Urban Organics
Delivers a box of organic produce and dry goods designed to last 1-2 weeks.
1395 Odlum St., 255-2004, www.urbanorganics.com

Good Cleaning Fun

Vicious Cycle Laundro & Leisurama

This licensed café allows you to do your laundry and socialize at the same time. You can also surf the net for $7 an hour. *2062 Commercial Dr., 255-7629*

Metropolitan Laundry and Suntanning

Get clean clothes and a tan in one stop. *1725 Robson St., 689-9598*

Photo: Mandelbrot

Walking in Chinatown

Photo: Robert Ballantyne

It was touch being Chinese in turn-of-the-century Vancouver. Newcomers had to fight to maintain some sense of tradition, at the same time making their way in a strange new land. The Chinese Freemason's Building at 1 West Pender Street neatly exemplifies these conflicting pressures. On the Carrall Street side, the building's façade is the picture of Edwardian conformity, while on the Pender Street side, the three-storey structure is exuberantly Chinese.

For those interested in these and other curiousities, the Chinese Cultural Centre offers a 90-minute guided walking tour of Vancouver's Chinatown, one of the largest in North America. Guides point out heritage buildings and landmarks, such as the "narrowest" building in the world and other architectural oddities. One can also participate in a guided tour of the Chinese Cultural Centre Museum and Archives, which uses artifacts and images to explore the history of the Chinese community in British Columbia from the Gold Rush to the present. In addition, take in the 45-minute slide show presentation "Legacy of the Dragon" and learn about the building of Chinatown (a great way to rest your feet after the walking tour). And since you will know doubt be starving after all of this, why not join in a tasty Chinese meal at a local Chinatown restaurant for only $10, including taxes and gratuities. In fact, all of the above events are moderately priced and combo packages are available. Call 687-7993 to book. There must be 10 people per tour, so the more the merrier!

The First Cut is the Cheapest

Hairstyling students at Vancouver Community College provide trims, cuts, colouring, and perms, all for about half the price of a full-service salon. Downtown campus, *250 W. Pender St., 443-8332*

kids' birthday places

Here are a few places to take the rugrats on their birthdays:

Burnaby Village Museum

A tad old-fashioned, but that's the appeal. Birthday party packages include hot dogs, drinks, treat bags, a tour guide dressed in period duds, and a ride or three on the vintage carousel.
6501 Deer Lake Ave., 293-6500

Greater Vancouver Zoo

Reserve a private train for a guided tour of the zoo. Admission starts at $10.50 for adults, $7.50 for kids. Peanuts extra.
5048 264th Street, Aldergrove, 856-6825

Kids Only Market

Many options, from puppets to magic to clowns.
Granville Island, 689-8447

Midnite Fairy Parties

Only for the seriously girly, the Midnite Fairy Party offers six guests (or more) an hour and a half with a storyteller inside an elaborate fairy castle. Guests are provided with appropriate costumes. Not available in the West End.
Port Moody, 989-1909; Maple Ridge, 463-3773

Playdium

The ultimate Power Play package includes 45-minute use of a private room and biddable Play Master (only tasks allowed are the fetching of hot dogs, pizza, and bottomless cups of pop), and time on all the fancy toys. Cost is from $17 per person for one hour of play up to $26 for two hours.
5E-4700 Kingsway, Metrotown, 433-7529

Whistler's for Kids

Visiting Whistler for some much-needed R&R? Send the kids off to day camp, where they can swim, canoe, sail or participate in field trips, theatre, arts & crafts, and games.

Resort Municipality of Whistler
604/938-3133

Tamwood International Camps
604/938-9843

Whistler Kids Windsurfing
604/932-3898

Whistler Summer KIDS
1-800-766-0449

Young Heart Tours
604/932-8815

WET KIDS AT PLAY

Water play parks are a fabulous invention, allowing kids to get soaked to their hearts' content, without the slightest danger of drowning (scraped knees are common, but rarely life-threatening). Two of the cities best-known water parks are at Kits Beach and Stanley Park. Slightly more secretive are the parks at Granville Island, located conveniently within eyesight of the outdoor patio at what used to be Isadora's and is now the Cat's Meow Restaurant, and Grandview Park, off Commercial Drive. Least-frequented and most secret of all, however, is the play park at Chaldecott Park, way off at 25th and Wallace.

Science World

A $190 deluxe package includes admission for eight children and eight adults, 90 minutes of free roaming time, 45 minutes in a private party room, food and drinks for all the munchkins, eight goodie bags, and a t-shirt for the birthday kid. *1455 Quebec St., 443-7505*

Watermania

Two water slides, a wave pool, a hot tub, and limitless opportunity to make endless amounts of noise. *14300 Entertainment Way, 448-5353*

kidding around

Here are some events and places around town where your little 'uns can find other little 'uns (and probably have a lot of fun, too).

Lynn Canyon Ecology Centre

Set in a 600-acre park amid stands of 100-year-old Douglas Firs, the Centre features displays, films, and guided walks, many with a kid-friendly emphasis. *3663 Park Rd., North Vancouver, 981-3103*

Pacific Space Centre

The Pacific Space Centre, located above the Vancouver Museum in Vanier Park, has interactive displays that allow kids and adults to explore the solar system, while virtual simulators take them on a trip to Mars. Once the kids have gotten excited about the concept of space, the Gordon M. Southam Observatory, just next to the Vancouver Museum, offers kids and adults the chance to see the real thing for free. *1100 Chestnut St., 738-7827*

Science World

Hands-on science is the speciality of this touch-and-play museum, in the silver geodesic dome on the shores of False Creek. Exhibits change regularly, so there's always something new to see, and there are plenty of enthusiastic volunteers to demonstrate and explain the intricacies of science in a fun and kid-friendly way. *1455 Quebec St., 268-6363*

secrets of the sea

A few things you didn't know about the Vancouver Aquarium:

Buy a Fish, Save a Rainforest

Feeling beset by a bout of eco-guilt? Buy an ornamental fish from the Vancouver Aquarium. They're just as pretty as the ones at pet stores, and because the aquarium is part of Project Piaba – a program that helps maintain a sustainable ornamental fish industry in Brazil – at least some of the cash will travel back south to Brazil.

Animal Adventures

Photo: Ross Demofter

Looking to lose your kids for the day? Take them on an Animal Adventure at the Aquarium's Marine Science Centre. Cost is a whopping $150 per child, but the fee includes admission to the aquarium, presentations with the Adventure Team, time with Marine Mammal staff as they prepare for the Adventure, and hands-on interaction with beluga whales. For the especially energetic child, tours of the shark tank and piranha pool are also available. Tours are offered every day but reservations and legal waivers are required.
659-3550 or 1-800-931-1186

Aquanauts and Young Biologists Club

Kids who like goo, ick, and squishy, squirting smelly forms of life can get involved with the aquarium on a regular basis. Children aged six to nine can join the Aquanauts, exploring the wonders of the natural aquatic world while getting gross and grubby taking part in a hands-on science club.
659-3550 or 1-800-931-1186

Picnic Pleasures

We asked some of Vancouver's best picnic suppliers about where they like to picnic, and almost all of them responded (we think someone at Capers needs a vacation):

Ecco il Panne
238 W. 5th Ave., 873-6888
2563 W. Broadway, 739-1314
Will put together a basket of top notch panini, rustic tarts, cookies, and desserts.

Favourite Spot:
1. Lighthouse Park
2. English Bay
3. Whytecliff Park

Meinhardt's Fine Foods
3002 Granville St., 732-4405
Order a customized picnic, $20 and up for two, or select items from the deli counter, pastry section and store. Sandwiches, salads, quiches, roti, chicken, Cornish game hen, roasts, cheeses.

Favourite Spot:
1. One hour up the 18-km. trail from Cypress Park parking lot there is a spot with a great view of the city
2. Jericho Beach
3. Spanish Banks

Lesley Stowe Fine Foods

1780 W. 3rd Ave., 731-3663
High-end, ready-to-roll picnic packages, $18 to $25 per person, or select items from the deli counter, the reach-in cooler with dips and snacks, the cheese cooler, the olive bar, and the bakery counter.

Favourite Spot:

1. Iona Island Park for watching big planes land and take off over the ocean
2. The foot of Angus Dr. below SW Marine, where there is a view out over the Fraser
3. Under the Arthur Laing Bridge

Tony's Neighbourhood Deli and Café

1047 Commercial Dr., 253-7422
Changing roster of panini made with crusty bread, grilled to crunchy perfection.

Favourite Spot:

1. Scenic Park in Burnaby (Capitol Hill): great view of oil refineries, Burrard Inlet, and Indian Arm
2. The switchback trails on the way to Lynn Valley
3. McDonald Beach Park on North Dyke Road on Sea Island

Capers

2285 W. 4th Ave., 739-6676
1675 Robson St., 687-5288
2486 Marine Dr., North Vancouver, 925-3316
Store and deli takeout. All kinds of breads, cheeses, fruits, baked goods.

Favourite Spot:

Too busy ever to leave Kitsilano

Vancouver is blessed (or cursed, depending on your point of view) with both a culture of dog-ownership (one in four Vancouver families owns a dog) and a population top-heavy with baby boomers.

MISCELLANEOUS
Dog Play

An Internet clearing house for all that is out there "lifestyle-wise," including Animal-Assisted Therapy, Dog Camps, Education, Earthdog Trials, Eventing, Flygility, Flyball, Flying Disc, Backpacking, Performance Art, Pet Facilitated Therapy, Skijoring, Socializing and Off-leash Play, and Weight Pulling. *www.dog-play.com*

FIDO

The Federation of Individuals and Dog Organizations helps reunite lost dogs with owners, organizes dog visits to nursing homes (animal-assisted therapy), trains dogs for people with disabilities (Pacific assistance dogs), and best of all, provides a dog info line that you can call with any and all questions about dogs. *681-1929*

Pet Psychic

Elaine Thompson will come to your house and give your pet a reading for the cost of gas and $1.50 a minute (usually takes only 10 to 15 minutes). She uses her telepathic skills to communicate with your pet and locate what ails them. Often, the reading points to a generalized biological area (like the stomach or chest), which can be explored further by a veterinarian. According to Thompson, this has worked so many times that veterinarians from all over Vancouver refer clients to her. *739-4854*

PET CAMPS
Camp Good Dog and Cat

Run by a qualified pet therapist and trainer, this camp provides fun physical work-outs and – for a small added fee – training and behaviour therapy. *515-CAMP; www.campgoodcat.com*

Camp Ruffin' It

Provides weekend adventures for people with their dogs. Located just north of Boston Bar in the heart of the Fraser Canyon, the 1,200-acre camp offers activities like the Tails of Steel work-out, a 5K Iron Dog competition, Flyball Workshops, a Nature Stroll & Tea, and workshops on obedience, dog sports, and canine craft-making. (Look, Fido made a little pottery dog dish, how sweet.) *www.campruffinit.bc.ca*

TRAINING
A+ Pooch

Offers Puppy Kindergarten for dogs under six months old. Consists of one-hour weekly group workshops that will provide the basics for a well-trained pet. *441 W. 6th Ave., 875-8585*

Hollywood North Canine Training and Talent Agency

Think your dog's got the right stuff for film or television? Why not sign it up for one of three levels of acting classes? The focus is on developing talent and then ensuring that the animals receive fair treatment once they're working. *571-916 W. Broadway, 738-1568*

Paws Ahead K-9 Sports Centre

For the dog that could use a little shaping up, or the show dog that needs to maintain its fine physique, the K-9 Sports Centre offers six-week programs that will get your dog running and jumping in a structured and knowledgeable setting. Classes are held in a large indoor warehouse space, and include obstacle courses and games which promote agility and mental fitness as well as physical fitness. *4025 E. 2nd Ave., Burnaby, 298-3647*

PET REMEMBRANCE

Special Friends Pet Cremation Service understands how special pets can be to their owners, so for approximately $275, they'll pick up your deceased pooch, cremate it respectfully, and return the ashes in a tasteful urn. Those looking for cheaper sentiment can drop off the ex-pet personally and get it back in-urned for only $185. *165 Riverside Dr., North Vancouver, 929-3491*

Photo: Blaine Kyllo

DOGGIE DELIGHTS

Chef Canine's School of Dog Cuisine

Three-part course taught by North Vancouver's Moneca Litton teaches students how to make 1. nutritious dog food; 2. tasty dog treats; and 3. birthday cakes and goodies for other canine occasions. Take all three and get a certificate. Then check yourself in for counselling. *985-7533*

The Dog's Kitchen

Johnny Tom started out in the wholesale produce business, which gave him all the ingredients he needed to fix up vegetarian chow for his own dog. Soon enough his friends started asking him to make them some. So he started the Dog's Kitchen, which will home-deliver dog food made according to his popular vegetarian recipes. *3345 Valley Dr., 738-3647*

Pet Food Supermarket

Around for over 25 years, it carries a wide selection of oganic pet foods. Also has toys and organic health products. 2949 Main St., 873-4117

Three Dog Bakery

Specializes in all-natural treats, like cookies, birthday cakes, and bon bons, that are low in fat and made without salt or preservatives. Also, check out the free brunch held every Sunday at 11 am - 4 pm, where your dog can sample items from the *The Three Dog Bakery Cookbook*. *2186 W. 4th Ave., 737-3647*

Woofles Doggie Deli

This little store creates their own 100% organic dog food that is so good, according to the owner, that humans could eat it. It will create custom order platters for doggie parties and doggie weddings (it happens!), as well as cookie jars that make great gifts at doggie birthday parties. It also sells one-of-a-kind items for your dog, such as sterling silver, 14 and 18-karat gold, diamond, and pearl jewellery. Gold items with diamonds start at $1,600 and gold with pearls start at $1,000. Its clientele includes big players in the movie industry and foreign dignitaries, plus that all-time ideal demographic, the rube with too much loot. *1496 Cartwright St., Granville Island, 689-3647*

A SPIRITUAL LABYRINTH

Every weekday morning, an eclectic assemblage of people can be seen tracing their way through the circles of a maze – or mandala – drawn on the floor of the hall at St. Paul's Anglican Church on 1130 Jervis Street. Newcomers are welcome, and indeed as a mere bystander you may take a look at the maze and say to yourself, "That's dead easy! I can do that." The trick, of course, is that the maze is a metaphor for a spiritual journey, and as you navigate the pathways you're supposed also to be finding inner peace. Which makes it a bit tougher.

piercing secrets

So you want to do the urban-tribal/marching-to-the-beat-of-a-different-drum thing and have a bit of metal inserted into your body? A professional piercing parlour is the place to go. Here's roughly what you can expect to pay:

First on Granville
1149 Granville St., 682-3937
Nipple: $45
Nose/face: $38 - $60
Tongue: $67
Genital: $50 - $80
Strangest request: Ankle, behind the archilles tendon

Insamsara Body Designs
848 Granville St., 681-8732
Nipple: $50 - $55
Nose/face: $44
Tongue: $72
Genital: $60 - $70
Strangest request: Pectoral pierce

Mack's Leathers
1043 Granville St., 688-6225
Nipple: $40
Nose/face: $35
Tongue: $57 - $70
Genital: $40 - $45
Strangest request: Back of the neck

Next!
1068 Granville St., 684-6398
Nipple: $72
Nose/face: $65 - $70
Tongue: $85 - $95
Genital: $72 - $150
Strangest request: Uvula

Sacred Heart Tattoo & Body Piercing
3734 W. 10th Ave., 224-1149
Nipple: $55
Nose/face: $33 - $44
Tongue: $72
Genital: $60 - 70
Strangest request: An insert or "pocket" just under the skin of the chest

The Naked Bunch

Wreck Beach, one of the world's most notorious nude beaches adjacent to UBC, is anything but a secret. There are even driftwood concession stands with naked men selling boiled hot dogs. But for those looking for a something perhaps a tad more clandestine, here are four options:

Lost Lake, Whistler
From Whistler Village, walk the valley trail west for about 10 minutes and you'll reach Lost Lake. The beach here is public and not for nudies. Carry on for five more minutes along the trail until you reach a wooden dock. This is the spot. Feel free to bare all and dive in, bearing in mind the water is glacier-cold.

Van Tan Club, Grouse Mountain
This old-fashioned nudist club is located southeast of Grouse Mountain on Mount Fromme. Head straight up Mountain Highway to the locked gate. Walk just past the gate until you see the sign. Beware of the dog (his name is Rex). Non-members can visit during periodic open houses. Volleyball, pool, sauna, and a terrific view. *980-2400*

high societies

There are societies and associations aplenty in Vancouver. What we find most curious and intriguing about these groups is their very existence: no matter how esoteric the interest, it seems, there are enough people out there who share it to warrant banding together formally. Here is a smattering of some of Vancouver's common-interest groups:

Clan Hay Society

Formed in 1951 by the Countess of Erroll, 31st Chief, for the promotion of this ancient clan throughout the world. Eligible to join are those bearing the names of Hay, MacGaraidh, De la Haye, Hayes, McGara, Erroll, Gifford, Leith, Beagrie, or descent from or marriage to one of these. 32nd Chief (present): Earl of Erroll, Lord Hay and Slains. Members are encouraged to attend the annual B.C. Highland Games where there is a Hay "tent." *2025 W. 5th Ave., 733-0796; www:dchdesign.com/CLAN_HAY/index.html*

Esperanto Society Of Vancouver

Broken English spoken. Meetings are held monthly. *704-1255 Main St., 331-1442*

Fools Society

Here's one whose potential membership seems unlimited. The Fools Society. Founded in Vancouver in 1980, it's actually a charitable, non-profit organization dedicated to promoting the art of clowning. The society offers public workshops, performances, and annual celebrations such as The Mad Hatter's Tea Party and the Fools' Day Parade. Membership is open to anyone with a sense of humour. *253-3207*

No Kidding!

Social group for couples and singles without progeny. Three to six social functions per month, lollipop free. *538-7736; www.nokidding.bc.ca*

Sexaholics Anonymous

A program of recovery for men and women who want to stop their sexually self-destructive thinking and behaviour. *875-6381 or 290-9643*

Brunswick Beach, Howe Sound

About three kilometres beyond Lion's Bay is the Brunswick Beach Turnoff (a sharp left turn from highway 99). Head to the water and take the trail to the beach. Watch for homeowners peeking from nearby windows, and the teenaged sons of boat owners swinging in close for a gander. Would-be nudists are advised to respect local residents and keep to the most secluded areas.

Pacific Canadian Association of Nudists

Social nudist club for gay and bisexual men of legal age. Monthly naked social events. Not a sex club.

www.p-can.org

Society for Creative Anachronism

Dungeons and Dragons for adults. Members believe in researching and recreating all aspects of the Middle Ages, from the music, heraldry, and hierarchy to needlework and jousting. That's the theory. In practice, being a Creative Anachronist means going out to a park dressed in padded armor and whacking the bejeezus out of another guy with a blunt wooden broadsword. If that's your cup of mead, call for details.
988-0304

Vancouver Japanese Sword Appreciation Society

For those who couldn't get enough of *Shōgun*: an organization of people interested in Japanese samurai swords, armor, art, and history. Meetings are held in the boardroom of the Vancouver Museum.
1100 Chestnut St., 943-7171

Vancouver Mycological Society

For people interested in mushrooms. Meetings are held on the first Tuesday of most months at 7:30 pm at the VanDusen Gardens classroom.
Oak & 37th Ave.; Mushroom Hotline: 878-9878

Vancouver Whisky Exchange (Guild)

"Objects of the Guild are to provide for the exchange among members of trade information concerning whisky held under seal of Her Majesty's customs and excise control in Britain, and to co-operate with the Happy Day Foundation in providing assistance to senior citizens in need of help, who are referred by other groups who, by their charter, are restricted from helping." Okay ...
307 Larchway Gardens, 2475 W. Broadway, 733-1584

Vancouver Chinese Motorsport Club

Meetings are on the first Tuesday of each month.
734-7656

Country Clubs

The Arbutus Club
2001 Nanton St. 266-7166
Facilities: Swimming, skating, tennis, squash, and racquetball
Entrance Fees/Dues: $22,000

Royal Vancouver Yacht Club
3811 Point Grey Rd., 224-1244
Facilities: Clubhouses at Jericho, Stanley Park, and seven stations on the coast
Membership: Sponsorship from four active members
Entrance Fees/Dues: $24,600 plus $60 monthly

Terminal City Club
837 W. Hastings, 681-4121
Facilities: Oldest club in town (est.1899) has dining and meeting rooms, claims a clientele of movers and shakers
Membership: Must be sponsored by two current members
Entrance Fees/Dues: $10,000 plus $135 monthly, yearly dues for those under 36 years of age are $5,000

café societies

People have traditionally gathered in cafés; perhaps it's the quest for java that gets people together in the first place. Whatever the reason, here are some funky places to meet while ordering your daily caffeine fix:

Café Deux Soleil

This Commercial Drive fixture is vegetarian and very kid-friendly. The stage doubles as a kids' play area during the day. That makes it a bad choice if you're looking either for bacon or peace and quiet, but a great spot for baked goods and an ever-changing menu of high quality veggie-stuff. Staff usually sport numerous facial piercings, which add to the visual interest. *2096 Commercial Dr., 254-1195*

Capers

The combination of nearby Duthie Books and the café portion of the organic supermarket Capers, with a open courtyard between, has proved to be a powerful force in Kitsilano. Residents have been known to spend entire days there, sipping organic Sumatra blend coffee, and munching chocolate oat bars and sandwiches made with crusty Tuscan bread. The crowd is the usual Kits combination of aging activists, BMW-driving yuppies, and mothers with kids in $400 strollers. Coffee's great. *2285 W. 4th Ave., 739-6676*

Delany's

In the last few years, Delany's has become a mecca for the West End's gay community to gather (and man-watch) before and after an evening's stroll along the seawall. On warm summer nights, the crowds trickle onto the sidewalk. *1105 Denman St., 662-3344*

The Grind & Gallery Coffee Bar

Always open, usually full, the Grind is ideal for those armed with books, a need to study, and money for only one cup of coffee. If you happen to arrive without a book, pick up a few mags and newspapers from the

---

University Women's Club

1489 McRae, 731-4661

Facilities: Clubhouse, library, meeting rooms, interest groups, ongoing events

Membership: Women who hold university degrees

Entrance Fees/Dues: $175 plus $370 annually

Vancouver Club

915 W. Hastings St., 685-9321

Facilities: Dining room, billiards room, meeting facilities

Membership: A nominator, seconder, three references

Entrance Fees/Dues: $5,000 plus $3,000 annually

Shaughnessy Golf and Country Club

4300 SW Marine Dr., 266-4141

Facilities: Golf course; building a fitness centre

Membership: Must be sponsored, with five references

Entrance Fees/Dues: $42,500 plus $235 monthly

well-stocked free reading rack, then spread them out over an available tabletop and tell anyone who asks you're in media studies. If they look doubtful, toss out a Chomsky and an institutional bias or two, then sit back and analyze your biscotti. *4124 Main St., 874-1588*

Joe's

A Commercial Drive institution. Decor is church basement basic – think aluminum chairs and bright fluorescent lights – but the atmosphere is strictly Joe's. Likely the only place in the city where you'd see alternative theatre types squeezed in with Latin-American immigrants to watch a heavyweight fight on the counter-top TV. And definitely the only place where the owner will tell you to keep your order to yourself while he watches the last two rounds. But when they're done, ask him about his 10-year bull-fighting career in Portugal. He'll tell you about his adventures, including the gore to his lower abdomen that netted him 47 stitches and 3 months in the hospital, but didn't stop him from bullfighting. The coffee, when you get it, is superb. *1150 Commercial Dr., 255-1046*

Seattle's Best Coffee Company

The place where the tech-heads in Yaletown juice up for long nights in front of the computer, Seattle's Best is also the place to catch some summer sidewalk culture. Conversations range from the benefits of the latest piece of online software to the newest colour of paint recommended by *Wallpaper**. The newly renovated Yaletown location now has a sister location in the South Granville strip. *1137 Hamilton St., 685-6511; 2706 Granville St., 734-2706*

Spiritual Quests

People are always searching for something.... Need some advice about what to search for? Here are some ideas:

Witches
Becoming as common as firewood, the B.C. Witch Camp *(P.O. Box 21510, 1850 Commercial Dr.)* teaches and practices wicca; the witch camp itself, usually held near Chilliwack, is held in July (training by Starhawk). Also of note are the Coffee Cauldrons on the third Saturday of every month at La Quena Coffee House on Commercial Drive, and the Witch Camp event line *(253-7195)* with information on the yearly festivals of Imbolc, Beltaine, Lammas, and Samhaine.

Photo: Blaine Kyllo

The Whip Gallery & Café

The Whip is the one place in the city where the wall art and the clientele match. The folks sipping and munching look like they could have produced the art hanging on the walls (and probably did). Young and angry isn't the look here; Whip customers have some success under their belts and are mellowing into their 40s and 50s. Food is above average, beer is excellent, and the coffee, well, it's there.
209 E. 6th Ave., 874-4687

looking for god in 7 strange places

In a city where the mother tongue of more than half the residents is something other than English, the most unusual place of worship might actually be the United Church of Canada, but that would be too dull. The places of worship in this list all have some unique feature other than their non-WASPishness that makes them worth a visit:

Basel Hakka Lutheran Church

The only church in Canada providing services in Hakka, a minority language of the Chinese mainland.
823 Jackson Ave., 255-5988

Ching Chung Taoist Church

A peaceful enclave in a difficult part of the city, this church, located on the second and third floors of a building at 233 Keefer Street, offers quiet meditative surroundings and free literature on Taoism. The Bioshi Rey Tsaang Temple, three blocks away at 514 Keefer, offers free vegetarian food at noon on Sundays.
681-6116

Chaotic Goddess Productions Weekly Women's Gathering

"Get in touch with your goddess self!" These gatherings offer intuitive games, drumming, goddess image and face painting, tribal chanting, and "experiencing the Sage Expression of all Emotions." *650-7061*

Scientology

We'd like to tell you some of the secrets of this religion, founded by American sci-fi author L. Ron Hubbard, but we're afraid we might get sued. You could always ask John Travolta, or just go down to their Vancouver headquarters *(401 W. Hastings St.)* and say you're looking for your help with your personality.

Kuan Yin Buddhist Temple

This temple's palatial architecture, bonsai garden, and immense white-and-gold statue of the Buddha Sakyamuni has generated so much interest from the public that the Buddhist management now offers guided tours for groups of 15 or more. Others are welcome to stop in and look around for themselves.
9160 Steveston Hwy., 274-2822

St. George's Greek Orthodox Cathedral

So many visitors have arrived over the years to see the lush interior and view the ornate gilt religious artifacts that the church has published a guidebook. Services are in Greek. *4500 Arbutus St., 266-7148*

St. Raphael's Old Catholic Church

The Pope may not approve of this church as it accepts Protestants, and one of old Catholicism's hallmarks is its non-acceptance of the 1870 decree making Popes infallible. Another reason is its cosmopolitanism; the Lord's Prayer is read each Sunday in English, French, German, Italian, Tagalog, Portuguese, Spanish, Sri Lankan, and Latin. Service begins at 11 am.

Shambhala Training Meditation Centre

Wednesday night open houses have introductory classes and meditation instruction at 7:30 pm.
3275 Heather St., 874-8420

Universal Buddhist Temple

This Buddhist temple is worth a look if only for the great eastern dragon fronting the entranceway.
525 E. 49th Ave., 325-6912

Cemetery Tours

Cemeteries. Though most folks are dying to get in, it's also possible to opt out — for a time — on the mortality and simply take a tour. Unlike Victoria, few local boneyards offer a full-on guided tour, but most are happy to have you poke about. Here are a few to try:

Capilano View Cemetery

Capilano View is the resting place of many a local quasi-notable, among them former West Vancouver Mayors John Lawson and Don Lanskil, long-time media celeb Jack Webster, and Thomas Sewell of Sewell Marina fame. Though still alive and kicking, David Suzuki has reserved a plot for himself and his family. Currently no guided tours are on offer, but they are being considered. All things come in time.
1490 W. 3rd St., West Vancouver, 925-7120

Gardens of Gethsemani

No guided tours, but the friendly Monseigneur can point out most of the notables, including the plots belonging to Catholic dignitaries such as Archbishops Johnson, Duke, and Carney.
15800 32nd Ave., Surrey, 531-2141

Ocean View Burial Park and Mausoleum

Those with a claim to fame in Burnaby's best boneyard include Kate Ryan, aka Klondike Kate, one of the first women to rough it through the bush to the Klondike gold fields; Chinese singer/movie star Yam Kim Fai; and Canada's first and only world heavyweight boxing champion (from 1906 to 1908) Tommy Burns.
4000 Imperial St., Burnaby, 435-6688

Valley View Memorial Gardens

Who says the funeral biz is low-tech? Out in Surrey, Valley View has one of Canada's first and nicest fully-interactive crematoriums.
14644 72 Ave., Surrey, 596-7196

Victory Memorial Park Cemetery

Valhalla for Canada's war vets. Call to arrange a tour if you're interested in finding out more.
2977 King George Hwy., 536-2268

Mountain View Cemetery

Lorraine Irving offers guided tours to markers of particular interest, including that of Vancouver's first mayor (Malcolm MacLean), first lifeguard (Joe Fortes), and first bizarrely murdered nanny (Janet Smith).
5455 Fraser St., 325-2646

Given Vancouver's multicultural landscape, it's not surprising that there are ethnic festivals of one sort or another virtually every month of the year.

Baisakhi (Indian New Year)

Held in mid-April, this festival celebrates the birth of Sikhism. There's a parade, complete with floats and marching bands, which wends its way to the temple at 8000 Ross Street. Afterwards there's a free (and very good) vegetarian buffet. Bring your lawn chair.

Caribbean Days

The Trinidad and Tobago Cultural Society sponsors this festival on the last weekend in July. It's a fabulous place to catch some really fine music.

Celtic Festival

The Celtic Festival programs music and dance at various venues throughout the city. And don't forget about the Celtic New Year celebration, Samhain.
434-3747

Chinese New Year

Fifteen days of drumming, dragon dancing, and firecracker-exploding in Chinatown. Because it celebrates the beginning of the new Chinese calendar, the date varies.

Janmastami Festival

This festival – which commemorates the appearance of Lord Krishna – is impossible to mistake. Look for tall, western-looking white girls in orange robes parading along Beach Avenue in the West End in August.

Moon Festival

This festival in August and September honours the moon goddess. The Chinese Cultural Centre at 50 E. Pender St. (687-0729) usually sponsors a concert of traditional Chinese music.

Powell Street Festival

On the first weekend in August, residents and descendants of the former inhabitants of Japantown gather in the old 'hood at Oppenheimer Park on Powell Street. There are displays of crafts and origami, as well as taiko music, martial arts, and kite-flying.
Powell Street Festival Society, 1101 W. Broadway, 739-9388

Attack of the Killer Tomatoes

What should you do if attacked by a man-eating 15-foot killer tomato? Should have watched the movie. For those who haven't there's still time to brush up on your tomato lore at Tomato, Granville Island's annual tomato fair. Held the second weekend in September, Tomato offers home-growers the chance to enter their round red killers in five separate categories: slicing; sauce and paste; specialty; heritage and multi-coloured tomatoes; miniatures; and biggest, roundest, reddest, most Sumo-like. (Contestants are asked to register at 666-6477.) There are also tomato games for kids, and booths where well-known chefs show off tomato recipes. As for the critical tomato self-defence secret, as serious bad-film buffs know, the only thing that'll kill a killer tomato is bad pop music. For the last invasion, a sweet and saccharine tune called "Puberty Love" did the trick, though nowadays, in a pinch, Britney Spears would probably do.

Gone to Seed

Wanna know the best place and time to spread your germs around? On the last Saturday in February at the VanDusen Botanical Gardens (5251 Oak St., 878-9274), when a seriously seedy crowd gathers at the normally well-heeled precincts of Oakridge for Seedy Saturday, the annual seed swap and sale. Aficionados from all over the Lower Mainland bring in all manner and type of seeds, some for sale, many others just for the swapping. Even more enticing than the free germs is the opportunity to spend hours engaged in earnest conversation with the Saltspring Island gardener who may well have the last existing varietal of the rare flowering purple something. Really.

DIY BIKE REPAIRS

PEDAL, Pedal Energy Development Alternatives, is a non-profit organization created to "promote the use of pedal powered technology ... as a form of transportation." This includes operating Our Community Bikes *(197 E. 17th Ave., 879-BIKE)* and The Bike Kitchen *(UBC, NE corner of SUB, 82-SPEED)*, small workshops where they provide the space and the tools so you can fix your own bike. They also offer courses and workshops, and, if you really want to pay someone, will do the repairs for you. *www.pedalpower.org*

Bike Repairs

When your bike is feeling under the weather, take it to one of the following:

A-1 Cycle
3743 Main St., 876-2453

Bike Doctor Bicycle Shop
163 W. Broadway, 873-2453

Bikeway Bicycle Shop
831 Commercial Dr., 254-5408

Cyclepath
1421 W. Broadway, 737-2344

Reckless
1810 Fir St., 731-2420

Urban Cycle
3578 E. Hastings St., 294-2453

gardener's goods

Like to garden with style? Here are a few places where you'll find everything you need to create a garden masterpiece:

Avant Gardener
2235 W. 4th Ave., 736-0404

Dig This Garden Shop
10-1535 Johnston St., Granville Island, 688-2929

Earthrise Garden Store
2954 W. 4th Ave., 736-8404

Art Knapp Figaro's Garden
1896 Victoria Dr., 253-1696

Art Knapp Urban Garden
1401 Hornby St., 662-3303

VanDusen Garden Shop
5251 Oak St., 257-8665

Photo: Blaine Kyllo

Unusual Grocery Stores

Photo: Mandelbrot

Granville Island Public Market

Not exactly a secret, but it is one of Vancouver's most popular public markets, and a major tourist desination. Parking is next to impossible during the summer.
1689 Johnston Street, 666-6655

Lonsdale Quay

This large market offers much the same fare as Granville Island. Easily accessible by Seabus for those who don't live on the North Shore.
123 Carrie Cates Ct., 985-6261

Park Royal Market

A fairly new addition to the Lower Mainland's oldest shopping mall.
2002 Park Royal South, 925-9576

Fujiya Japanese Foods
You'll find everything you need to home-cook delicious Japanese food, as well as great take-out sushi, at a reasonable price.
912 Clark Dr., 251-3711;
100-8211 Westminster Hwy.,
Richmond, 270-3715;
203-403 North Rd., Coquitlam,
931-3713

Galloway's
Specializes in hard-to-find items for cooking and baking, including spices from A to Z, prepared nuts and fruits, specialty flours, and imported jams and crackers. Check out its website to see if it has what you're looking for:
www.gallowaysfoods.com.
702B-6th St., New Westminster,
526-7525; 25H-777 Dunsmuir St.,
Pacific Centre Mall, 669-3036;
904 Davie St., 685-7927

Gourmet Garage

Called a "gourmet food Costco" by some, this grocery store is run by Caren McSherry of Caren's Cooking School and operates on the same principle of bulk buying for better discounts. However, both the quality of service and ambiance is more like a traditional grocery store.
1856 Pandora St., 253-3022

South Seas Trading Company

Located within the Granville Island Market, this is the place to shop for all your South Asian cooking staples such difficult-to-find items like kaffir lime leaves, Thai basil, mangosteens, rambutans, and young ginger. Also, experimenting is easy because items tend to be clearly marked with instructions for use. You'll also find some great bargains. *681-5402*

T & T Supermarket

You'll also find all of your Asian cooking essentials here, and then some. However, the live seafood bins, which can include frogs and turtles, are not for everyone.
181 Keefer Place, 899-8836, and 5 other locations

Robson Public Market

This conveniently located market is popular with West Enders.
1610 Robson St., 682-2733

Photo: Blaine Kyllo

Westminster Quay Public Market

Catch a cool breeze off the Fraser River as you shop.
810 Quayside Ave., New Westminster, 520-3881

Chinatown Night Market

You'll find an exotic selection of imported clothing, knick knacks, fake luxury goods, art, and food items at the Chinatown Market. It is located where Keefer and Pender Street meet, between Main and Gore, and is open throughout the summer from 6 to 11 pm.

designer food markets

Choices

Carries a wide selection of gourmet groceries, both conventional and organic, as well as all-natural vitamins. Also has an espresso bar.

Photo: Blaine Kyllo

627 W.16th Ave., 736-0009; 3493 Cambie St., 875-0099; 1202 Richards St., 633-2392

Lesley Stowe Fine Foods

A great source of take-out desserts and packaged foods such as preserves, oils, coffee, and tea.
1780 W. 3rd Ave., 731-3663

Meinhardt's Fine Foods

Here, the gourmand will find all they need to satisfy their refined palate under one roof.
3002 Granville St., 732-4405

Urban Fare

The spot for yuppies, guppies, and woopies (well-off older people). Located at the foot of Davie Richards

Photo: Blaine Kyllo

Street, this gourmet market flies in $100-plus bread from France every second day; it travels by Concord to New York and is then "Fed-exed" to Vancouver. Also a great source of prepared and packaged meals for those with a tight schedule as well as a sit-down cafeteria-style restaurant. And, rumour has it, it's a great place to meet people.
177 Davie St., 975-7550

Kaplan's Delicatessen & Restaurant
Authentic '40s-style Jewish deli boasts over 265 different items on its menu, including showpiece sandwiches.
5775 Oak St., 263-2625

Max's Bakery & Delicatessen
A cozy and comfortable meeting place that sells comfort food for eat-in or take-out.
3105 Oak St., 733-4838; 521 W. 8th Ave., 873-6297

Photo: Blaine Kyllo

Chocolatiers

Bain's Chocolates & Candy

An expert chocolatier whose shop resides in a heritage house off of Main Street.
151 E. 8th Avenue, 876-5833

Chocolate Arts

Chocolate creations that look so good, you won't want to eat them. But do, because these people make great chocolate.
2037 W. 4th Ave., 739-0475

Daniel Le Chocolat Belge

Chocolate delights with an emphasis on fresh. 1105 Robson St., 688-9624, and 4 other locations

Dutch Girl Chocolates

Dutch treats made from world-famous Belgian chocolate.
1002 Commercial Dr., 251-3221

House of Brussels Chocolates Outlet

A great resource for both chocoholics and chocolate buyers, these people sell seconds and bulk chocolate at anywhere from 10 to 50 percent off.
208-750 Terminal Ave., 687-1524

Purdy's Factory Outlet Store

As the name suggests, you can get bulk discounts here and seconds are only $11 a pound.
2777 Kingsway Ave., 454-2700

bakeries

All India Sweets and Restaurant

Famous for its colourful yogurt-based and coconut desserts, as well as its tasty samosas.
6507 Main St., 327-0891

Angus Bakery and Cafe

Specializes in French-inspired confections and an assortment of nut loaves. 3636 W. Broadway, 733-9955

Broadway Bakery

At this Greek bakery in Kitsilano, Jerry Zorbinos serves up great bread at prices that definately rival his competitors. His large round wholewheat karavele is only a dollar, the substantial flax bread is $1.45, and his sesame seed buns are between $1.50 and $1.80 a dozen, depending on the size.
3273 W. Broadway, 733-1422

Calabria Bakery

A great place to go for fresh biscotti and ondi.
5036 Victoria Dr., 324-1337

Ecco Il Pane Bakery & Bistro

Afficionados of bread, particularly Tuscan and Casa. Also, bistro serves daily specials that are sure to please.
2563 W. Broadway, 739-1314 and
238 W. 5th Ave., 873-6888

I Love Bagels

This family-run open-style kitchen serves 15 varieties of hand-rolled bagels, smoked meat, and Matzo boards.
105 East 12th St., North Vancouver, 986-3578

Jock Bakery

A great Scottish bakery! Makes bonny bridies, pasties, Aberdeen rowies, and burr.
8289 Oak St., 263-0563

La Vienne European Bakery

Specializing in European-style cakes and pastries, including fruit danishes and a to-die-for Viennese chocolate-coffee cake.
116 Davie St., 669-6658; 101 Robson St., 647-1112

Liberty Bakery

A little out-of-the-way on Main Street, but worth seeking out. *3699 Main St., 709-9999*

New Town Bakery and Restaurant

A Chinatown gathering spot where locals and tourists can enjoy steamed buns and other Chinese baked delicacies. *158 E. Pender St., 689-7835*

Serano Greek Pastry

Serves up authentic spanikopita and baklava so good it'll knock you off your diet. *3185 W. Broadway, 739-3181*

Siegel's Bagels

These award-winning bagels can be found in your local grocery store, but to get the Tuesday half-price special, you'll have to visit one of their stores. *1883 Cornwall Ave., 737-8151; 5671 No. 3 Rd., Richmond, 821-0151; 1689 Johnston St., Granville Island, 685-5670*

Solly's

You can get more than just bagels at this traditional family owned and operated bakery. Created in the style of eastern neighbourhood bakeries, the authentic Solly's specializes in Jewish baked goods including babka, blintzes, knishes, and rugoleh. They also have cinnamon buns, unique pastries, and much more.
*189 E. 28th Ave., 872-1821;
2873 W. Broadway, 738-2121*

Butchers

Auld Scottish Larder
Vancouver's best known source of authentic Scottish meat items.
4022 Hastings St., 294-6616

Caffe Moka
Wanting to taste some exotic game meat? Talk to Rena or Augusto at this bistro, and get some pheasant, buffalo, cariboo, or even muskox, for your next dinner party.
350 Nanaimo St., 255-3330

Calabrian Meat Market
Carries a great selection of Italian style meats.
5223 Victoria Dr., 324-0118

Cioffi's Meat Market & Deli
Pasta, meat, oils, and cheese delights imported from Italy.
4156 Hastings St., 291-9373

Freybe Thrift Shop
Prices vary weekly, but you'll always find a good deal on deli meats, sausages, and tenderloin. Bring the kids because Rudy the German butcher is sure to have a treat for them. Open Wednesday to Saturday only.
716 E. Hastings St., 255-6922

Terra Breads

Famous for its savoury sourdoughs.
*2380 W. 4th Ave., 736-1838;
Granville Island Public Market, 685-3102*

Uprising Breads

An east-side favourite since 1976, specializing in
wholesome yet delicious baked items. *1697 Venables
St., 254-5635*

Jackson's Meats

Around since 1911, it offers
a great selection of fresh meat
and poultry.
*2717 Granville St., 738-6328;
2214 W. 4th Ave., 733-9165*

fishmongers

Angel Seafoods

Reportedly the city's best source for rare and imported
seafood. *1354 Grant St., 254-2824*

Antonia's School of Fish

Commercial Drive's favourite fishmonger.
1439 Commercial Dr., 254-9922

Peter Black and Sons Butchers

Specializes in olde world delicacies
like haggis, black pudding, and
cured bacon.
*3M - 2002 Park Royal South,
W. Vancouver, 922-5116*

Granville Island Seafoods

6-1669 Johnston St., Granville Island, 682-7178

The Lobster Man

Not just lobsters, but live crabs, oysters, clams, and
more. *1807 Mast Tower Rd., Granville Island,
687-4531*

Vancouver Community College Butcher Shop

You'll find discounts of at least 20
percent at this student-operated
butcher and deli.
250 W. Pender St., 443-8351

Steveston Landing Fish Co.

Conveniently located on the Fraser River, right beside
the mooring dock of the fishing boats. *3800 Bayview
St. Unit #101 and 102, Steveston, 275-4746*

Sasamat Seafood Market

4513 W. 10th Ave., 224-4640.

Save-On Seafood

43 W. Hastings St., 681-2677

Seasonal Seafood Market

264 E. Hastings St., 685-6024

Seven Seas Fish Market

2328 W. 4th Ave., 732-8608

Waggott Seafoods

7M Park Royal South, W. Vancouver, 925-4140

direct from the farm

Here are just a few of the many farms in and around Vancouver that you can visit and buy really fresh produce:

Chu Lin Farm

Field cucumbers, English cucumbers, carrots, several varieties of lettuce, including endive and escarole, celery, green onions, a variety of herbs, zucchini, and rhubarb. Open 9 am to 6:30 pm daily.
17535 40th Ave., Surrey, 574-0268

Fook Shing Farm

The usual salad vegetables, but specializes in Asian veggies like sui choy, bok choy, Shanghai bok choy, yin choy, Vietnamese spinach, yan choy, and gai lan. Open 9 am to 7 pm daily.
4890 S.E. Marine Dr., Burnaby, 431-8518

Farmers' Markets

East Van Farmers' Market

While others buy wilted Mexican veggies from the supermarket, wise marketers are lining up for the first shot at the leek tops on the dot of 9 am at Trout Lake Park beginning Victoria Day weekend. This annual farmers' market features such local produce as Karl Haan's yellow, pink, and orange tomatoes, baby minuza and spinach from Langley Organic Growers, exotic funghi from Richmond Specialty Mushrooms, and locally grown, ruby-red strawberries. Saturdays 9 am-2 pm, from mid-May to mid-October.
3350 Victoria Dr., 879-3276.

Hop-On Farms

Radishes, green onions, carrots, three kinds of lettuce (romaine, leaf, and butter), and herbs like basil, cilantro, parsley, dill, and watercress. Open 9:30 am to 7 pm daily (closes at 6 pm on weekends).
5624 S.E. Marine Dr., Burnaby

Krause Farms

Corn, pickling cucumbers, blackberries and blueberries. Open Monday to Saturday from 8 am to 8 pm. *6179 248th St., Surrey, 856-5757*

Surrey Farms

Raspberries, blueberries, strawberries, as well as vegetables. Open 8 am to 7 pm daily.
5180 152nd St., Surrey, 574-1390

W & A Farms

Potatoes, dill cucumbers, carrots, broccoli, beans, beets, and cauliflower. Open 8 am to 5:30 pm daily.
17771 Westminster Hwy., Richmond, 278-5667

Westham Island Herb Farm

Fifteen cooking herbs plus carrots, potatoes, artichokes, beets, field cucumbers, English cucumbers, zucchini, and bush beans. All but the potatoes and artichokes are organic. Open 9 am to 5 pm daily.
4690 Kirkland Rd., Delta, 946-4393

Willow View Farms

Squash, carrots, potatoes, pumpkins, onions, corn, Italian prunes, and pears. Open Monday to Saturday 9 am to 5:30 pm.
288 McCallum Rd., Abbotsford, 604/854-8710

Yellow Barn Country Produce

Field and pickling cucumbers, potatoes, green and red onions, beets, broccoli, Swiss chard, purple and yellow beans. Open 8:30 am to 9 pm daily.
39809 No. 3 Rd., Abbotsford, 604/852-0888

Coquitlam Farmers' Market

Similar to the one in East Vancouver, but smaller. Sundays, 9:30 am - 1:30 pm in the Coquitlam Rec Centre parking lot.
633 Poirier St., 461-5387.

West End Farmers' Market

Located at Lord Roberts Elementary School at the corner of Bidwell and Pendrell St., you'll find a variety of locally grown and prepared produce. Open Saturdays from 9 am to 2 pm from mid-May to the end of October.
879-3276

index

index

index

index

index

SHAWN BLORE was born in Santa Barbara, California – just a hop, skip, and jump down the West Coast – but lengthy detours in Ottawa, Amsterdam, and Moscow kept him from reaching Vancouver until 1994. In the half-decade since, he's immersed himself in Terminal City's unique culture, becoming a self-declared expert on all things strange, unusual, and secret about the place. A journalist and magazine writer, Shawn has been published in *The Globe & Mail, Saturday Night, Elm Street, The Georgia Straight, BC Business, Canadian Geographic*, and *Vancouver Magazine*. He's been nominated for numerous awards, and has won a Western Magazine Award, a National Magazine Award, and a Jack Webster Award.